Edinbu[rgh]
THE WAL[K]

mica

Text © Roddy McDougall & Elizabeth May 2022
Photographs © Roddy McDougall, Elizabeth May, Rab Anderson, Tom Prentice 2022

ISBN: 978-1-9993728-4-2
A catalogue record for this book is available from the British Library

Previous page: Edinburgh Castle from Salisbury Crags

Maps are derived from Ordnance Survey OpenData™
© Crown copyright and database right 2022

Roddy McDougall and Elizabeth May are married and have been working on *Edinburgh The Walk* for several years.

Roddy was born and brought up in Edinburgh, within a few hundred yards of one of the seven hills. A History graduate of the University of Edinburgh, he's a former journalist. He's a keen walker, a member of the Long Distance Walkers Association and has completed more than 20 long distance walks and coastal paths in the UK.

Elizabeth is a Fifer by birth who studied Geography at the University of Edinburgh. A former chartered surveyor, she has a life-long interest in urban development and a love of city walking and exploring – with a particular interest in researching working class housing in the 19th century.

For our parents Eileen and Tom McDougall and Edith and Harry May

Published by **Mica Publishing**, Glasgow & Edinburgh
Printed & bound in India by Replika Press Pvt Ltd

Distributed by Cordee, 11 Jacknell Road, Dodwells Industrial Estate, Hinkley, LE10 3BS
(t) 01455 611185   (e) sales@cordee.co.uk   (w) www.cordee.co.uk

Edinburgh
THE WALK

Roddy McDougall & Elizabeth May

mica

Introduction 6
Using This Guide 9

Section 1 12
BIRTH OF THE CITY: Edinburgh Castle to Leith
8.5km; 5.25 miles

Section 2 50
HARBOUR TO HARBOUR: Leith to Granton
8km; 5 miles

Section 3 80
WATER & WILDERNESS: Granton to Maybury
Road   10km; 6.25 miles

Section 4 100
WESTERN HEIGHTS: Maybury Road to
Balgreen tram stop   7km; 4.25 miles

Section 5 114
HEALTHY SUBURBS: Balgreen tram stop to
Greenbank   8km; 5 miles

Section 6 132
SOUTHERN HILLS: Greenbank to Nether
Liberton   8.5km; 5.25 miles

Section 7 148
COAL & CANDYFLOSS: Nether Liberton to
Portobello   11km; 6.75 miles

Section 8 166
CROWNING HEIGHTS: Portobello to the
Palace of Holyroodhouse   8km; 5 miles

References 190

- **S** Section Start
- **F** Route Finish
- Route
- Alternative Routes & Variations

5

INTRODUCTION

The castle, towering above the refurbished Ross Fountain in West Princes Street Gardens

Edinburgh – as anyone who's lived there or just visited for a few hours will know – is one of the most beautiful cities in the world. Wherever you are, there's a breathtaking view nearby: across the Firth of Forth to the hills of Fife, the classical Georgian terraces and crescents of its New Town, or the imposingly grand Edinburgh Castle and Arthur's Seat which dominate so many views of the city beneath them.

Edinburgh is one of Britain's greenest cities with nearly half of its area taken up by open spaces, so it came as something of a surprise (certainly to us) to discover that there isn't a long-distance walking route linking them all up.

London, however, has the 'Capital Ring', a 125.5km (78 miles) route circling the inner suburbs and taking the walker through many areas of woodland and park. The aim of *Edinburgh The Walk* is to establish a similar circular route for the city.

The actual route is defined by three main objectives:

- Visit all of Edinburgh's famous 'seven hills'
- Join up as many green spaces (natural and man-made) as possible
- Encourage visitors and residents to visit lesser known parts of the city

Catching the sun on Cramond beach

INTRODUCTION

Yachts at the mouth of the River Almond

In choosing where to start and end the route we decided to adapt one of the main tourist walks, the Royal Mile. The Royal Mile is the unofficial name for the road which runs east from Edinburgh Castle downhill to the Palace of Holyroodhouse.

Edinburgh The Walk, also starts at the castle, where Edinburgh's story began, and ends at Holyrood, but takes the more adventurous walker through 69km (43 miles) of glorious cityscape, coastline, river, parkland and hills, with wonderful views along the way.

As written, the walk circles the city in an anti-clockwise direction, allowing the drama of seeing Arthur's Seat from all sides during earlier sections of the route, to build to a fitting conclusion with an ascent in the final section, and the opportunity to look back over the route in its entirety.

Edinburgh may not have had its own 'Capital Ring' until now, but it has had an excellent network of cycleways, existing walks and trails criss-crossing the city, many of which have been utilised to create **Edinburgh The Walk**.

Among these are former suburban railway lines, sections of the John Muir Trail and part of the Water of Leith Walkway, the Edinburgh Coastal Trail and the River Almond Walkway.

As well as visiting the summits of Edinburgh's 'seven hills', Castle Rock, Calton, Corstorphine, Craiglockhart, The Braids, Blackford and Arthur's Seat, the route includes more than 30

The tower of the Nelson Monument and colonnades of the unfinished National Monument on Calton Hill, with the snow-capped Ochil Hills beyond

INTRODUCTION

The River Almond and cottages on Dowie's Mill Lane, from the Old Cramond Brig

of the city's parks, woods and open spaces.

Inevitably, given our aim of following the spirit of the 'Capital Ring' to come up with a circuit around the city, several of Edinburgh's well-known green spaces have had to be omitted, to prevent the route becoming too winding and unwieldy.

Regrettably, areas such as The Meadows, Hermitage of Braid, Colinton Dell and Inverleith Park have not made the final walk. However, we're confident these omissions will be compensated for by the creation of a very

The sun rising over Arthur's Seat from Stevenson's 'Rest and Be Thankful' on Corstorphine Hill

satisfying route which will appeal to both visitors and residents, taking them to areas they might not be familiar with.

Edinburgh has developed in response to the landscape in which it sits. In addition, the city has been the stage for many of the great dramas of Scottish and British history and the cradle of what became known as the Scottish Enlightenment. Indeed, it is not too fanciful to say that the very landscape of the city played a part in the ideas of the Enlightenment, given the contribution to the science of geology by Edinburgh thinkers.

This walk through the wonderful landscape surrounding the city is further enhanced by the addition of geological, historical, architectural and cultural details. To prevent this detail distracting the walker from the route descriptions, it is included in a variety of panels adjacent to the main text.

However you decide to approach this walk we hope you find something in it to surprise and delight you, whether you're a long-time Edinburgh resident or a first-time visitor to this wonderful city.

USING THIS GUIDE

The Route
The route is a total of 69km, (43 miles) and the terrain can be quite rugged. Sadly it is not accessible for the less able-bodied or those in wheelchairs, as there are stairs and hill paths. However, there are also some long sections of tarmac cycle and footpaths which are accessible and can be explored.

The route is tackled in **Eight Sections,** most of which are about 8km, (5 miles), with the longest 11km, (6.75 miles). Each of these makes an enjoyable linear walk in itself. The start and finishes of each are accompanied by public transport details from and back to the city centre (see public transport on p11).

These **Eight Sections** lend themselves ideally to completion over four days – walking two sections, totalling some 16km or 10 miles a day. Alternatively, the whole could easily be done over three days – with two longer days of three sections and a shorter day of two.

A more ambitious approach would be to tackle it over two days – of four sections each – and around 32km or 20 miles per day. It is, of course, also possible to split the walk any other way you choose and there may even be some physically fit souls who would be up for the challenge of completing the circuit in a single summer's day, taking advantage of the city's 17 hours of June daylight. It would also offer an excellent challenge to runners.

Attempting the steep ascent and descent from Arthur's Seat in anything other than good daylight is not recommended, so anyone walking the route in a day would require a very early start, along with adequate food and water for the route, and a good foot massage at the end!

Alternative Routes & Diversions
The outdoor landscape is always changing and that is certainly true of a busy and dynamic city like Edinburgh where housing developments are always underway. At the time of writing, housing is being built at Granton (**Section 2**), the Cammo Estate (**Section 3**) and Little France (**Section 7**). It is entirely possible that this might lead to temporary diversions at a later date and, if so, please follow the recommended routes which will be clearly indicated.

It's also important to point out that natural occurrences such as mud slides, rockfalls and path maintenance can all cause routes to be temporarily closed. As noted in the text, there are also occasions (the Edinburgh Festival in August and over New Year) when city

Portobello Promemade and beach on the Firth of Forth

USING THIS GUIDE

The rocky ascent route leading to the summit of Arthur's Seat requires care and concentration

centre paths may be temporarily closed and diversions indicated.

Weather & Fitness

While this is a city walk it is not totally an urban walk. The mostly coastal part between Granton and Cramond in **Section 2** can be battered by strong winds and horizontal rain straight off the North Sea – even on days when the sun was shining brightly earlier.

The same goes for the hill tops, particularly Arthur's Seat, where the weather can change suddenly. Many sections cross treeless open ground, where finding shelter will not be easy.

While some paths are tarmac, many others are just compacted earth and they can be very muddy and slippery, even on a dry day.

There are many steps on this walk, some of them wooden and others old and uneven stone ones, which will be slippery when wet.

Finally, the summit of Arthur's Seat tackled in **Section 8** involves scrambling up rocks and a very steep descent. If fitness or conditions prevent an ascent, then it is possible to skirt the summit via the alternative route along the pavement of Queen's Drive, which is clearly described on p184.

So, be prepared for all weathers, no matter what the season, wear supportive footwear with good grip, don't attempt any sections that are unsuited to your fitness and always carry some water.

Other Users

Many of the paths along the route are shared with cyclists, joggers and dog walkers. Some of the more urban sections are on the pavements of roads, with quite a few busy road crossings. There are also a few short stretches on minor roads where there will be cars. In short, keep your wits about you.

Refreshments & Toilets

Facilities have been listed in the text where available, but for a city walk, some sections will take you surprisingly far from toilets, cafes

USING THIS GUIDE

and restaurants. For some sections it is worth taking a little food and drink.

Public toilets are listed on the Edinburgh council website *www.edinburgh.gov.uk/leisure-sport-culture/public-toilets* Availability was severely restricted during the Covid-19 pandemic, but it is hoped that many toilets previously open to the public, such as those at every council sports and leisure centre, will reopen and be listed again on this website in the future.

If relying on a food or drink stop suggested in the text then it is advisable to check the opening times before setting out. Some pubs may not be open in the mornings and small local cafes may shut mid-afternoon. Every effort has been made, post-pandemic, to update information but circumstances always change.

Public Transport

One of the plus points of an urban walk in a city like Edinburgh is that a bus stop is never too far away and plans can easily be changed, particularly if the weather turns nasty.

Each section starts and ends with public transport (bus and tram) details, from

Edinburgh's trams and buses provide essential links to and from each Section of the route

and back to the city centre. Again the recommendation is to check these before travelling.

The Lothian Buses website gives interactive details of bus routes, numbers and bus stop names, along with a journey planner, timetables and costs *www.lothianbuses.com/maps-and-times/network-maps/*

There is also a Lothian Buses app available for iPhone from the Apple App Store and for Android from Google Play Store.

Maps

The maps in this guide are based on Ordnance Survey OpenData. To these have been added a green arrow **S** showing the start of the section and a red arrow **F** showing the finish. The route followed by each section is shown by a white, red and yellow line ▭▭▭ while a white, green and yellow line ▭▭▭ shows alternative routes and variations. A magenta line ▭▭▭ shows the route in the preceding and following sections.

To aid easy cross-referencing between maps and the text, many street names have been emboldened in the text and have also been added to the maps. Red bullet numbers **1** have been added to the text at geographical points in the physical walk description.

The numbers and emboldening are not significant in themselves (in that they do not indicate a sight of specific interest), they are just there to help the walker keep tabs on where they are on the map.

Although this is an urban walk, it is always helpful to have an up-to-date map. For some this will be paper and for others it will be digital mapping on a mobile phone. A mobile signal is available for almost all of the walk. There are lots of digital mapping apps that offer Ordnance Survey and other mapping and GPS for mobile phones.

In some locations, such as Cammo Estate in **Section 3** and on Corstorphine Hill in **Section 4**, the paths can be confusing and trees significantly restrict visibility. In addition to the directions, a compass either on your phone or a physical one, could prove helpful.

11

Looking west down Princes Street from the top of the Nelson Monument on Calton Hill

Section 1
BIRTH OF THE CITY

Route: Edinburgh Castle to Leith
Distance: 8.5km; 5.25 miles
Grade: Easy urban walking, several sets of steps, hill ascent and descent on tarmac paths
Access: Edinburgh Castle Esplanade is accessed from Princes Street via The Mound, Mound Place, Ramsay Lane and Castlehill or from the Old Town via the Royal Mile

Edinburgh's complex landscape and the ingenious engineering solutions required to expand the settlement from the Old to the New Town are explored at the start of this section. The route then passes through the first of the city centre parks and green spaces, key elements in the city's unique urban landscape and 1995 listing as a UNESCO World Heritage site, to end at Leith on the Firth of Forth. Once a separate town, but now part of Edinburgh, this ancient port remains a distinct community with its own history and character

Section 1 BIRTH OF THE CITY

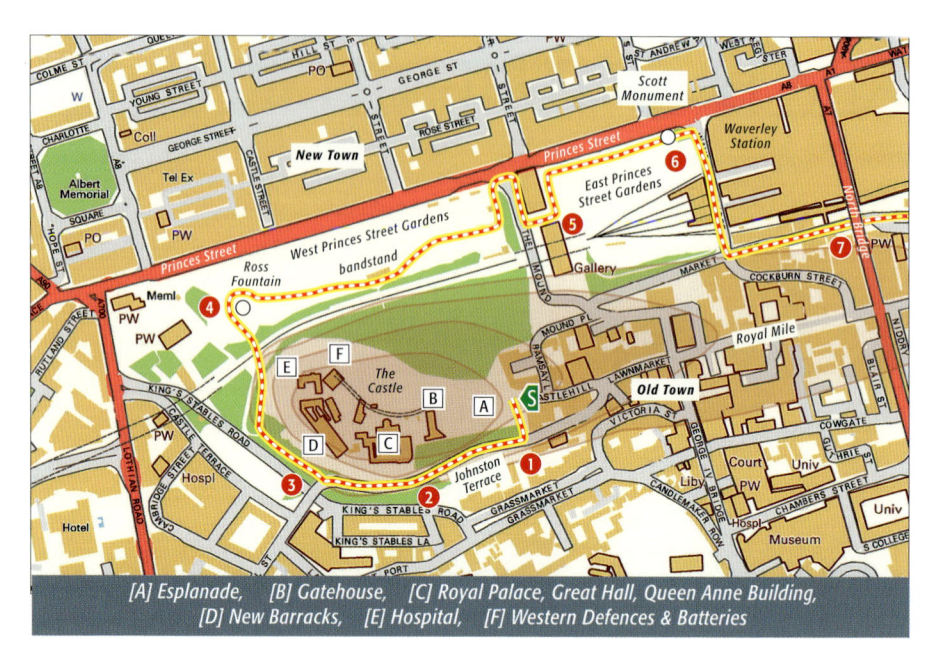

[A] Esplanade,   [B] Gatehouse,   [C] Royal Palace, Great Hall, Queen Anne Building,
[D] New Barracks,   [E] Hospital,   [F] Western Defences & Batteries

S Start on **Edinburgh Castle Esplanade**, just outside the castle entrance. During and in the run up to the Edinburgh Festival in August, there is no access to the Esplanade because of the temporary stands which are erected for the Edinburgh Military Tattoo.

There are a few small cafes and takeaways near the Esplanade (some are tucked away down small alleyways or 'closes' and require searching for) and if beginning the walk early in the morning, they might not be open, especially on Sundays

The Esplanade offers a fine vantage point for views north across Princes Street Gardens to the New Town, the Firth of Forth and beyond, and south to Blackford Hill, the Braid Hills and the Pentland Hills on the horizon. It connects Castle Rock to the Old Town and is the closest point you can get to the summit of the rock, without paying a fee to enter the grounds of the castle. At 131m Castle Rock is the first of the seven Edinburgh hills to be climbed on this walk.

The ridge of land that runs east from the Esplanade towards the Old Town, and on which the Old Town is built, is a 'crag and tail' feature. During the last ice age, an ice sheet flowing from the west scoured a plug of hard volcanic rock clean of the soft rock that surrounded it, save for that in the lee of the plug which was protected from the eroding ice, leaving this distinct, rocky hill with its attached ridge. Humans have exploited this natural, defendable site for centuries, with a town developing on the ridge beyond.

In terms of the castle's history, the Esplanade (from the Latin *explanare* meaning to make level) is a relatively modern part created in the mid-18th century when spoil from building the new City Chambers was used to fill a dip in the land between the town and the castle, leaving a rough parade ground. This was built up higher, paved and walled between 1816 and 1820 to mark Britain's victory over Napoleon, and turned from a functional military space to a venue where ceremonies could be held against the backdrop of the

Section 1 BIRTH OF THE CITY

GEOLOGY & DEFENCE

340 million years ago, when this part of Scotland sat south of the equator, it was a large, submerged volcano. As it ceased to be active, the magma in volcanic pipes cooled to form a hard dolerite rock. Millenia passed, continental plates shifted and the remains of the volcano were overlain with sedimentary rocks and subjected to erosion by ice over several cycles. The last ice age was approximately 12,000 years ago and during it a massive ice sheet crossed the region from west to east; the softer sedimentary rocks were easily eroded by the ice but the hardened magma in one of the volcano's pipes resisted its force and remained as Castle Hill after the ice melted.

Humans began to make use of this hill as a defensive site in prehistoric times with the first stages of a castle built 1,000 years ago. Scotland has had a turbulent history leading to the castle being under siege an estimated 26 times, making it the most besieged place in Britain. Notable among these has been the Lang Siege of 1571-73 when civil war engulfed the country after Mary Queen of Scots was imprisoned in England and forces loyal to her (led by Kirkcaldy of Grange) held Edinburgh for more than a year before surrendering the town and retreating to the castle.

Forces loyal to Mary's infant son James VI (led by the Earl of Morton) brought in English help – 1,000 English soldiers, 300 cavalry and 27 cannons – and began a 10-day bombardment, the like of which the castle had not seen before or since. During this, the medieval St David's and Constable's towers were destroyed, changing the look of the castle.

castle. The castle contains the Honours of Scotland (the Scottish Crown Jewels) and the National War Museum, and since 1950 has hosted the Edinburgh Military Tattoo. It attracts more than two million visitors a year.

Leave the Esplanade by its south-east corner and turn right down the steps of **Castle Wynd North**.

Edinburgh Castle, the Half Moon Battery, Gatehouse and Esplanade. The castle sits on top of its rocky 'crag', whose grass covered 'tail' leads east to the Old Town

Section 1 BIRTH OF THE CITY

> 👬 *There are public toilets partway down Castle Wynd North. However, public toilets are generally very scarce in Edinburgh and you often have to visit a cafe or pub in order to access one*

At the foot of the steps is **Johnston Terrace**, a road cut into the south side of the rock below the castle as part of a plan by Thomas Hamilton of 1827, which aimed to better connect the self-contained medieval town to the surrounding land, through making roads with gentler gradients, and to allow expansion beyond the confines of the medieval town.

❶ Cross Johnston Terrace to the top of the continuation, **Patrick Geddes Steps**, and look over the low stone wall on the right. This is Johnston Terrace Garden, somewhat improbably, the first open green space of this walk. The area is managed by the Scottish Wildlife Trust and at just 0.7 hectares is their smallest site. Sadly, due to past problems with vandalism, it can only be visited by prior arrangement or on Open Garden Days; access is from a gate on Patrick Geddes Steps.

By the late 19th century, when the urban area had spread and the Old Town had become an overcrowded slum, home only to the poor, concern began to grow about the lack of access to open spaces. In 1909-10 a committee under the guidance of Patrick Geddes conducted a survey of the Old Town to look for possible sites for small 'pocket' parks. Over 70 sites were identified by the committee on gap sites and derelict ground. It

PATRICK GEDDES

The view of the Old Town as something to be saved and cherished can be attributed to the 19th century visionary town planner and environmentalist Patrick Geddes. In 1880 at the age of 26 he became a lecturer in Zoology at the University of Edinburgh, having initially studied geology. At this time, many saw wholesale demolition as the only solution to the problem of the Old Town's slums.

Geddes took a radically different view advocating that, despite the poor conditions, this area should remain residential, and because of its great age, the fabric of the old buildings and layout had a cultural significance to the city and should be retained.

He developed the idea of 'conservative surgery' – taking out selected buildings to allow more light in while refurbishing the remaining buildings in a sympathetic style. Part of this philosophy involved providing parks for the Old Town residents, which he considered good for health and the soul. The available space was limited, so these parks were very small.

Geddes believed the classes should not live separate lives and he purchased slum property in James Court off the Royal Mile and made it his own family home. Through his position at the university he was instrumental in converting several other old tenements off the Royal Mile into student accommodation.

He became one of the foremost town planners of his day and was knighted in 1932. Today he is better known overseas for his work than in Edinburgh. His contribution to the city was acknowledged in 2012, with a statue of him in Sandeman House Garden off the High Street.

Section 1 BIRTH OF THE CITY

Johnston Terrace, south of the Esplanade, was constructed under an Act of 1827 to improve access to the Old Town

is not known how many parks were eventually created, but around eight are thought to have survived. As part of Geddes's holistic vision, children from nearby Castlehill School helped to tend the gardens where vegetables were grown for use in teaching the girls cooking. Access was controlled and Lady Superintendents oversaw playtimes in the afternoons.

Don't go down Patrick Geddes Steps, but turn right to continue gently downhill on Johnston Terrace beside the wall, passing a long building on the left which was built in the early 1870s as married quarters for soldiers.

Just past this is **Granny's Green**. Formerly this was used as a public drying ground for laundry. The drying poles are still there. Then in 2001 the steps down to the Grassmarket were constructed. In 2012 this increased access led to an initiative very much in the Geddes spirit, when the Patrick Geddes Gardening Club laid it out as a memorial garden to him.

Turning towards the castle, the junction between the hard volcanic plug of the 'crag' on the left and the softer rock of the 'tail' on the right, lies directly below the curved wall of the Half Moon Battery.

❷ This is roughly where a wall, known as the **Flodden Wall**, was constructed to protect the growing Old Town in the 16th century, running down to the valley below to a gate called the West Port. There was a small

THE CASTLE AS A ROYAL RESIDENCE

Royalty used Edinburgh Castle as a residence from the time of Queen (later Saint) Margaret, the wife of King Malcolm Canmore, who died there in 1093. Her son David I (reigning from 1124-1153) established it as a principal royal residence and made Edinburgh a Royal Burgh. Later James II, following the murder of his father at Perth in 1437, made Edinburgh the capital of Scotland. The castle remained a royal residence on and off till 1633. Charles I was the last monarch to stay there but he only stayed for one night prior to his Scottish coronation.

Section 1 BIRTH OF THE CITY

The Royal Palace, right, and Great Hall dominate the south side of Edinburgh Castle

postern (gate) here but no road.

Beyond the line of the wall and perched high on the rock – looking almost part of it – stands the **Royal Palace** (mid-15th to early 17th century) with its many small windows and the **Great Hall** (early 16th century) with its four large windows. Both buildings date from a time when the castle's primary function was as a royal residence.

❸ Cross back to the castle side of Johnston Terrace and continue to where the road bends left. Before a bus shelter, go through a gate in the railings on the right and enter **Princes Street Gardens** following a path ahead. As the path descends, the sheer height of Castle Rock becomes apparent. Note that this path and part of Princes Street Gardens may be closed for seasonal events. At such times, follow the sign-posted diversions to resume the walk at the foot of The Mound.

To the left in the valley is King's Stables Road, which passes under Johnston Terrace in

THE CITY'S DEFENCES – THE FLODDEN WALL

Completed in 1560, this wall was built to defend the compact settlement of about 57 hectares, which had developed in the valley south of Castle Rock, against a possible English invasion after the Scots had been defeated in the Battle of Flodden. An earlier wall known as the King's Wall had enclosed a smaller area.

The wall came down from St David's Tower, which was as high as a modern 10-storey building and dominated the city skyline. This 14th century structure was destroyed in 1573 during the Lang Siege, having been the royal living quarters for over 100 years. Only the lower parts of that tower now remain, buried among later structures.

As it turned out the invasion did not happen at this date and piecemeal demolition of the wall – and the later extension called the Telfer Wall – began after the threat of Jacobite action receded post 1745. Some small sections of the wall remain in Greyfriars Churchyard, the Grassmarket, Drummond Street and the Pleasance.

THE CASTLE – A MILITARY GARRISON

Over the years the physical fabric of the castle has changed in response to new military thinking and technology, and to repair damage done during the continued periodic sieges. From 1660, when the newly restored Charles II established a permanent garrison at the castle for his new standing army, the changes predominantly reflected this new role.

With the Act of Union in 1707, Edinburgh was designated as just one of four Scottish castles to retain a permanent garrison. No other building quite epitomises this military function than the massive six-storey block called the New Barracks. Designed to house 600 soldiers, it was constructed between 1796 and 1799 during the revolutionary wars in France, when the military presence in Edinburgh was increased.

On completion it was heartily disliked, Walter Scott felt that its utilitarian appearance was out of place on the "romantic" site of Castle Rock, calling it a "vulgar cotton mill". In 1923, when the garrison moved out to new barracks at Redford on the south-west side of the city, there was even talk of demolishing it, and yet it is now impossible to think of the castle's silhouette without it.

a short tunnel. These flatter lands at the base of the rock have had royal uses since the 14th century. The Royal Stables were on the eastern section of the road, but where there is now a multi-storey car park, was a tiltyard or 'Barras' where jousting tournaments were held in medieval times.

The construction of Johnston Terrace allowed the area to develop and the Barras site (long used for other purposes) was laid out as Castle Terrace Gardens. This garden was destroyed in 1962 when the car park was built. Prior to the construction of the New Town, King's Stables Road was the route out to Queensferry and the north. To the right, perched high on Castle Rock, is the rectangular massive of the **New Barracks** of 1799.

Turning first to face north and then east the views open out of Princes Street and Princes Street Gardens. Princes Street was part of James Craig's famous plan for Edinburgh's New Town adopted in the 1770s. It was originally meant to be wholly residential but is now the capital's premier shopping street (although many older residents say that its glory days are long past).

The castle's Western defences on the left with the – at the time of construction – unpopular New Barracks on the right, described by Sir Walter Scott as a "vulgar cotton mill"

Section 1 BIRTH OF THE CITY

Ross Fountain "grossly indecent and disgusting"

THE NOR' LOCH

Cut by the ice and probably always badly drained and marshy, the valley on the north side of Castle Rock was flooded in the 15th century on the orders of King James II to create a body of water known as the Nor' Loch, to strengthen the city's northern defences. This omitted the need for a defensive wall on this side of the city, save for the small section and a tower protecting St Margaret's Well.

Most of the time the city was not under siege, so the loch had many other uses, an important domestic one being for the washing of clothes. Another, allegedly, was the ducking of suspected witches.

By the 1760s the Nor' Loch was seriously foul and polluted and the decision was taken to drain it (a slow process) beginning with the eastern part; the western part was drained later between 1813 to 1820.

As the path forks, keep right hugging the base of the crags (noting where the ice sheet encountered most resistance to the hard dolerite rock formed by the cooling magma, at best managing to crack and tear it to produce this sharp, jagged cliff face), to reach path crossroads. Keep ahead and cross a bridge over the railway into the main section of Princes Street Gardens.

Princes Street Gardens occupy the western end of the ice-cut valley which once contained the Nor' Loch. The gardens are actually two separate entities, West Princes Street Gardens and East Princes Street Gardens, with different development histories; this part is **West Princes Street Gardens** which covers 12 hectares including the grassy lower slopes of Castle Rock.

By the time the New Town was being promoted in the late 1700s, the Nor' Loch was noxious and had outlived its defensive role, so the decision was taken to drain it. In 1818 a private consortium called the Princes Street Proprietors took a lease over the land from its owners the Crown Estate and spent considerable sums of money to lay it out as a garden. Such private gardens were common in the New Town (and several survive) but this one always had a degree of public access.

It was open on Christmas Day and New Year's Day. A guidebook from 1875 notes that the hotels on Princes Street could give access and that, in the summer, a military band played in the park once or twice a week when the public also had access. Pressure for greater public access culminated in the town council taking over the park in 1876 (it also acquired Castle Terrace Gardens and created access gates on King's Stables Road).

The shape of the valley has been modified over the years with the slope on the north (left) side made steeper in the 1880s when Princes Street was widened and an earth embankment on the south side was made to conceal the railway from the view of the houses on Princes Street – a condition of the railway company's Act of Parliament.

The view of the castle from here is defined by the jagged low walls of the 18th century

Section 1 BIRTH OF THE CITY

defences – from west to east the **Western Defences**, **Mills Mount Battery**, **Argyle Battery**, and **Low Defence**s – built in response to the threat of attack from Jacobite forces. When the rest of the city fell to Jacobite troops without a fight in 1745, the Governor of the Castle was able to hold out by bombarding the Jacobite troops in the city. This was the last time the castle saw military action and ended the long phase of its history involving attacks and sieges.

The park's current layout largely dates from the 1880s to the designs of Edinburgh City Architect Robert Morham. It is the very model of a Victorian public park with its paths, planting, fountain and bandstand, all surrounded by railings. There is even a park keeper's cottage.

❹ A fine collection of statues and memorials adorn the park. Keep ahead to visit the newly restored **Ross Fountain** then take the main path running east along the valley floor towards the Ross Bandstand, where the path splits.

> 🚻 There are public toilets at the back of the Ross Bandstand

Take the right-hand path round the back of the bandstand. On the right, a pedestrian bridge over the railway used to connect to the wilder parts of the gardens on the slopes of Castle Hill, giving access to the ruins of St Margaret's Well and the Medieval Welltower. However, due to the unsafe condition of the ruins, it is currently closed. Keep to the path round the bandstand to rejoin the valley floor path and turn right (east) towards The Mound.

High above on the right, by the Castle

MR ROSS & MR ROSS

It is a strange coincidence that two men named Mr Ross have gifted major facilities to Princes Street Gardens. The first was Mr Daniel Ross who gifted the fountain. A wealthy gunsmith, he bought the statue at the International Exhibition in London in 1862. It then had to be dismantled and shipped to Edinburgh. There was much discussion as to where this gift should be put and by the time it was finally unveiled in 1872, Ross was no longer alive to see it in place.

The richly detailed design incorporates four allegorical female figures representing science, arts, poetry and industry, topped by a naked woman holding a cornucopia. On the lower level, eight mermaids surround lion head waterspouts, while in between, cherubs and faces adorn the basins. All rests upon a base of Craigleith Sandstone. This hard building sandstone was quarried at many locations around Edinburgh including a large quarry at Craigleith, east of Corstorphine Hill (Section 4), which was subsequently infilled for a retail park.

Its distinct French style by Jean-Baptiste Jules Klagman was not to everyone's taste; Dean Ramsay of nearby St John's Church called it "grossly indecent and disgusting; insulting and offensive to the moral feeling of the community and disgraceful to the city". In 2017-18 a £1.9 million restoration was carried out by the Ross Development Trust which included restoring it to a bright colour scheme.

The present Ross Bandstand was gifted in 1935 by William Henry Ross, businessman and chairman of The Distillers Company, and replaced an earlier Victorian iron bandstand dating from 1877. It is also the subject of a plan by the Ross Development Trust, but this is a more challenging scheme than the restoration of the fountain as it aims to provide a new theatre and a visitor centre in this most sensitive of locations. Although architectural practice wHY won the design competition in 2017 with a structure dubbed 'the Hobbit House', the plans seemed, at the time of writing, to have stalled pending further public consultation as to both the nature of the development and the future management of the park.

Section 1 BIRTH OF THE CITY

Patrick Geddes's remodelled Old Town buildings on Ramsay Garden

Esplanade, stands an attractive group of colourful buildings. Not entirely as old as they seem, these are collectively named **Ramsay Garden** and are another example of the impact Patrick Geddes had upon Edinburgh's Old Town. They include a core of 18th century buildings which by the late 19th century had seen better days. Geddes believed that the Old Town had suffered from the loss of middle class citizens with the building of the New Town a century before and thought that it was necessary to attract them back.

He remodelled these prominent buildings, primarily to attract university professors. The redesign, in a distinctive Arts & Crafts fantasy style, was done in stages and must have looked startling amidst the dour grey stone when first completed in 1893 to the designs of S.Henbest Capper and Sydney Mitchell.

At the red sandstone park keeper's cottage, follow the path as it doglegs left uphill then turn right and up steps past the floral clock to exit the garden onto **The Mound**. Turn left, cross over The Mound at the lights and turn right past the long colonnade of the **Royal Scottish Academy** (1820s) to a pedestrian

THE MOUND – CONNECTING EDINBURGH'S OLD AND NEW TOWNS

The Mound was constructed in the 1780s to facilitate access from the Old Town to the New Town, which was then being developed to James Craig's plans, from a more westerly point than the existing North Bridge. Much of the purported million and a half cartloads of soil used to build up the ground on which the roadway now stands came from digging out the foundations and basements of the New Town houses and it took the best part of 50 years to reach its full height, only to be tunnelled through a decade later for the railway line. Although The Mound was no bar to the railway it did scupper Craig's proposal for an ornamental canal to run along the valley floor after the Nor' Loch was drained.

Section 1 BIRTH OF THE CITY

way separating it from its younger sister the **Scottish National Gallery** (1845) beyond. Both are by William Henry Playfair whose taste for neo-Grecian architecture added to the city's sense of itself as the Athens of the North.

Looking ahead, is another Playfair building, New College with its soaring twin gate towers (1846-50). As that site was in the Old Town, Playfair deemed a neo-gothic style appropriate. The route of the roadway up The Mound and its connection with the Old Town was decided by Thomas Hamilton's 1827 plan and it is his planning, combined with Playfair's architecture, that is important in enabling these two distinct urban landscapes – the Old and the New Towns – to sit side by side in harmony. These Playfair building are all grade A listed.

5 Turn left and follow the pedestrian way between the galleries to a terrace. Ahead is a fine view over East Princes Street Gardens towards the Scott Monument and clock tower of the former North British Hotel (now The Balmoral), with the elegant spans of North Bridge beyond. Turn left on the terrace, then right through the gate into **East Princes Street Gardens**.

Looking south across East Princes Street Gardens to the twin gate towers of Playfair's New College

William Henry Playfair's neoclassical Royal Scottish Academy on The Mound dates from the 1820s

Section 1 BIRTH OF THE CITY

Scott Monument, Balmoral Hotel (formerly the North British Hotel) and East Princes Street Gardens

> 🚻 🍽 *Making a further right turn at the gate into East Princes Street Gardens and descending the steps, gives access to the cafe and toilets at the newly expanded National Gallery of Scotland*

East Princes Street Gardens is much smaller than its westerly sister at just 3.4 hectares, partly because of the space taken up by the multiple railway lines emerging from Waverley Station. While it contains fewer monuments than the west gardens, it is dominated by the enormous gothic presence of the **Scott Monument**. This spire was erected as a memorial to the writer Sir Walter Scott, a man who did much to create the modern image of Edinburgh and indeed Scotland.

At 61.11m (200ft 6in), it is one of the largest monuments to a writer anywhere in the world, and is open to any member of the public who wishes to tackle its 287 steps (currently a £5 fee). The gothic style is unusual in Edinburgh and despite the presence of many quarries locally (including one right underneath it called Bearford's) the stone is Binny Sandstone from a quarry near Ecclesmachan, West Lothian. During restoration in the 1990s it was decided that the stonework would not respond well to cleaning, leaving it with a somewhat mottled appearance with soot encrusted old stone and bright patches of repaired and replaced stone.

The monument was constructed from 1840-6 to the designs of George Meikle Kemp a self-taught architect who won a competition for this commission. Unfortunately, he did not live to see it completed, accidentally drowning in the Union Canal during construction. The Carrara marble statue of Scott (and his dog Maida) is by Sir John Steell and there are subsidiary statues placed around the structure of three Scottish monarchs, 16 poets and 64 characters from his novels.

❻ Sticking to the high path, walk past the Scott Monument and go through a gate to reach **Waverley Bridge**. Turn left to the junction with Princes Street and cross over at

Section 1 BIRTH OF THE CITY

the traffic lights. Turn right and walk downhill past the entrance to Waverley Station and Waverley Mall to reach a pedestrian and vehicle access road on the left, just before The Booking Office pub.

Previously called Canal Street, this ramp leads down into the station. Before the original railway companies amalgamated and the station was rebuilt in the 1890s, it had the Edinburgh, Perth & Dundee Railway Station on its north (left) side and the North British & Edinburgh & Glasgow Railway Station on its south side. **Waverley Station** takes its name from Edward Waverley, the lead character in Walter Scott's historical novels, and reinforces the impact of his writing in shaping the psyche of early Victorian Scotland.

Look ahead across the expanse of the station's glass roof to the dramatic silhouette created by the North Bridge slung between the former North British Hotel (now The Balmoral) and the buildings of the Old Town. The vastness of the station disguises how broad the valley, which used to contain the Nor' Loch, is at this point. This eastern section of the Nor' Loch was drained earlier than the western section, after Edinburgh town council acquired land to build the North Bridge in 1763 and begin the expansion into the New Town.

Keep straight ahead on Waverley Bridge to a crossroads with a mini-roundabout and turn left down **Market Street**. On turning here note Cockburn Street winding uphill ahead. This was cut through old closes running off the High Street in 1860 to create the first direct vehicular access from the High Street in the Old Town to Waverley Station. Passing along Market Street, its very name and that of The Fruitmarket Gallery to the left, recall the function of this area as the site of the city's meat and produce markets for nearly two centuries following the draining of the Nor' Loch.

SIR WALTER SCOTT

At the time of his death in 1832 Walter Scott was a superstar of a writer with a huge public profile (hence the huge memorial) yet financially ruined. A lawyer by profession he only published his first novel, Waverley, at the age of 43 after gaining a reputation as a poet. Initially, it was published anonymously due to his worry that his father considered writing novels trivial. He is credited with inventing the genre of historical fiction and rehabilitating the reputation of Highland culture which had been vilified following the 1745 Jacobite uprising. After the publication of Waverley, Scott's output was prodigious – a further 24 novels, three more long poems, two books of short stories and four plays.

Scott was granted permission to search for the Scottish Crown Jewels (known as the Honours of Scotland) which had been mislaid since royalty had abandoned the custom of visiting Scotland for a separate coronation. He found them in Edinburgh Castle, and in response George IV, already a fan of his writing, made him a baronet and invited him to stage-manage his visit to Edinburgh in 1822. This was a big deal as it was the first visit to Scotland by a reigning monarch in almost two centuries.

Scott was financially ruined by a banking crisis of 1825-6 when the printing firm in which he was a partner collapsed. He vowed to write himself out of debt and although he died from epidemic typhus before seeing this achieved, his works continued to sell after his death and the debts were soon cleared.

Section 1 BIRTH OF THE CITY

Calton Hill and the Nelson Monument, right, over the vast glass canopy of Waverley Station

NORTH BRIDGE

The concept of building a bridge here was central to the expansion of Edinburgh out of its cramped site on the tail of Castle Rock. The 160m long, three-span iron bridge seen here is the second bridge on this site. It was constructed from 1894-97, to the designs of City Architect Robert Morham. The contractor was Sir William Arrol & Co who also built the Forth Rail Bridge.

The earlier bridge was begun in 1765 and was quite a feat of engineering in the days before the invention of structural ironwork, due to the required height and the length it had to span. This bridge was very elegant with three high stone arches visible with smaller multi-storey arches supporting the ends. These subsidiary arches became hidden behind later buildings – which rose five storeys from the valley floor to the bridge level and a further four above that. The roadway was a generous 12m wide. It was constructed from stone from Bearford's Quarries (located below the Scott Monument and Princes Street) and Maidencraig Quarry.

As the Nor' Loch had been drained before construction, there was ample space on relatively flat land beneath it for new meat, fish and fruit markets to be located there. The designer and contractor for the first bridge was City Surveyor William Mylne whose reputation was destroyed when the nearly complete bridge suffered a partial collapse, killing five workmen. The cause of this calamity was at least in part because Mylne had assumed the ground of the valley floor to be firm and stable, whereas sections of it were unstable accumulations of earth and rubbish thrown into the loch over the centuries.

Section 1 BIRTH OF THE CITY

WAVERLEY STATION

In a pivotal space of two years from 1846 to 1848, three railway companies built termini for their railway lines on the drained land under the North Bridge and in the process Edinburgh became vastly better-connected, fuelling further commercial growth. First to open was the North British Railway's North Bridge Station for its line from Berwick-upon-Tweed, followed two months later by the station for the Edinburgh & Glasgow Railway.

This company had been the first to open a station in Edinburgh four years earlier but opposition to the line along the valley of the drained Nor' Loch had meant initially it had to terminate at Haymarket further west. In 1847 Canal Street Station was opened to serve the Edinburgh, Leith & Trinity Railway Company (later known as the Edinburgh, Perth & Dundee Railway) for its line, which connected with the ferries crossing the Firth of Forth.

When the North British Railway's 1849 line from Edinburgh to Hawick (axed in the early 1960s and partly reopened in 2015) was extended through to Carlisle in 1862, crossing the border country whose history and traditions had been such a feature of Sir Walter Scott's work, it was unofficially called the 'Waverley' line after Scott's Waverley novels.

In 1868 the North British Railway took over its smaller rivals and from then, the three stations were run as one. Eventually in 1892 work began to demolish the older station buildings and create a single large station, in tandem with the rebuilding of the North Bridge, whose new design with longer iron spans freed up more land on the valley floor. The final unifying piece, the great glazed roof, was complete by 1908. Between 2011 and 2014 this roof was reglazed – all 34,000 square metres of it!

On the right and before the bridge, is the City Art Centre, which was created in 1980 by Edinburgh City Architects from a fine iron-framed warehouse circa 1900. Just beyond is the arched entrance to the narrow, steep and straight stairs of Fleshmarket Close (immortalised in Ian Rankin's Inspector Rebus novel of the same name) heading uphill to the High Street. A short distance further on The Scotsman Stairs wind up inside a stone tower with grilled windows to **North Bridge**.

❼ Keep ahead under the bridge and emerge into **East Market Street,** and more views across Waverley Station roof to Calton Hill. Here was the site of a lost garden at the eastern end of the Nor' Loch. Roughly where platform 11 is now was a physic garden from 1676 to 1763. Under the stewardship of James Sutherland plants were grown to supply botanicals to Edinburgh's physicians. Sutherland published an important index of the plants in the garden by the title of *Hortus Medicus Edinburgensis* and was made Professor of Botany on the strength of his work. His collection of plants was moved to a new site on Leith Walk (and combined with the collection from the physic garden at Holyrood Palace). In 1820, this garden was moved to Inverleith where it remains as the Royal Botanic Gardens.

Further down East Market Street on the right, are bold stone arches, now repurposed for shops and cafes, which support **Jeffrey Street**, a route engineered in 1867 as part of the city's Improvement Act of that year. Here, as part of the 1890 revamp of Waverley Station, a pedestrian footbridge was erected running from Jeffrey Street across the roof of the station to connect with Calton Road to the north.

This was closed in 1958 and the structure largely removed in 2009 apart from a short raised section of wall on East Market Street which supported one of the metal legs, and a small section of stone steps and ornate metal pedestrian bridge at the Calton Road end, which still provides an entrance to Waverley Station.

27

Section 1 BIRTH OF THE CITY

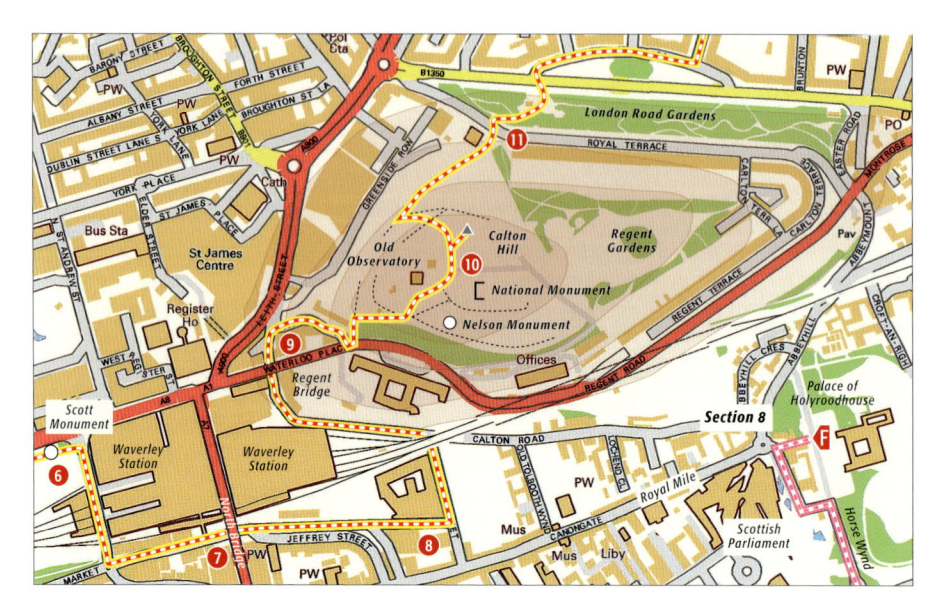

Walking and cycling groups are calling for a reinstatement of this bridge, which would be historically appropriate, as it is roughly on the ancient route from the Netherbow Port on the Royal Mile, skirting round the base of Calton Hill to reach Leith.

Prior to the construction of North Bridge and The Mound, there were no routes across the valley or the loch between this one and King's Stables Road seen earlier on the route.

8 Beyond the arches, on the left, is an office block for City of Edinburgh Council (2007, BDP architects) incorporating extensive roof gardens. The block is on land which was formerly a goods station, created as part of Waverley's 1890s expansion. Continue along East Market Street to a junction with New Street.

On the right is the former Canongate School (1900, R.Wilson, architect to Edinburgh School Board) which now has an aparthotel with a contemporary ground floor extension.

Straight ahead, a new pedestrian square has been created as the centrepiece of a large mixed-use redevelopment scheme named New Waverley. Sibbald Walk, the pedestrian route through the square, is named after physician Sir Robert Sibbald (1641-1722), the Geographer Royal and creator of the city's first botanic garden which was on land nearby.

Turn left down **New Street** (a relative term, for this street certainly predates the railway by many decades) where the redevelopment continues. To the right are new UK Government offices on the site of a large bus depot dating from the 1930s. This, in turn, replaced what had been Edinburgh's first gasworks which opened in 1817 – one of the earliest anywhere – making town gas from coal. Its tall slender chimney was a distinctive landmark on old photographs of the city centre – belching out smoke and adding to the polluted air of 'Auld Reekie', as Edinburgh became known. One of the uses for this new fuel was for street lighting. There were previously oil lamps along Edinburgh's streets but the first gas lamps appeared on nearby North Bridge in 1819. From 1881 these began to be replaced by electric lighting on the principal streets, but gas lighting remained on some backstreets into the 1950s.

Walking downhill, there appears to be another castle ahead, but it is actually St Andrew's House, a 1930s government office block (Thomas Tait Grade A listed), above a

Section 1 BIRTH OF THE CITY

The roof gardens of the 2007 City of Edinburgh Council offices on East Market Street

REGENT BRIDGE – GATEWAY TO A THIRD NEW TOWN

By 1800 the streets on James Craig's New Town Plan were largely built up and Edinburgh's population and wealth were growing, giving rise to demands for more 'modern' housing beyond the Old Town. Building on Calton Hill might not seem an obvious place to expand but developers other than the city's council were already planning developments to the west and north of Craig's plan.

These developments would become known as the Second New Town and the council backed development on Calton Hill and eastwards was to be the Third New Town. A plan by William Henry Playfair was eventually chosen for this.

The success of this expansion scheme depended upon bridging the deep valley. The city commissioners chose the classical design of Archibald Elliot and Robert Stevenson was appointed engineer. It was Stevenson who proposed the idea of preserving views from the bridge, which Elliot achieved with the Corinthian screens to the sides of the bridge in a Greek revival style.

What is not apparent from the modern view is how wide the valley is – over 90m – while the visible arch is only just over 15m. Hidden from view by buildings of great height rising up from the lower road on either side are stacked smaller arches. The arch has very pleasing proportions being roughly as high as it is wide. The impressiveness of this structure is recognised with category A listed status.

The bridge was opened in 1819 by Prince Leopold of Saxe Coburg, the son-in-law of the Prince Regent (subsequently George IV), after whom the bridge was named.

29

Section 1 BIRTH OF THE CITY

"Choose life" – the Black Bull pub, made famous in the film Trainspotting

'castle-like' wall which was built as the boundary of the 19th century complex of prisons which once stood there.

Directly opposite the point where New Street meets Calton Road, and below the railway bridge, is the entrance to Jacob's Ladder, a flight of 140 steps cut into the rock and dating from the 18th century. Recently reopened after a £150,000 refurbishment, they lead up to Regent Road, east of St Andrew's House, and offer a good view over the station to North Bridge and south-east to Salisbury Crags.

Turn left on **Calton Road** and continue round the north side of the station. Ahead on the hill is the distinctive castle-like structure of the Governor's House of the former Calton Hill Prison. This quiet corner of the city was once a small medieval settlement called Low Calton, and later home to a glorious medieval building complex, Trinity College Church and Hospital. Somewhat ironically, this genuine gothic structure was being demolished (to make way for the railways) around the time that the Victorian neo-gothic Scott Monument was being built. Some of the old stonework is incorporated in Trinity Apse church on Trunk's Close off the High Street.

Having now walked around most of Waverley Station its scale can be fully appreciated. On the left, the high stone wall with mock arches dates from the 1890s rebuilding. Straight ahead, as the road bends round to the right, are the stone steps and elevated iron walkway which once connected with the pedestrian bridge over the station to Jeffrey Street.

Follow the road as it bends right. Ahead is the monumental **Regent Bridge** which carries **Waterloo Place** over the valley. This audacious piece of engineering now seems a little over the top as it serves a relatively quiet stretch of road. However, when it was built it was designed to be the key to opening up a large swathe of land for developing Edinburgh's Third New Town.

Section 1 BIRTH OF THE CITY

The bridge spans the valley between Multrees Hill and Calton Hill, two of Edinburgh's original seven hills. The peaks nowadays considered to be Edinburgh's seven hills were quite distant from the limits of the town when the term was coined, and it was more central hills, now mostly obscured by building – Multrees, Sciennes, St John's and St Leonard's – which made up the seven, along with Abbey Hill, Castle Rock and Calton Hill – see also p138.

9 As the road heads gently uphill to the junction with Leith Street, look out for a short flight of stairs on the left leading to **The Black Bull** pub. This spot features in the opening sequence of the Danny Boyle film *Trainspotting*, when Renton (played by Ewan McGregor) runs down them to the soundtrack of the famous 'choose life' monologue, backed by the beat of Iggy Pop's *Lust for Life*.

Just past the Black Bull, and before the junction with Leith Street, take a sharp right turn up the steep **Calton Hill** with its old cobbles. The ascent gives the opportunity to look back to see the most recent development on Multrees Hill, the rebuilding of the Edinburgh St James shopping centre. Higher up are some late 18th century houses which predate the Regent Bridge.

The last house on the left, the two-storey Rock House, was for some years the studio

The austere classical buildings of Waterloo Place, looking west towards Princes Street and the Scott Monument, from the Regent Bridge

of the pioneering Victorian photographers Robert Adamson and David Octavius Hill, some of whose work can be seen in the Photography Centre of London's Victoria and Albert Museum.

At the top is a T-junction with **Regent Road** to the left and Waterloo Place to the right. This is the start of the A1 road south to London, although it's now relatively quiet due to the modern bypass south of the city and mainly used for parking tourist buses.

Firstly, look right down Waterloo Place to see the vista over Regent Bridge towards the Scott Monument and Princes Street, noting the

---

CALTON HILL PRISONS

Edinburgh city acquired part of Calton Hill in the 18th century and it was to prove useful space for expansion, initially for the location of institutions for which there was no room in the cramped Old Town. The earliest of these was the 'Bridewell', a house of correction based on the London model. Started in 1791 to designs of Robert Adam, it predated the building of Regent Bridge. At that time Edinburgh's jail was the Old Tolbooth on the High Street but by the early 19th century this was no longer fit for purpose and in 1817 a much larger felons' prison was built on Calton Hill, next to the Bridewell. The Governor's House is all that remains of this prison, (both were designed in a gothic style by Archibald Elliott). A third prison, this one for debtors, was added to the complex around 1825.

By 1887 the three separate institutions were amalgamated into one, known simply as The Prison – a grim place with a harsh regime. Together these buildings perched on the side of the hill with an appearance to rival Edinburgh Castle. All but the Governor's House and some sections of retaining wall were demolished in 1930 when St Andrew's House was built.

Section 1 BIRTH OF THE CITY

austere classical style of the design which is very typical of the period in Edinburgh. This was the view that was intended to form the 'gateway' to the city for those approaching along the road from London.

The walls that line the road here enclose the Old Calton Burial ground, which was cut in two by Regent Bridge and the new road. This is worth a visit as it contains the graves and memorials of many leading figures of the Edinburgh Enlightenment and includes the 27m high Political Martyrs Monument (1844 Thomas Hamilton). Immediately across the road is the frontal face of St Andrew's House seen earlier from New Street.

Turn left then left again and continue the ascent of Calton Hill via a flight of steps. Take a second flight on the right, then follow the path uphill heading for the tower of the **Nelson Monument**. Calton Hill is another volcanic 'crag and tail' where the hardness of its rock and resistance to the moving ice sheet has created its shape. At 106m it is lower than Castle Rock but still forms a very distinct peak.

CALTON HILL – ITS MONUMENTS

Collectively, the buildings on Calton Hill are a monument to Enlightenment Edinburgh being started between 1775 and 1828. The largest structure is the old observatory which is the product of primarily three architects over three phases. The first section, the gothic tower built in rubble, is a rare remaining building by architect James Craig who produced the plan for the New Town. The original grander scheme – in which Robert Adam had a hand – was to house a telescope belonging to Thomas Short, but this floundered amid money troubles and legal wrangling, although Short did run a scaled down observatory till his death in 1807. The domed classical temple building (see photo p34) was completed in 1818 to the design of William Henry Playfair when new life was breathed into the observatory project by the formation of the Edinburgh Astronomical Institution (it became a Royal Observatory after the visit of George IV in 1822).

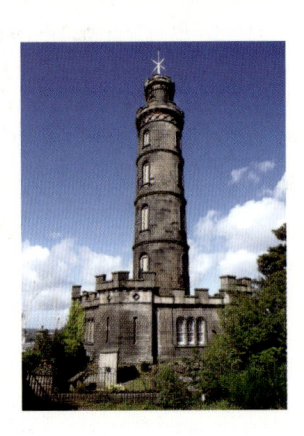

An important function of the observatory was accurate timekeeping and, as part of this, the neighbouring Nelson Monument was used to site a ball which would drop at 1pm each day. Visible from ships in Leith harbour, this saved ships' captains having to visit the observatory to set their chronometers before setting sail. On the south-east corner, the small classical pavilion of 1826 was also designed by Playfair – it is a memorial to his uncle the mathematician and natural philosopher John Playfair, a giant of the Scottish Enlightenment.

As Edinburgh industrialised – particularly the expansion of railways – the air quality became too poor, the Royal Observatory moved to Blackford Hill (see Section 6), and the vacated site was taken over by Edinburgh council for a new City Observatory. The poor air quality also necessitated adding a sound time signal – the One o'clock Gun fired from the castle.

In the third phase, in the 1890s, City Architect Robert Morham added the large copper dome on the north-east of the complex in yellow Binny Sandstone. The observatory closed in 2009 when the Astronomical Society of Edinburgh moved out and the buildings found a new use. A £4.5 million project has transformed the site and opened it up for public access.

Section 1 BIRTH OF THE CITY

At the top is a junction of paths. Keep ascending straight ahead on the left-hand of two paths to reach an open tarmacked area between the domes of the old **City Observatory** and the colonnade of the **National Monument**.

10 The flat surface at the top of this hill is a feature called a glacial pavement, an area scoured level by boulders carried in the ice, some of which were left behind when the ice melted and are now arranged around the tarmac. While this is the hill's highest natural point, continue north down the stepped tarmac path, then right to the lower trig point beyond, which has great views over north Edinburgh to Leith and across the Firth of Forth to Fife.

On this hill there are 8.9 hectares of public open space, which the City of Edinburgh purchased in 1723. It is studded with a picturesque collection of late 18th and 19th century monuments and buildings, which Patrick Geddes called "a museum of the battle of styles". A strange collection, together they form a wonderful skyline when viewed from other parts of the city. The old City

---

The tall tower commemorates Admiral Lord Nelson's 1805 victory at Trafalgar and was begun in 1807, but also suffered funding troubles, not being completed till 1816. It was designed by Robert Burn and is modelled on an upturned telescope.

In 1819 the idea was raised of a memorial to the Scottish soldiers and sailors who died in the Napoleonic Wars. After some public discussion and fundraising, building began in 1822 on a replica of the Parthenon in Athens, exact in all its external details and dimensions; a project which eventually resulted in only the 12 columns visible today.

Architect C.R.Cockerell worked with Playfair on the design and the foundation stone was laid during George IV's visit in 1822. The sandstone came from Craigleith Quarry, where the nature of the rock meant suitably large blocks could be cut, each block reputedly requiring 12 horses and 70 men to haul it the 5km from the quarry.

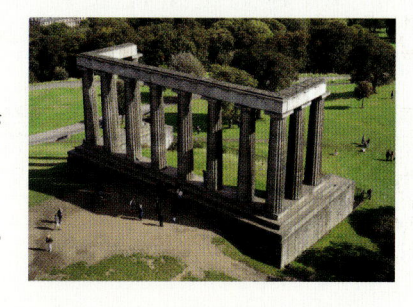

The architrave, which tops the columns, was formed from blocks cut from the largest single stone ever quarried at Craigleith. It measured 41.5m by 6m and weighed 1,524 tonnes and, after cutting these blocks from it, there was still stone left over which was shipped to London for use on Buckingham Palace. The money for this hugely ambitious project was all being raised by public subscription as the work proceeded, but dried up as the memories of the war faded and a banking crisis (which started in 1825) began to bite deeply. The abandoned structure soon acquired the nickname 'Edinburgh's Disgrace'. However, through time, its incompleteness has added extra drama to the skyline and helps reinforce the notion of Edinburgh as the Athens of the North.

Completing the collection is another distinctive monument to the now largely forgotten figure of Dugald Stewart, which was constructed after his death in 1828. This comprises a round Greek temple supported by nine slender columns (see photo p35). Stewart was another giant of the Enlightenment. He was a Professor of Moral Philosophy and became the first to teach Political Philosophy at a university. Among his pupils who went on to be influential in their own right were Lord Palmerston and Sir Walter Scott. This memorial was also designed by Playfair.

Section 1 BIRTH OF THE CITY

The City Observatory's central building, designed in 'classical temple' style by William Henry Playfair in 1818

Observatory complex has recently undergone extensive restoration and conversion works to create the Collective, a centre for contemporary art with free entry (restricted opening times).

> *There are public toilets within the Old Observatory and a kiosk selling takeaway food and drinks*

A new restaurant with a distinctive pyramidal roof, has been built on the north-eastern corner of the compound (booking required). It replaces a derelict, domed pavilion and provides a very modern addition to the architectural ensemble.

Return to the tarmac path between the trig point and the old observatory. Turn right and descend a stepped path. At a junction of paths keep ahead down another section of steps to a T-junction. Go left here and on down to a second T-junction of paths at a stone wall.

Down the steep slope to the left, in the shadow of the hill, is a district called Greenside. Here, there developed a densely populated area which, by the 1950s, was deemed to have become a slum. Over the next decade it was demolished and the population moved to new estates on the city's periphery. It remained a gapsite for over 30 years before being redeveloped.

Turn right and descend the path beside the stone wall to reach the road where Blenheim Place becomes Royal Terrace.

(11) Royal Terrace to the right is a continuation of Regent Terrace which has made its way round the east side of Calton Hill on the level from Regent Bridge. In the triangle created by these streets, and east of the public land on the hill, lies one of Edinburgh's private New Town gardens – Regent Gardens.

While the space around the monuments at the top of the hill was always accessible to the public (and even in past times used as a drying green for laundry), this substantial 4.8 hectare garden was, and still is, only accessible to subscribing key-holders. The public open space coincides with the hard volcanic 'crag' (basalt with some dolerite), while the housing and private Regent Gardens are on a softer sandstone which forms the 'tail' of the hill.

Section 1 BIRTH OF THE CITY

Looking west to the castle from the Duguld Stewart monument on Calton Hill

35

Section 1 BIRTH OF THE CITY

Royal Terrace – integral to Playfair's design for Edinburgh's Third New Town

Cross over Royal Terrace noting the grandeur of its classical houses, then walk a little to the left and turn right onto a path into the gardens ahead. This pleasant little spot is **London Road Gardens** (originally known as Royal Terrace Gardens). Its design was integral to the classical planning of this area and the land was leased from Heriot's Hospital by the council in 1893.

Descend the tarmac path rightwards to pass to the right of a diminutive classical pavilion of 1836 which was the Gardener's Cottage and is

FAILURE OF THE THIRD NEW TOWN

The timing of the third New Town was not good. Work started on the side of Calton Hill where three grand terraces – Royal, Carlton and Regent – were built and private gardens laid out. They took decades to complete and by the time the lower sections north of London Road were being offered to builders, the scheme was in trouble.

There was, by now, serious competition for high-end occupiers from developments in the west end such as the Moray Estate which were proving more popular. As a result, little of William Henry Playfair's planned grand layout stretching down to Leith was actually built.

Hillside Crescent, along with Windsor and Brunswick Streets, did get some buildings to classical designs although the modest scale of the houses in these side streets shows the builders knew that catching the very highest quality occupant was now a lost cause. Whether there was demand for further development here on the north-eastern fringe was a moot point as the banking crisis, which had financially ruined Sir Walter Scott, intervened and halted further development.

Section 1 BIRTH OF THE CITY

AN 'UNCONFORMITY' IN BUILDING

The abrupt change in architectural style from the Classical of the Regency period to the later Victorian tenements of the late 19th century can be seen all around Edinburgh. It is almost like an unconformity in geology, where two strata of rocks of vastly different ages occur side by side. This came about as a result of the financial crash of 1825-6 which had long term consequences for Edinburgh. While investment in house building dried up, population was still on the increase as people migrated in from rural areas (and Ireland), so increasing the density of population in the Old Town and causing old housing to slide into overcrowded slums.

The change in style of development had a bearing on open spaces too. The Classical style often incorporated communal private gardens into street layouts, but land economics often worked against this in later Victorian times and the city was required to provide land for public parks. Where open space was left by developers, it was often for new organised sports such as bowling.

now a restaurant of that name. Prior to the development of this area, which was known as Upper Quarry Holes, there were quarries here, at one time worked by a builder called William Jamieson who will be encountered again later in the walk. Being distant from the town, these quarries were also a favourite site for duels.

On reaching the main road (where **Leopold Place** on the left becomes **London Road** on the right), cross over and head slightly left to enter **Hillside Crescent**. The small Hillside Crescent Garden was purchased by the council in 1952, along with Royal Terrace Gardens. Originally private for the use of local householders only, the social mix of the area had changed by the 1890s and there was a pressing need for more public parks and gardens. Together, these two gardens cover just under 10 hectares. Like Royal Terrace Gardens, Hillside Crescent Garden was laid out as part of William Henry Playfair's Third New Town Plan, as were the roads radiating to its north.

Look out for number 11 Hillside Crescent, an original Playfair house built for Mr Allen of Hillside, one of the three landowners who jointly agreed to feu their land for the third New Town scheme, the other two being Heriot's Hospital and Trinity Hospital.

Here the route leaves the dramatic volcanic scenery behind for now and crosses onto a coastal plain, a landscape created from material deposited when the area was under water in a past geological era. It also leaves behind 'Classical Edinburgh' with its porticos, colonnades and ironwork balconies to enter the Edinburgh of the later 19th century.

House building in Edinburgh virtually came to a standstill in the wake of the 1825-6 banking crash and by the time building on any scale had resumed in the city in the 1870s-80s, styles had changed dramatically, although the tenements on the next section of Hillside Crescent (by John Chesser 1880s) nod to Playfair's style with porticos and columns.

Take the third left into **Wellington Street**. The

Regent Gardens – key-holders only

Section 1 BIRTH OF THE CITY

Mural in Montgomery Street Park

handsome tenements here have full height bay windows and date from the 1890s when building in this part of Edinburgh had revived. In the years between the building phases seen here, this district was utterly transformed by the arrival of the railways, bringing industry in their wake.

12 At the end of Wellington Street cross **Montgomery Street** and enter a small park through a gate on the right. This little park was originally laid out as a recreation ground and bowling green, which provided a buffer zone between the more aspirant tenements for the clerking class of Wellington and Montgomery Streets and the more working class streets, which had been built earlier, immediately to the north.

Cross the park diagonally right to emerge on **Elgin Street** at the junction with Elgin Terrace. Here in a little triangle between Elgin Terrace, Elgin Street and Brunswick Road, once stood four rows of tenements built to accommodate workers at the large North British Railway's Leith Walk Goods Station on the north side of Brunswick Road. This little enclave of closely packed streets was known as Chinatown because of the density of the population, rather than because it had Chinese families

living there. The individual flats were small – just two rooms – and, lacking basic facilities, were demolished under slum clearance around 1970. Latterly the goods yard became a Post Office distribution depot but has now been redeveloped as flats.

Walk left up Elgin Terrace, turn right into **Edina Street** and follow it to Middleton's pub on the corner of Easter Road. **Easter Road** was the main route from Edinburgh to the Port at Leith until the opening of the North Bridge in 1772. By then, a stagecoach service had been operating along the route for more than 150 years – the first regular stagecoach service in Scotland. However, the building of tenements along its length dates mainly from the early years of the 20th century.

> *To the right, Easter Road has a small selection of pubs and cafes*

Turn left and walk north up Easter Road, then cross over right into **Bothwell Street.** At the top of the building on the left, note the name Andrew Whyte & Son Ltd, a large printing and wholesale stationers who moved here in 1898, and on the right the typical

Section 1 BIRTH OF THE CITY

working class plain-fronted stone tenements circa 1880s.

⑬ Follow Bothwell Street as it bends left, then cross the pedestrian **Crawford Bridge** to **Albion Terrace**. The bridge spans a section of the North British Railway line that once led west to the Leith Walk Goods Station, then on to Granton and round to Leith docks. East of here was a large and complex junction of lines and railway sidings. The bridge's name is possibly a connection with the Leith biscuit manufacturers Crawford's who were major employers in the area up to the closure of their Elbe Street factory in 1970.

Built in the 1920s, this bridge provided a convenient shortcut for local workers but may have been an early attempt to show how the controversial enlargement of Edinburgh in 1920 to take in Leith, could benefit the smaller town. At this date, Leith's population was 80,000 compared to Edinburgh's 320,000; Leith's council fought hard to retain its independence but ultimately failed.

Close proximity to the railway encouraged industrial premises and working class housing and the area built-up rapidly. Straight ahead, the handsome former Norton Park School, now a business centre, was built for the expanding population. In the 1950s its staff and pupils made a film called *The Singing Street* to record, for posterity, the street games and songs of local children, capturing the end of an era (viewable on YouTube).

Turn right into **Albion Road** and follow it round to Easter Road Stadium, home of Hibernian, one of Edinburgh's two Scottish Premiership football teams (the other being Heart of Midlothian who play at Tynecastle Park in Gorgie in the west of the city), another indication that this area was home to a working-class community.

Around the stadium a few buildings remain from the area's industrial past. On the right, the red sandstone building facing the stadium has

The former Norton Park School on Albion Road – creator of the 1950 film The Singing Street

Section 1 BIRTH OF THE CITY

James Dunbar's former lemonade and soft drinks works on Lochend Butterfly Way

RB&Co above the main door and was once part of Redpath Brown & Co structural engineering works, which located here in 1896. Beyond the stadium on the left, an access road leads to the former lemonade and soft drinks works of James Dunbar. The southern end of the stadium is still known as the Dunbar End.

Continue past the stadium. The route has now crossed out of Edinburgh into Leith, to reach a crossroads, and turn left into **Lochend Butterfly Way**. The development site here is called The Butterfly but it has nothing to do with nature; the land was formerly covered by a complex railway junction on the North British Railway's network which, on plan, looked like the shape of butterfly wings. On the left, a low stone wall, in front of part of Dunbar's Works, was the former edge of railway land and is the only clue to the land's former use.

Follow this road as it bends right. Then, where it turns left, go right onto a path and follow this downhill into **Lochend Park** to reach the loch's edge.

14 Turn right and go anti-clockwise around the loch, keeping left at the next junction to remain at the lochside, where the path is squeezed between the water and a cliff topped by Lochend House.

This park was originally the gardens of the house and open grazing meadows. It was acquired by Edinburgh council (on a lease) and opened as a public park in 1907, securing

---

LOCHEND CASTLE & HOUSE

Lochend House dates from around 1820 but incorporates some stonework from Lochend Castle, a much older structure, probably from the 16th century. This older stonework is what can be glimpsed through the trees from the lochside. The De Lestalric family, who have given their name to the surrounding area of Restalrig, had some sort of fortified house on this eminently defendable site as early as the 14th century.

Restalrig was a barony and an important settlement in its own right. Several owners of this property have played a part in Scottish history, including Robert Logan who was a supporter of Mary Queen of Scots but who later fell from grace over political conspiracies. After the council acquired the house, it was used as a clinic before lying empty for some years.

Section 1 BIRTH OF THE CITY

> ## LOCHEND DOVECOT
>
> *This structure dates from the 16th century when it was built to house pigeons, kept both for food in winter and to use their droppings as manure. Unusually, there is also a chimney, leading to the suggestion that it was used to burn clothes and bedding during times of plague.*
>
> *Centuries later this modest structure found a new use as a boathouse for the Humane Society who had a presence here to rescue skaters who fell through the ice. Skating has a long history in Scotland and it was in Edinburgh that the world's first skating club was formed, with records dating back to 1778. At that time the climate of northern Europe was in the grip of a short, intensely cold period known as the Little Ice Ages and, as the area around Edinburgh was studded with little lochs, it is perhaps not surprising that skating became a popular winter exercise. The small hexagonal building nearby is a pumping house for Leith's 18th century water supply; both it and the dovecot are listed buildings.*

8.5 hectares of open space for the residents of a district that was becoming very densely developed. Local lore has it that the loch is bottomless and it is certainly unusually deep (it may be a post-glacial feature called a 'kettle hole' like Loch Leven in Fife). For safety reasons, it was partly infilled in the 1960s to reduce its depth and surrounded by a fence. The water level of the loch is maintained by natural underground springs and, from 1753 to 1771, it was the sole source of a piped water supply to Leith. Today the loch is home to a wide variety of wildfowl.

Continue round to where the path opens out again to reach a play area and turn right to Lochend Dovecot ('doocot' in Scots) and a fine view of Arthur's Seat nestling in the distance behind the loch. After the doocot, take the path to the right to exit the park onto **Lochend Road South**, turn left and then take the second left into **Hawkhill Avenue**.

15 The area here is largely one of inter-war council housing; the utilitarian appearance is down to the timing of construction when the generous central government subsidies, which had been introduced in the post WWI 'Homes

Lochend Dovecot and loch, with Holyrood Park and Arthur's Seat in the distance

Section 1 BIRTH OF THE CITY

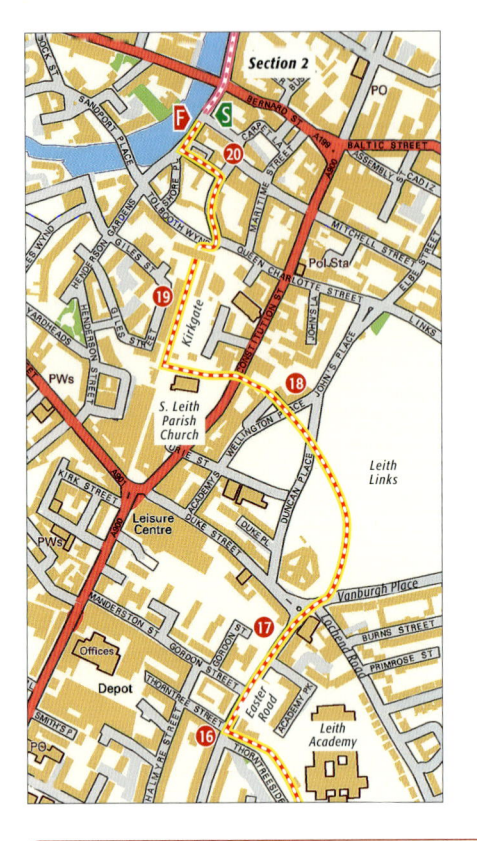

Fit for Heroes' housing drive, had been withdrawn. To continue to provide affordable housing – and remove slums in the Old Town – the city had to abandon building cottages on garden city principles and return to higher density blocks of flats. The design of these flats is likely to be down to the City Engineer Adam Horsburgh Campbell.

Walk up Hawkhill Avenue and cross at a pedestrian crossing to take a path, signposted **Restalrig Railway Path**, which zigzags down to the right to a T-junction. Two railways once crossed here but never connected. The North British Railway's branch to Leith Central ran south-north in a cutting (now filled in but old stone walls still mark its former boundaries) having come up the west side of Lochend Park, while the Caledonian Railway's freight-only Leith New Lines crossed it east-west. Turn left onto this path, signposted for **Leith Academy**, Easter Road and the Foot of Leith Walk, and continue in a north-westerly direction, following the route of the Caledonian's line.

The competition in the late 19th century between the North British and the Caledonian companies, and the subsequent demise of the suburban railway network, has given north Edinburgh a legacy of non-road routes which

---

LEITH & EDINBURGH – A COMPLICATED RELATIONSHIP

The harbour at Leith came under Edinburgh's ownership in medieval times and Leith was the underdog in this early relationship. Edinburgh was not just a burgh it was a Royal Burgh, so its freemen enjoyed the most liberal trading rights, including the right to sell goods abroad. Leith men could own ships but could not trade their cargo within the town, so it had to be taken to Edinburgh to be sold by Edinburgh merchants.

These rules were relaxed over the years as the medieval gave way to the mercantile age – particularly under Cromwell's Commonwealth. Leith gained burgh status in 1833 following the Great Reform Act. At this date, development of its new docks led to huge financial problems and Edinburgh seemed happy to cut the ties.

Independence for the new burgh did not get off to a good start as badly drafted legislation left Leith with no ability to raise money. Although this difficulty was resolved a few years later, ongoing money worries were a contributory factor in Leith once again losing its administrative independence in 1920, when it was fully absorbed into Edinburgh (despite Leithers rejecting the move by a large margin in a referendum). Although now formally part of Edinburgh, Leith's residents would argue that it very much retains its own identity.

Section 1 BIRTH OF THE CITY

> ## LEITH, A FORTIFIED TOWN
>
> *In 1544 the strategic importance of Leith in relation to Edinburgh became clear as the English began a brutal invasion, later named by Sir Walter Scott as the "Rough Wooing". This invasion was intended to force Scotland to agree to a marriage between Edward, son of England's Henry VIII, and the infant Mary Queen of Scots, (Mary I of Scotland).*
>
> *English soldiers under the Earl of Hertford landed further west at Wardie and marched on Leith to seize the port, thereby allowing greater numbers of troops and supplies to be brought in for an attack on Edinburgh. Four years later, Mary of Guise, the widow of James V, moved the Scottish Parliament to Leith and ordered a massive defence be built to prevent a repeat of the invasion which she feared would happen after a marriage treaty had been agreed between the infant Queen and the Dauphin of France.*
>
> *These defences ran roughly along the line of modern-day Bernard Street, Constitution Street and Great Junction Street, with a short stretch north of the Water of Leith running down to the seafront. This massive wall, although an earthwork, was built to the latest continental military designs under Monsieur De'Esse, the commander of the French troops. Mary of Guise had invited the French to Leith to protect the catholic Auld Alliance as the pro-Protestant forces in Edinburgh intensified. Leith was then besieged through 1559-60 by English troops dug in on the Links. With the siege came famine and the south-west quarter of the town was burnt down. But the defences held, the siege only ending when Mary of Guise died and a surrender and removal of the wall was negotiated under the Treaty of Edinburgh.*
>
> *Within a century religious strife was once again tearing Scotland apart as Charles I attempted to impose the Episcopalian version of protestantism on Scotland. His opponents found themselves in common cause with the English Parliamentarians in the Civil War but, following the beheading of Charles I, this common cause was broken.*
>
> *In 1649, anticipating Oliver Cromwell's New Model Army would now invade, the Scots rebuilt the defences at Leith and constructed a long dyke from the town up to Calton Hill (it later became Leith Walk). After the Scottish army was defeated at the battle of Dunbar in 1650, Leith was occupied and ruled for the next eight years as part of the English Commonwealth and Cromwell built a new Citadel at Leith (on the west side of the Water of Leith).*

have been well-utilised for paths and cycle routes. This line was a late part of the network, built to bring coal from West Lothian to the docks, which was only completed in 1903 and closed in 1973. Its retention, and use as a path, provides a valuable ribbon of green through the surrounding urban area. This path was given a substantial upgrade in 2012 and is now a well-used cycle route.

The path curves round enclosing the playing fields of the new Leith Academy (1991 Lothian Region Architects) but it cuts through an area that was previously industrial. To the left was Dobson & Molle's St Clair printing works, then the huge St Ann's Maltings, while to the right was a sawmill. The latter two both had direct rail connections. Old maps show the historic name for this area as Nether Quarryholes, indicating stone working in the area before the development of these other industries.

16 Emerge back onto **Easter Road** and turn right. Keep to the right-hand side of the road but note Gordon Street, the second street on the left. For enthusiasts of railway architecture, a stretch of handsome red sandstone railway arches survives a short distance down this street. These arches, and those beyond in Jane Street across Leith Walk, carried the Leith New Lines, the continuation of the Caledonian's

43

Section 1 BIRTH OF THE CITY

The incongruous central block of flats in pale brick, mark the point where the railway lines into Leith Central Station crossed Easter Road on a wide metal girder bridge

line. In recent years it has been mooted that this elevated line could be utilised to make a park in the style of New York's High Line Park, in the process improving the cycle route network.

🔟 A short distance further on, there is a Tesco supermarket on the left. This was the site of the huge **Leith Central Station** railway terminus built in 1903 by the North British Railway at the end of a branch line from

> ### LEITH CENTRAL STATION
>
> *Opened in 1903, Leith Central Station was built by the North British Railway at the same time that the company was rebuilding Waverley Station. Like Waverley, it was topped by a huge ridge and furrow glass roof. The tracks came into the station from the south-east, crossing the bottom of Easter Road on a metal lattice girder bridge, breaking through pre-existing buildings (see photo above) and arriving at a high-level above a lower concourse. The main station access was on the other side, at the corner of Duke Street and Leith Walk, where some of the station buildings, including the distinctive clock tower, have been retained.*
>
> *Always too big and grand for what was effectively a suburban branch line, traffic dwindled further when Edinburgh expanded to take in Leith in 1920 and the two separate tram systems were merged to offer more convenient travel between the two centres. The station closed to passengers in 1952 but continued in use as an engine depot for a further 20 years.*
>
> *The vast derelict station shed achieved notoriety in the 1980s when it became a shooting gallery for heroin addicts and is pivotal in Irvine Welsh's novel Trainspotting in a scene where the author implies a parallel between the pointlessness of the hobby of trainspotting and the 'hobby' of drug-taking.*

Section 1 BIRTH OF THE CITY

HISTORIC LEITH LINKS

'Links' indicates a landscape of sandy hummocks by the sea which is covered in rough vegetation. However, the sense of this park as being by a sandy shore has long since been obliterated by the building of the docks

Long a place of recreation, the sands were the scene of horse racing and the Links also have a long association with golf; Charles I and James VII (II in England) are noted as having played here while staying in Edinburgh. The Honourable Company of Edinburgh Golfers, dating back to 1744, was originally based on the Links and here they produced 13 Rules of Golf which were subsequently adopted by the Royal and Ancient Golf Club of St Andrews. At this time, Leith was also a fashionable seaside resort with good sea bathing and the Links are flanked with handsome classical terraces from the subsequent decades.

Further back, during the Siege of Leith in 1560, the English army dug trenches here when they came to the aid of the Scots in a bloody battle to expel the French who, under Mary of Guise, had held Leith for 12 years. It was also the site of mass burials during the 1645 plague outbreak.

In 1888 the natural terrain of the Links was flattened to create a formal Victorian park, with walks and avenues of trees as part of a wider Leith Improvement Plan. Two mounds were left, Giant's Brae to the west of the park and Lady Fife's Brae to the east, as, at the time, they were thought to be gun emplacements dating from the Siege of Leith (now doubted); these mounds, like the mature trees, add topographical interest to what could otherwise be a flat and featureless landscape. The formal park was much smaller than the Links had been in previous times but still provided a much needed open space as the town industrialised.

Waverley. As already seen, the line came up the west side of Lochend Loch, passed under the Caledonian's railway line at Hawkhill, then through what is now the new Leith Academy site to cross Easter Road into the station. An incongruous modern infill block of flats opposite the car park entrance marks where the lines crossed the road on a metal girder bridge. The train shed covered the whole of the supermarket, the soft play area and the car park. The high stone wall on the north side of the car park shows the delineation between the faced stonework above platform level and the unfaced stonework below.

Continue in a northerly direction to the roundabout at the bottom of Easter Road. Ahead is the imposing former Leith Academy building designed in 1931 by Reid & Forbes. The site was previously occupied by John Watt's Hospital, an endowed charitable institution built in 1862 for 'destitute aged men and women'. Prior to the construction of Watt's

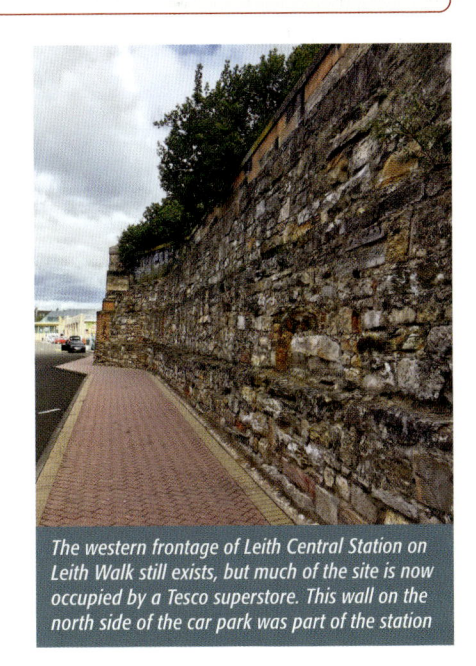

The western frontage of Leith Central Station on Leith Walk still exists, but much of the site is now occupied by a Tesco superstore. This wall on the north side of the car park was part of the station

45

Section 1 BIRTH OF THE CITY

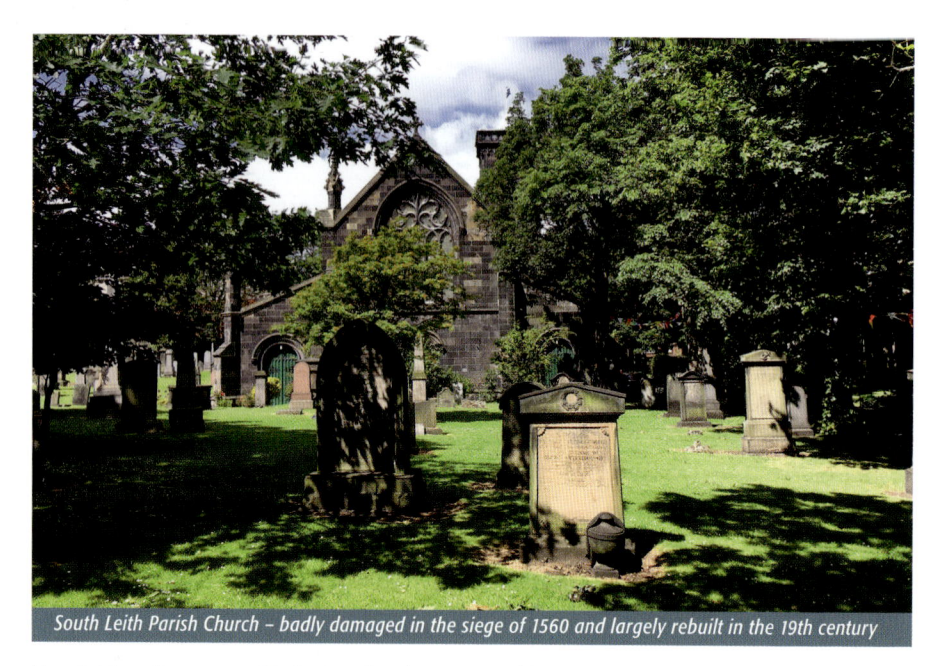

South Leith Parish Church – badly damaged in the siege of 1560 and largely rebuilt in the 19th century

Hospital the site was notable for housing the first clubhouse for the Honourable Company of Edinburgh Golfers. In 1831 the club got into financial difficulties and was forced to move east to Musselburgh and later Muirfield.

Keep right to cross **Lochend Road**, then continue round to **Vanburgh Place** facing the park with its elegant houses dating from the 1820s and cross at the traffic lights to enter Leith Links. This pleasant open park covers approximately 20 hectares. Three paths radiate out from the park entrance. Take the middle one, passing a large earth mound known as 'Giant Brae', then the second path on the left to head towards a large stone building. Cross **Duncan Place** to reach **John's Place** at the junction with **Wellington Place** and pass to the left of this building.

18 This and the adjoining building are both bonded warehouses, which were once very common in Leith. The older of the two dates from 1862 and is the one with the oversized rope moulding above the door; the neighbouring one is from 1898. Together they give a flavour of the industrial and commercial architecture of Leith in its economic heyday.

Continue ahead down Wellington Place to **Links Lane**, a narrow path with a stone wall on its right. This emerges onto **Constitution Street**. Cross slightly left and enter through the gates of **South Leith Parish Church**. As the route crossed Constitution Street it traversed Leith's medieval walls and its new tramline.

Cross the churchyard on the path to the right of the church. The colonnades to the right contain Commonwealth War Graves from WWI. In the closely built up medieval town, the churchyard would have been a rare bit of open space. The church started in the 15th century as a chapel dedicated to St Mary and only became the parish church in 1609. What remains today is smaller than the original, which suffered damage from bombardment in the siege of 1560 and, by the early 19th century, was in a sorry state. The steeple was no longer standing straight and was demolished in 1836. Ten years later, there was a major rebuilding of what remained, including a new square tower to the designs of Thomas

46

Section 1 BIRTH OF THE CITY

Hamilton. The church is now category A listed.

Exit the churchyard onto a broad paved footpath, the remains of the medieval thoroughfare of Kirkgate. From ancient times until the 1950s this was one of the most important streets in the town – a bustling thoroughfare full of shops, pubs and even a theatre. The utter transformation of this area of the town by slum clearance and comprehensive redevelopment is hard to comprehend by anyone who did not know the area before. While we may look with hindsight at photographs of old Leith and lament the loss of such an ancient place and its medieval relics, back in the post-war years the housing conditions of the poor were of highest importance. Questions were even being asked in Parliament by Leith MP James Hoy in 1957 as to why plans for radical slum clearance were progressing so slowly.

On exiting the churchyard, one of the few surviving old buildings on Kirkgate can be seen opposite. This is the category A listed **Trinity House** dating from 1818 and designed by Thomas Brown. Built on the vaults of the 16th century hall of the Incorporation of Masters and Mariners, the oldest but not the only guild in medieval Leith. There were also guilds for maltmen, brewers, sledders, carters, craftsmen and corn meal men and merchants. By the 19th century the guild initiated formal training schemes for mariners. Turn right here down the broad avenue flanked by low ranges of post-war flats. (Turning left would lead to the modern shopping mall called the Newkirkgate, 10 minutes).

19 Continue straight ahead. The 11-storey behemoth looming in front is **Linksview House** by Alison & Hutchison (1964-7) designed as part of the replacement housing for the slum clearance scheme. Climb the steps onto the windswept and neglected podium and, keeping to the right, follow the path which passes under the block of flats, to emerge on **Tolbooth Wynd** on the other side.

The name Tolbooth Wynd relates to a building which stood on this site between 1564 and 1824 – the Leith Tolbooth, a sort of

Trinity House on Kirkgate is now a Maritime Museum celebrating Leith's long seafaring history

Section 1 BIRTH OF THE CITY

Leith's medieval Kirkgate culminates at its northern end, with the 11-storey Linksview House

medieval town hall – marking this as the administrative centre of the bustling medieval town. There was a market behind the Tolbooth, just west of where the podium is now.

On Tolbooth Wynd there is a small play area in front of the block, which was created by the demolition of old property. An often overlooked part of post-war urban planning was the desire to create little pocket parks to provide open spaces for inner city residents. In its conception, this little park is a close relation of the pocket parks that Patrick Geddes created in Edinburgh's Old Town in the late 19th century, an example of which was encountered on Johnston Terrace at the start of this section.

Turn right on Tolbooth Wynd and follow it round, then left down **Water Street** to reach the pale coloured and pantile roofed 17th century merchant's house on the corner of Burgess Street.

[20] Lamb's House, also known as Andrew Lamb's House, was gifted to the National Trust for Scotland by the Marquess of Bute in 1958. In 2010, the category A listed building was sold to Groves-Raines Architects who have restored and refurbished it. Back in the 17th century,

there were several other grand merchant's mansions in this part of Leith and a flavour of this prosperous period of the town's history remains.

By the mid-19th century this once prosperous and bustling part of town had sunk low despite the flourishing docks and was described by a contemporary source as "buildings… huddled together without order or

The 17th century Andrew Lamb's House

Section 1 BIRTH OF THE CITY

regularity and the streets and lanes are, for the most part, narrow, crooked and filthy". It was a similar story to Edinburgh's Old Town but Old Leith had no equivalent of Patrick Geddes to save it from destruction.

Turn left in front of Lamb's House and follow **Burgess Street** to the Water of Leith and the broad quayside called **Shore**.

> 🍽 Here, stretching north along Shore, is a selection of pubs, restaurants and cafes if a toilet stop is required

Before 1806, when the first of the enclosed docks opened, it was here on the quays of Shore that all cargoes were loaded and landed; this was the harbour. Indeed, in medieval times, this was the only place where it was permissible to load and unload ships, as it was here that the Edinburgh officials, much to the chagrin of the Leith merchants, examined the cargoes and assessed them for taxes. Now quiet and picturesque, this area once bustled with ships and commerce. Like much of Leith it suffered from the loss of local industries but has been revived in recent decades. Much of what seems old has been restored or even reinstated, so all is not quite as it seems.

While the river is the heart of Leith, it also originally divided the town into two areas, North and South Leith. Section 1 has travelled through South Leith, which was always the larger of the two. Section 2 will explore over the bridge into North Leith. 🇫

> 🚌 Lothian bus 22 back to Princes Street from the stop at the south end of Shore, just down from its junction with Henderson Street, Tollbooth Wynd and Sandport Place. Alternatively, Lothian bus 35 goes to the Royal Mile from the stop on Shore south of the Bernard Street-Commercial Street bridge over the Water of Leith. The 36 leaves from the same place to Stockbridge and the West End

POST-WAR SLUM CLEARANCES

After a century of industrial development and population growth, housing in the old centre of Leith was overcrowded and insanitary. There were some attempts at improvement from the 1880s (when among other things Henderson Street was cut through old lanes). In the idealistic years after WWII, came a more concerted attempt to improve housing conditions of the poorest Leithers on a much larger scale, by using the planning principles of slum clearances and comprehensive redevelopment.

The 11-storey Linksview House explains much about the aims of these policies. Not only were the old tenements of Leith overcrowded and lacking in such basic amenities as bathrooms and private toilets, but they were densely packed, with a lack of open spaces. The planners, in advocating blocks such as this, were trying to square the circle. They wished to give every family more space within their homes to allow for bathrooms and two or three bedrooms, as well as creating outdoor spaces where children could play safely.

The ideal was a family house with a garden in the tradition of the garden suburb but, so dense was the population in Leith, it was just not possible to rehouse everyone on the footprint of the demolished old properties. The only way to make space, both within and outside the flats, was to pile them up high. Even in building high, the overall population had to be reduced and many Leithers were rehoused outside the core of the district in new, large, peripheral housing schemes during the town's many post-war slum clearance schemes.

Linksview House was category A listed in 2017 being considered as "among the best of Scotland's post-war mass urban housing schemes".

'Fish and Boat' sculpture at the entrance to Commercial Quay, Leith docks

Section 2
HARBOUR TO HARBOUR

Route: Leith to Granton
Distance: 8km; 5 miles
Grade: Easy flat walking, much of it along the routes of disused railways. Many of the paths are shared with cyclists. There are few cafes or toilet facilities, except at the start
Access: Lothian bus 22 from Princes Street, buses 35 from the Royal Mile or 36 from Stockbridge and the West End to Leith (*Shore bus stop*)

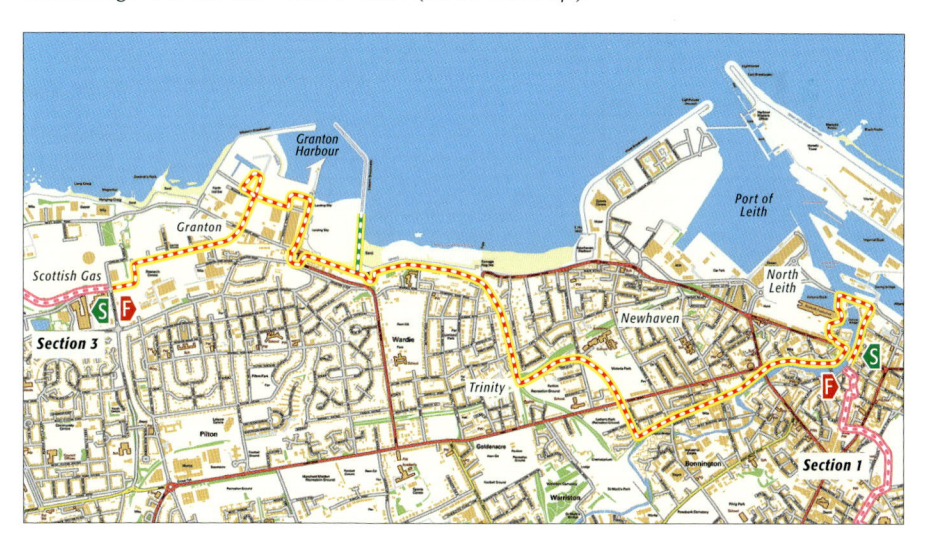

Having reached Leith and the coast, the route heads west. The shoreline is extensively built up between Leith and Newhaven, and although the latter is an ancient settlement with its own small harbour and history, it currently has no significant green spaces. As a consequence, the route initially turns inland at Leith and follows the areas of green space created from deindustrialisation – the north bank of the Water of Leith and the network of old railway lines around Trinity – before rejoining the coast to encounter a partially infilled harbour and an expansive area of urban regeneration

To start Section 2, head north along **Shore**, with the Water of Leith on your left. Cobbles maintain the air of an ancient place and the buildings are a mixture of restorations, Victorian rebuilds and new infill flats. Of note on the right is The King's Wark just before the junction with Bernard Street. The current building dates from the 18th century (restored 1975 and category A listed), but the royal connection dates back to medieval times when James I established a residence, storehouse and arsenal on the site. The building passed through several owners and uses; in the 16th century it was the tolbooth and at one point it

51

Section 2 HARBOUR TO HARBOUR

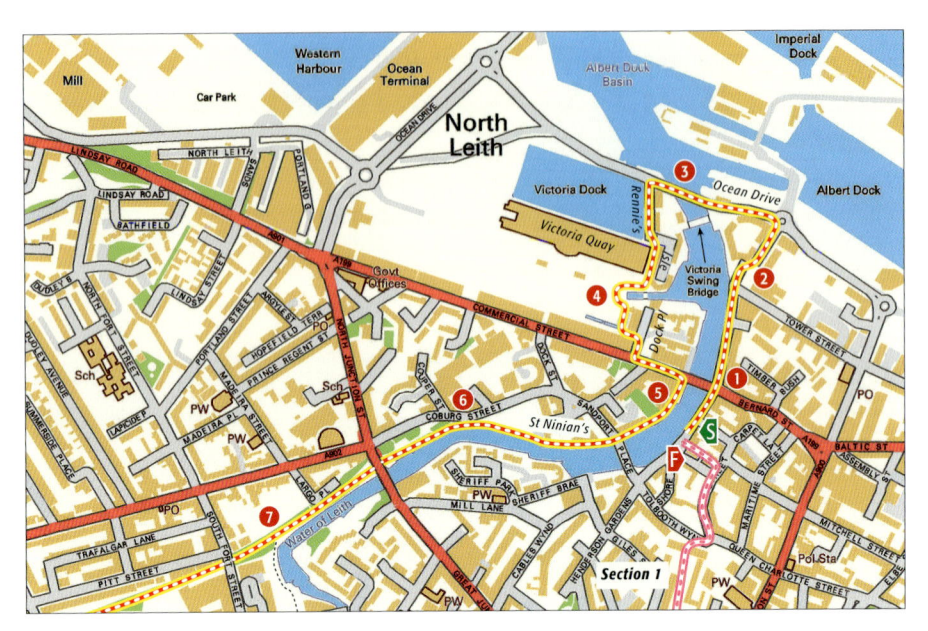

also included a Real Tennis court.

Cross the main road, **Bernard Street**, beyond which Shore has an almost continental air. This road has been the focus for Leith's regeneration since the inception of The Leith Project in the late 1970s, although some long-term Leith residents may feel the protection of 'heritage' and provision of upmarket eating places has not met their needs.

❶ The first of the low-gabled buildings, with the ironwork ship and large lantern (a replica) over the door, is The Old Ship Inn. This was one of three inns which catered for the needs of Edinburgh travellers arriving and departing by ship before the age of stagecoach and steam train. This old inn burned down and was rebuilt in sympathetic style in 1888. It now houses The Ship on the Shore seafood bar and restaurant. Beyond the archway, the next building has a carved doorpiece inscribed 1678 and was the New Ship Inn (the upper floors were subsequently rebuilt). The third inn on Shore was the Britannia but it is now gone.

The archway between the inns has the curious name **Timber Bush**, a modern corruption of Timber Bourse, bourse being French for market. The site was the exchange for the timber trade which for centuries was carried on between Leith and the Baltic States. Leith was always the main connecting gateway for the Auld Alliance between Scotland and France (including importing wine), but it was also the premier port for trade across the North Sea. A fine collection of warehouses survived in the Timber Bush till the 1980s when a fire destroyed over half of them. Look out by the waterside for a plaque commemorating the spot where George IV landed on his historic visit of 1822.

The next building along, **Maritime House,** only dates from the 1950s, but again the doorpiece of an earlier building has been incorporated. The lampstands are not original, but the cobbles closest to the river have a stretch of railway track embedded in them, part of the dock rail network that connected the two banks of the river via a drawbridge.

A round stone tower stands at the corner of Shore and **Tower Street** and is one of the oldest buildings in Leith. Category A listed, Leith Signal Tower dates from 1686 and was originally a windmill, built to grind rapeseed oil

Section 2 HARBOUR TO HARBOUR

LEITH'S EASTERN DOCKS

After a couple of decades of debate and inaction, the Leith Dock Commissioners constructed a series of docks on reclaimed land on the east side of the Water of Leith, in response to developments in ship construction as sail gave way to steam. First was Albert Dock (1869, designed by the engineers A.M.Rendel). This was larger and deeper than any of the western Georgian docks and had a wider entrance lock. The Edinburgh Dock was constructed to the east of this in 1874-81 (named for Prince Alfred, the Duke of Edinburgh, who performed the opening ceremony); the retaining wall used rubble rock quarried at Craigmillar (see p153).

As shipping tonnage increased, a further 32 hectares were reclaimed north of the Albert Dock, from which the Imperial Dock was excavated and opened in 1902. This was the biggest dock so far with 8 hectares of open water and a 12m depth. Dock trade peaked on the eve of WWI when exports were dominated by coal from the Lothian coalfield, but fish, finished goods such as cloth, pig iron and steel were also crucial. Imports were more varied and reflected the needs of local industry – grain, hemp, hides, tallow, timber, esparto grass (for papermaking), wine and wool, as well as tobacco, fruit and tinned meat.

at a time when this was an exposed windy site on the shoreline. The builder was the master stonemason Robert Mylne who worked on Holyrood Palace among other projects and was also the grandfather of William Mylne the architect/builder of the first North Bridge.

❷ Keep straight ahead across a plaza. In the middle of this stands a memorial commemorating the role of the Merchant Navy, which suffered proportionately higher losses than the armed services in WWII. Designed by Benjamin Tindall Architects and sculpted by Jill Watson, it was unveiled by the Princess Royal in 2010. It is appropriately sited in front of a large baronial style building which was built in 1885 as an establishment for

Memorial to the seamen of the Merchant Navy at the plaza between Shore and Tower Place

53

Section 2 HARBOUR TO HARBOUR

The former Northern Lighthouse Board ship Fingal, now repurposed as a luxury floating hotel and restaurant

seamen of all ranks when ashore; now restored and repurposed as a hotel and restaurant.

Pass to the right of the memorial and proceed through the contemporary metal gates, which have been added to the posts of the old dock gates, into **Tower Place** and reclaimed land. The shoreline here did not form a natural harbour other than the shelter provided by the mouth of the Water of Leith, beyond which there was a large sandbar. The building of enclosed 'wet' docks began around 1800 on the other side of the river, while the first dock basin on this side was opened in the 1860s. The third and last phase of dock building created the Western Harbour lock gates and was only undertaken in the 1960s.

Continue along Tower Place past modern flats on the left and the former Dock and Harbour offices (1892) on the right, to reach a

LEITH'S MERCHANT FLEET

The names of the great shipping lines of Leith are now all but forgotten. George Gibson & Co – dating back to 1797 and initially North Sea trade but, after the opening of the Suez Canal, routes to the far east. James Currie & Co – mostly trading with northern English and Baltic ports. William Thomson & Co – known as the Ben Line, not the most ships but the biggest tonnage as it operated larger ships primarily for trading with the Far East. Christian Salvesen – large general trade but specialist whaling fleet from the 1860s. James Cormack & Co – mostly traded with the Russian ports of Riga and Archangel.

Other smaller companies traded with the Orkney & Shetland Islands, Belfast, Amsterdam, Iceland and America. Between them these companies lost nearly 50 ships to enemy action in WWI and this slowed down the growth of the docks.

Section 2 HARBOUR TO HARBOUR

> ## THE MODERN PORT
>
> Leith is now part of a larger grouping called Forth Ports (which despite its name also includes Dundee and Tilbury on the Thames), and continues to be the largest enclosed deep-water port in Scotland. But it has been Grangemouth – with its superior road connectivity – which has claimed the bulk of the container trade and Leith has had to seek other business in addition to its core services.
>
> It has proved a popular port for cruise ships and after Robb's shipyard closed, its site on the Western Harbour was used to build the Ocean Terminal Shopping Centre in 2001 and the decommissioned Royal Yacht Britannia – now a tourist attraction – is now moored alongside. The western side of the port is now undergoing land reclamation and residential development.

mini-roundabout and turn left along **Ocean Drive**, following the new tramline. The water to the right is the Alexandra Graving Dock (1894-6 P.Whyte), now home to the Fingal, a Northern Lighthouse Board ship repurposed as a hotel. Behind that is the Prince of Wales Graving Dock (1858), the first dock on the east side of the river. Like the Alexandra dock it originally had gates allowing it to be drained to facilitate ship repairs. The pumps for draining this dock were contained in the Italianate building behind (1863 A.M.Rendel), and now the Forth Ports offices. The docks on the east side of the Water of Leith are still very much operational and largely intact, despite a small section of the Edinburgh Dock being filled in. Sadly none of the original quayside sheds have survived.

❸ Cross the Water of Leith on the modern road bridge with the **Victoria Swing Bridge** (1874 A.M.Rendel) now to the left. Constructed of riveted wrought iron bow trusses, its hydraulic mechanism allowed it to swing open. The small red sandstone building to the right (1896 P.Whyte) held the machinery for the bridge and for draining the Alexandra dock. The bridge carried a footway and a railway, connecting the docks on the east and west sides of the river, while at the same time still allowing ships to navigate up the Water of Leith. When constructed, its 37m clear span made it the longest swing bridge in Britain. Upstream of the swing bridge is the small inner harbour and downstream is the much

When completed in 1874, the Victoria Swing Bridge was the longest of its type in Britain

Section 2 HARBOUR TO HARBOUR

Looking back to Shore from the Victoria Swing Bridge, with Leith Signal Tower on the left

SHIPBUILDING AT LEITH

Shipbuilding in Leith ceased in 1984 after a long history – the last yard working was Henry Robb, while one of the first recorded shipbuilders was John Corton in 1439. In 1818, shipwright Thomas Morton, who could not afford to construct a dry dock, patented a cradle slipway for hauling large ships out of the water; it was a significant invention and helped his business flourish for decades.

In 1837 Menzies, a business started in 1664, launched a wooden hulled paddle steamer the SS Sirius which, the following year, became the first ship to cross the Atlantic using only steam. It was in a race against the mighty Great Western, but the much smaller Sirius, only designed for crossing the Irish Sea, managed to arrive a day ahead of its bigger rival. Although Sirius cut more than 21 days off the crossing time, the Great Western started four days after it, so in fact made a much faster crossing.

Leith yards never built really big ships; generally coastal shipping vessels and ferries were their mainstays, but the development of the Western Harbour did permit the construction of ships of considerable size. At this site, the yard of Ramage & Ferguson, founded in 1877 and known for luxury yachts, built the SY København in 1921 for the Danish government. Despite the date, this was a sailing ship and the largest sail ship ever built in Britain.

The Henry Robb yard started in 1918 on the Western Harbour and eventually bought out many of its older competitors – Hawthorns (which had recently acquired Morton's yard), Cran & Somerville and Ramage & Ferguson as the industry slumped in the interwar years. Then in 1963 it also took over the historic Menzies's yard. The last ship to be built at Robb's yard was the ferry boat MV St Helen.

Section 2 HARBOUR TO HARBOUR

larger outer harbour. At the far end of the swing bridge on the inner harbour side was the location of the historic Menzies shipbuilding yard, now the site of modern flats.

Cross the road bridge and turn left down **Rennie's Isle**; the name references John Rennie (the elder) the engineer who designed the Georgian section of the docks here on the west side of the Water of Leith. The body of water to the right is the Victoria Dock (1851, J.M.Rendel) and the monolithic office block overlooking it is **Victoria Quay** by architects RMJM. Opened in 1996 by the Queen it was originally built to house the Scottish Office of the UK government, but following devolution in 1999 it is now the offices of some 2,000 civil servants of the Scottish Government. In the distance, across the water, is the Ocean Terminal shopping centre on land formerly occupied by shipbuilding yards.

When Rennie's Isle ends, keep ahead on the signposted Water of Leith Path, and pass between the government offices and flats to emerge at a paved area with a small swing bridge ahead. This bridge crosses the entrance to East Dock, the first of the enclosed wet docks, which, with the growth of the dock system, came to be known as **East Old Dock**. It was infilled in 1974.

This early swing bridge (1806 J.Rennie and R.Walker) along with the hand winches, capstans and the lock gates is an exceptionally rare example of this type of dock structure. Do not cross over but go right then left along the edge of the car park enjoying the view of the bridge to the left. Note the large smooth paving blocks. These are the tops of the dock walls of the East Old Dock and are all that is left to show where it was.

Ahead is a wall of warehouses, now repurposed for flats, with restaurants on the ground floor. These buildings (also J.Rennie with J.Patterson), were multi-storey warehouses for the Carron Iron Company; built at the same time as the dock. Like the two swing bridges passed, the warehouses are category A listed.

❹ Turn left again on approaching the warehouses (the stretch of water in front of them is purely ornamental), and past another dock gate topped by a metal arch signed **Commercial Quay** and the 1997 'Fish and Boat' sculpture,

Victoria Quay houses a large proportion of the Scottish Government's civil servants

57

Section 2 HARBOUR TO HARBOUR

1806 cast-iron swing bridge over the entrance to the now infilled, East Old Dock

LEITH'S WESTERN – GEORGIAN DOCKS

John Rennie (see also Section 3, p94), had a plan to build three connected dock basins parallel to the shore stretching along to the fishing harbour at Newhaven, where there would be a deep-water entrance untroubled by the sandbar which caused problems at the river entrance. Simultaneously a long pier was to be built projecting out from the east bank of the river to stop sands blocking the harbour entrance.

In the end, only two of the proposed dock basins were built – East Dock (East Old Dock) which opened in 1806 and West Dock of 1817 – each roughly giving two hectares of enclosed water and 7m deep (along with a graving dock). A western pier was added to the scheme, the eastern pier was made longer and a long straight breakwater was built. These changes were considered a cheaper solution to the problem than building the third dock.

Despite trimming back Rennie's plan the undertaking nearly bankrupted Edinburgh, which had borrowed heavily to fund the scheme, just as a great financial crash occurred. However, the cost-cutting proved short-sighted and by the 1830s the dock trade had slumped. The sandbar problem persisted and there was ongoing resentment between Leith and Edinburgh, centred on the seeming reluctance of Edinburgh to invest in up-to-date dock infrastructure, while happily pocketing all the tolls and charges. Matters were partly resolved in 1826 when ownership of the docks was vested in a Board of Commissioners (later reorganised) made up of representatives from both Edinburgh and Leith.

Finally, embarrassed by Queen Victoria choosing to land at Granton Harbour when she visited Edinburgh in 1842, expansion plans were resurrected. Works began in 1847 to the designs of J.M.Rendel and the Victoria Dock was opened in 1852. No bigger than the two earlier docks, it did have wider entry gates and deeper water.

Section 2 HARBOUR TO HARBOUR

and into **Dock Place**. This was once a busy spot as a freight-only railway line came from the dockside warehouses, running here at street level, heading to the Water of Leith, then crossing that on a drawbridge. The bridge was removed around 1910.

Turn right and walk to the junction with **Commercial Street**. Cross over at the lights on the right, noting the expanse of warehouses stretching along the street, then walk back left with a fine view of the neo-classical Custom House (1812 R.Reid, category A listed) on the other side of the road.

Just before **Bernard Street Bridge,** which heads back over the Water of Leith to Shore, turn right down **Commercial Wharf**. Bernard Street Bridge is modern, being the third bridge on this spot. The original was a drawbridge built in 1805 at the time of the first enclosed dock. This connected the main centre of South Leith with the docks, but still allowed ships to pass upriver. It was replaced around 1900 with a wider swing bridge which allowed the tram lines to be extended to Newhaven. In turn it was also replaced with the current fixed bridge in the 1950s, by which time boats were no longer using the river and the trams no longer running. In an echo of the past, trams have returned to Leith but rather than utilise this bridge, the tramline to Ocean Terminal and Newhaven crosses the river further north.

❺ Keep ahead along Commercial Wharf past an early 19th century warehouse known as **The Cooperage**. Just beyond this is a small patch of tree-fronted grassland, the site of a dry dock constructed by shipwright John Sime in 1771 – look closely to see the edge of the dock marked out in stone. This dry dock was built on the site of glassworks which had been destroyed by fire in 1747. Leith was the scene of the first glass production in Scotland in 1663 (before which it was all imported). It

The former warehouse of The Cooperage, reflects Leith harbour's long connection with the whisky trade

Section 2 HARBOUR TO HARBOUR

The 17th century steeple of St Ninian's Church and adjoining manse

was always an uncertain industry as glass was a heavily taxed luxury product, but it employed several hundred men in the town at its peak. Beyond this there is a striking modern building on Ronaldson's Wharf (1995 Fraser Brown Mackenna).

The stone bridge ahead was once a drawbridge, built around 1780 to replace the medieval bridge of 1486 at the same spot; formerly known as the Upper Drawbridge but now called **Sandport Place**. Even after the building of the docks the quays here on the inner harbour and beyond continued to be commercially important and used by substantial ships necessitating an opening bridge. The date of removal of the central metal and wood section with its drawbridge mechanism is not confirmed but it would have been redundant from 1969. At that date major changes to the harbour, including the installation of lock gates at the entrance to the Western Harbour, effectively made the river non-tidal keeping the water level artificially high.

Cross the road and continue on the now signposted Water of Leith Walkway. Just past some 1980s industrial sheds is a light-coloured, harled building with a curious steeple. This remarkable survivor is the remains of the largely 17th century former **St Ninian's Church** and its adjoining manse. The church and Quayside Mills next door have been restored in recent years. The clock face on the steeple is a reproduction, with the original in the National Museum of Scotland. This quiet corner was once the heart of old North Leith. An inscription carved on a lintel reads BLESSED AR THEY YAT HEIR YE VORD OF GOD AND KEIP IT LUK XI 1600.

❻ Beyond Quayside Mills and a block of flats comes the small green space North Leith Burial Ground on **Coburg Street**. The grandparents of the Victorian Prime Minister William Ewart Gladstone are buried here as is Lady Anne MacIntosh, the only woman in Scotland

Section 2 HARBOUR TO HARBOUR

The central section of Sandport Place Bridge once housed a drawbridge mechanism

to raise a clan in support of Bonnie Prince Charlie during the 1745 rebellion. On the opposite bank of the river, modern flats occupy the site of the former Leith Engineering Works. Between the closure of the works and their demolition, locals recall a novel use for the large shed as a ballroom and venue for professional wrestling.

Beyond the burial ground, the green strip narrows then opens out again. This space was the site of a coal depot on the North British lines, (formerly the Edinburgh Leith & Granton Railway). The line ran from here in a tunnel to Citadel Street where there was a goods station serving the Old East and West Docks. Fortunately this former railway land has been spared redevelopment and contributes another pocket of green space for North Leith. Now know as Coalie Park it is a good place for observing ducks and swans on the river.

NORTH LEITH

Always the smaller of the two Leiths, North Leith was the centre of the town's shipbuilding industry before the development of the western pier and its associated yards. The land and settlement belonged in medieval times to Holyrood Abbey and originally did not have a church. St Ninian's was built by Abbott Ballantyne (who built the original bridge over the Water of Leith) of Holyrood Abbey in 1493 as a chantry chapel.

After the Reformation it became the parish church for the newly created parish of North Leith in 1606, after which it was substantially rebuilt. By the early 19th century, as the town was prospering and growing, this old church became overcrowded and a new one built on Madeira Street a little to the west, on a site which was in the open fields when construction began. However, it soon became surrounded by a grid of fine wide streets in what was at the time described as Leith New Town, only partially completed when the banking crisis of 1825 intervened to halt building – as it did with Edinburgh's Third New Town.

Section 2 HARBOUR TO HARBOUR

Keep right to go under **Great Junction Street Bridge**, opened in 1818. In 1868 as part of the changes instituted by the North British Railway when it acquired this line, a passenger station was built just west of the bridge, allowing a quick service to the centre of Edinburgh. A stone wall to the right delineates the railway land, while the station's single platform was to the left.

❼ At the next path junction the Water of Leith Walkway swings left beside the river. Keep straight ahead on the line of the old railway, following signs for Cycle Route 11 to Craigleith and Haymarket and pass under **South Fort Street Bridge**. On the left, between the old railway and a meander in the river was an extensive area of industry served by rail sidings. This included a sugar refinery, foundry, iron works, corn and grain stores, and an oil cake mill; now largely replaced with modern light industrial sheds.

Before passing under another bridge, this one carrying **Newhaven Road**, note the platforms that remain of another suburban station. About 200m beyond the bridge there is a junction of paths marked by a cycle route post; a point known as **Stedfastgate**.

❽ Turn right here onto another cycle route – Victoria Path – signposted to Victoria Park,

Trinity and Newhaven. In making this turn the walk switches from the line of the North British route (from North Leith) to the Caledonian Railway's line (the Leith New Lines which have weaved across from the east side of Leith).

At Stedfastgate the Caledonian's line crossed the North British on a viaduct with no connection between the different railway lines. Following the removal of the tracks, landscaping has drastically altered the appearance of this spot. However, some stonework from the Caledonian's metal truss bridge can be spotted on the right before the turn, and one of the stone piers remains to the left beside the river.

On turning, look for a modern housing scheme over to the left, which was built on the site of the huge Chancelot Flour Mills.

Just after turning note on the right the remnants of the Catherine Sinclair Memorial Fountain which once stood at the junction of Princes Street and Lothian Road to provide water for horses. A plaque on the wall marks the opening of this stretch of path in 1983.

Follow the path north along the cutting in which the railway ran. Either side of the cutting, rows of tenements were squeezed in around 1900 as suburban development took off in this locality – development made

---

CHANCELOT FLOUR MILLS

When the Scottish Co-operative Wholesale Society decided to set up an operation to mill its own flour in the 1890s, Leith was so densely developed that this was as close as it could get to the docks with a large enough site for its ambitious plans. The co-operative society had been in existence since 1868 serving as wholesalers for many of Scotland's small retail cooperatives.

The state-of-the art facility – a steam powered roller mill, which just 40 operatives could run day and night (except Sundays) – was designed to keep the cost of its produce low. There were two main blocks. The front office faced Dalmeny Road. This had a vaguely French styling, with five storeys and a central clock tower rising to 56m. Behind was a plainer mill-granary block but equally high and with a chimney even higher than the clock tower.

The site had its own siding on which trains could come direct from the docks on the North British's line. One thousand Co-op members from around the country came to the opening ceremony. A spectacular explosion and fire brought the mill's working life to an end and it was demolished in 1971. A new Chancellot Mill now stands at Leith Western Harbour.

Section 2 HARBOUR TO HARBOUR

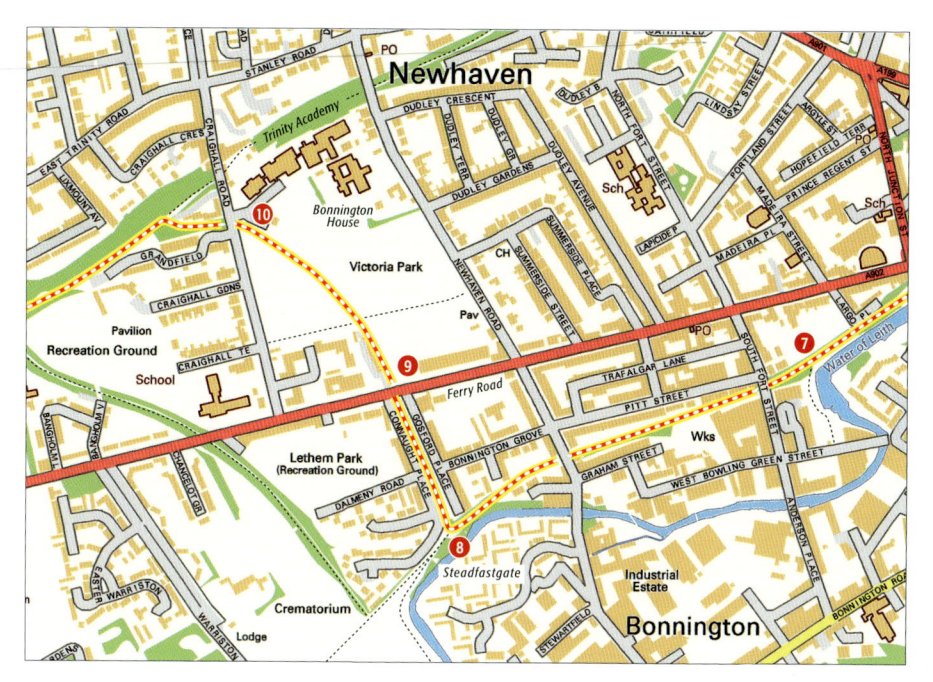

possible by the railways and the new suburban stations. Behind the tenements on the left is a small park previously known as Chancelot Park, now Letham Park, where Leith Football Club played their matches for a few years at the start of the 20th century.

9 Keep ahead as the path goes through a short tunnel under **Ferry Road** and emerges into **Victoria Park**. This 7.3 hectare park, like so many of Edinburgh's suburban parks, has its origins as the grounds of a small mansion house, Bonnington Park House of 1789. Although much altered and renamed **Bonnington House**, this still stands to the north-east of the park and is now a children's nursery. The house and grounds – which formed the eastern half of the park – were purchased from the estate of wealthy businessman Richard Raimes, (owner of a chain of pharmacies), by Leith Corporation for £16,621 in 1897. It opened as a public park the following year, with the name Victoria Park in commemoration of the Queen's Diamond Jubilee. What is now the west side of the park was then owned by the Caledonian Railway, whose Leith New Line had a cutting and a junction where the railway divided with branches heading east to Leith and west towards Granton.

By 1913 land had been purchased west of the railway and a bridge linked the two sides of the park. The original park layout was every bit the suburban Edwardian park, with a bandstand, bowling green and a drinking fountain of 1899 donated by the Leith Horticultural, Industrial and Sports Society and a statue of King Edward VII by John Stevenson Rhind. The park was transferred to Edinburgh when it incorporated Leith in 1920 and five years later the city authorities created the access from Ferry Road. It is not known when it lost its bandstand.

In the 1970-80s the cutting in the park was filled in (Leith New Lines having closed in 1966), to knit the divided parts back together. In 1983 the whole area was relandscaped to give it its present form, which is very much that of a community park with children's play

Section 2 **HARBOUR TO HARBOUR**

area and all weather sports pitches. Allotments have been constructed on the site of the redundant bowling green; these are used by pupils of nearby **Trinity Academy** to educate them about growing food, nature and biodiversity in an echo of Patrick Geddes and the Johnson Terrace Garden seen in Section 1. A mobile drinks kiosk is often open but there are no public toilets.

10 Curve gently left following the line of the mature trees which trace the upper edge of the former railway cutting. Maintain the same general direction following Cycle Route 15, to dip back down to the cutting and pass under the bridge that carries **Craighall Road**.

As the suburbs began to develop, the Caledonian Railway Company tapped into the potential for commuter traffic by adding a station on Craighall Road and a new passenger terminus a short distance from the goods station at Leith. Passenger services from Leith to Princes Street began in 1879 and were an important part of the city's suburban network until, with dwindling use, they ceased in 1962. Freight service limped on for a few years after.

At a T-junction with another railway path (Hawthornvale Path) turn left onto Cycle Route 14 to Granton, which picks up the route of the Caledonian's older Leith line. In approximately 300m there is a crossroads of paths called **Five-Ways Junction** where the Caley's line to Leith crossed the original Edinburgh Leith & Newhaven's line to Trinity.

11 Turn right here, signposted Cycle Route 13 to Wardie Bay, Lower Granton and Granton. Again this is a turn the trains could not make as the lines ran at different levels. The Caledonian's line was slightly elevated on an embankment and the Edinburgh Leith & Granton (later North British) line was in a cutting (just at the spot where the original 1840s line from Waverley and the 1860s line via Abbey Hill junction joined together). By the mid-1980s the tracks had been lifted and in

Entering the long Trinity Tunnel under East Trinity Road

64

Section 2 **HARBOUR TO HARBOUR**

the following years all remains of the two railways removed.

The walk now follows the route of the Edinburgh Leith & Newhaven Railway Company's original line to the Trinity Terminus which opened in 1842. The railway proposers' original intention was a line terminating at Newhaven to provide a better connection with ferries than was then provided by the stagecoaches, with a branch to Leith Docks. However, they had to change their plans as developing steamship technology opened up a great debate on the need for a new harbour on the north Edinburgh shore. Before construction even started, the proposed route of the line was shifted west aiming to terminate close to a proposed new harbour at Trinity.

12 Soon a tunnel going under **East Trinity Road** is reached. This tunnel is 133.5m long and was opened in 1842 (engineers T.Grainger & J.Miller), seeing its last train as late as 1986. The ends (portals) are beautifully detailed with a horseshoe shape. The tunnel does not seem to have been required for any reasons of difficult topography. The whole line was sunk in a cutting to cope with the steep gradient from the city centre to the shore. At this point it must have been cheaper to tunnel under the few existing houses than buy them up and demolish them to make way for a cutting. Land had been fued here for housing in the 1820s but not much was built before the banking crash. Tunnels have been almost as important to Edinburgh's development as bridges. On this line alone there were two other major tunnels as it progressed up to Canal Street Station (now Waverley) under Rodney Street and under Scotland Street – again to cope with the twin issues of the steep gradient and existing property.

Emerging from the tunnel, continue ahead under a bridge carrying **Lennox Row**, to pass

65

Section 2 HARBOUR TO HARBOUR

The former Trinity Station with its raised platform is now a private house

the former Trinity Station building (now a private house). This was the second Trinity Station. The first was built closer to the shore to allow passengers to walk down a lane to board ships at the chain pier, east of the current junction between Trinity Road and Lower Granton Road, which had been built in 1821. By the time the line to Trinity opened, the location of the new harbour had been settled and it was not to be at Trinity but further west at Granton.

Having reached Trinity in 1842 an extension was constructed curving west over Lower Granton Road towards the proposed Granton Harbour. The terminus there opened in 1846 when this new Trinity Station was built and the old station turned into a coal depot. The chain pier was destroyed in a storm in 1898. To reflect this extension, the railway changed its name from the Edinburgh Leith & Newhaven Railway to the Edinburgh, Leith & Granton Railway.

❸ Keep on the path curving downhill to emerge at the junction of **Trinity Road** and Lower Granton Road. Exiting from the path note the stone wall to the right, all that remains of the railway bridge which carried the railway over this road junction onto a high embankment. Cross Lower Granton Road at the lights and head left onto a tarmacked path by the seafront, known as **McKelvie Parade**.

With the railway embankment gone and the road junction realigned, this spot looks radically different to how it did for nearly 150 years. The sea views were previously obscured by the embankment and there was a tricky Z-bend in the road for the buses and, before that, the tram cars to navigate. The view east is now dominated by new development at Leith's Western Harbour and the view west by new development at Granton Harbour. Looking across the Firth of Forth to the Kingdom of Fife, the Craigkelly TV transmitting station sits on Binn Hill, a volcanic neck, behind the town of Burntisland. The firth is peppered with islands of volcanic rock the largest of which is Inchkeith, clearly seen to the north-east.

Head west along the shoreline path beside the stone wall. Here several blocks of tenements from the last quarter of the 19th century are a reminder that in the days of the railway and the

Section 2 HARBOUR TO HARBOUR

chain pier, this was a busy commercial quarter and the small square would have provided a much-needed green space.

The gentle indent in the coastline here is **Wardie Bay**. The surface rocks are shales famous for their fish fossils, several of which were named and classified by the Swiss-American geologist Louis Agassiz in the 1830s (see p141-2).

Another prominent 19th century scientific thinker, Charles Darwin also explored the marine life along Edinburgh's shoreline when he attended the University of Edinburgh for two years in the 1820s. He heartily disliked his medical studies; however, his time was not wasted as he joined several student societies which at that date were forums for new ideas and vigorous debate including one for nature studies. Through this, he visited the shore collecting specimens; he also took a course at the university on the then new science of geology which influenced his thinking.

So despite abandoning his studies without qualifying, Darwin took from his time in Edinburgh ideas that helped to inform his theory of evolution, particularly the idea from geology that the earth was far older than the age religious thinkers had calculated. Because of the importance of the fossil finds here the shore is a site of special scientific interest (SSSI).

Where the tenements end, look up to the left to see a fine regency terrace perched high above, which dates from 1828 before the railways arrived. Now partly hidden and looking like three separate houses, this is in fact a terrace, the original design being symmetrical to look like a classical country house. This terrace was built on a prime spot enjoying views over the Forth to Fife, part of a trend for villas to be built in Trinity in Regency times as prosperous Leith merchants began to desire summer houses away from the crowded town.

14 The far right of the three houses is the **St Columba's Hospice Education Centre**, part of the large modern hospice complex that overlooks the coast here. Incorporated into the modern buildings is an older house called Challenger. This was designed in 1825 by William Henry Playfair – responsible for many of the neoclassical buildings in the New Town, plus some monuments on Calton Hill – in his signature classical style. It was renamed Challenger when it was the home of Sir John Murray who accompanied the Challenger Expedition of 1872-6 on a journey sailing around the world compiling marine charts.

Between the terrace and the modern

SIR JOHN MURRAY

John Murray, now something of a forgotten figure, was a pioneer in the field of oceanography. Like Charles Darwin before him, he enrolled at the University of Edinburgh to study medicine but abandoned his course to go to sea on a whaling ship. While at sea he began making detailed observations and collecting marine specimens. He returned to Edinburgh in 1868 and resumed his studies, this time in geology.

Four years later he took up a post as a naturalist aboard a survey ship called Challenger. Returning from its long mission he took up residence here in Wardie, renaming his house after the ship, and spent more than a decade writing up his notes from the voyage. He also set up the UK's first Marine Laboratory at Granton. One of Murray's many scientific achievements was being the first to note the existence of the Mid-Atlantic Ridge and of ocean trenches.

He also observed deposits derived from the Saharan desert in deep ocean sediments. Several marine species and natural phenomenon are named after Murray as are laboratories at the University of Edinburgh and a Scottish Environment Protection Agency research vessel.

Section 2 HARBOUR TO HARBOUR

Brick cottages on Wardie Square, built for workers at the Duke of Buccleuch's Granton Harbour. Brick is an unusual building material for Edinburgh, but the duke also owned a nearby brickworks

complex, a bollarded road descends to the main road. This is part of Boswall Road which references Captain John Donaldson Boswall, a retired naval captain who owned the Wardie & Windlestrawlee Estates in the early 1800s.

This path has been upgraded in recent years as a cycle route which continues to Granton. At pedestrian lights, cross the road by the former Wardie Hotel and continue west. Crossing Wardie Steps the route moves onto the land belonging to the Duke of Buccleuch. Next is a long terrace of workers' cottages,

CAPTAIN BOSWALL

A man of some rank, Captain Boswall decided to develop his estates bordering the shore at Trinity in the 1830s. At that time there was much public discussion about how to solve the problem of Leith docks. Boswall was a Leith Docks Commissioner so could have been expected to back the expansion scheme, but instead he backed a scheme for a new harbour at Trinity in the hope of it increasing the value of his estate.

So positive was he of this scheme's success that he placed an advert in the press to the effect that his land was available for "such…buildings as the increasing trade and intercourse by steam navigation may require, on the establishment of the great steam packet landing place". Sadly for him, the Trinity Harbour plan did not proceed.

Boswall also tried to exploit the coal under his land. Coal is associated with the local rock formations, the Wardie Shales, and was known to have been mined in the 1600s, although outcrops at the shoreline had long since been worked out. An engineer's report helpfully found two coal seams under Boswall's land which he then leased for mine working. Unfortunately, after investing in the plant and machinery, the lessees found the coal seams unworkable and took Boswall to court for misrepresentation.

Section 2 HARBOUR TO HARBOUR

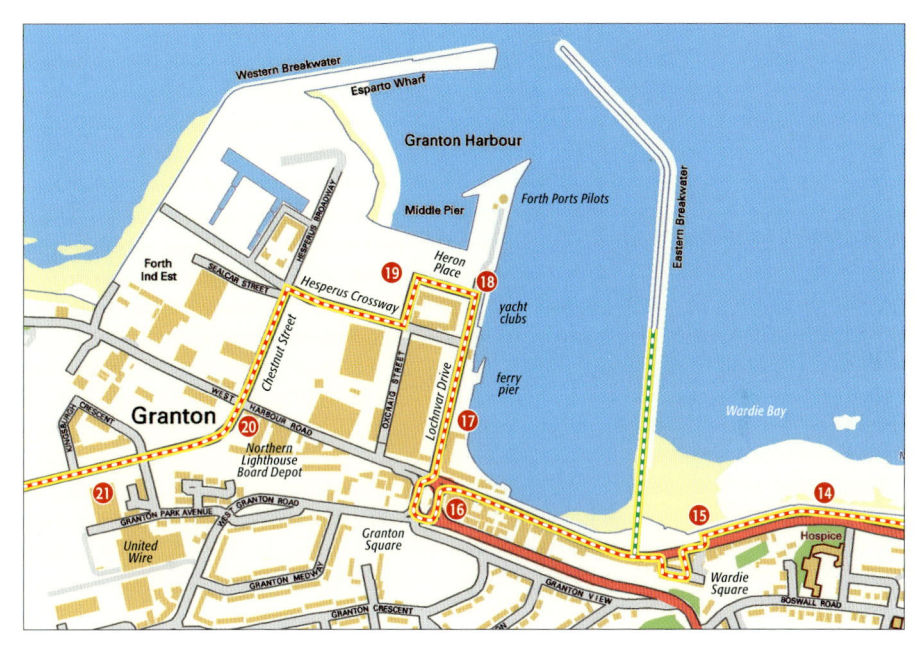

dating from the 1840s and, most unusually for Edinburgh, built in brick (the duke owned a brickworks not far from here).

15 Walk past the front row, called East Cottages, then turn left up **Wardie Square** to where a row of more Scottish looking harled and painted cottages face a back row of terraced brick. Follow the square round to exit back onto main road. When the duke began his developments at Granton, housing was required for dock builders and workers on what was then a quiet and remote stretch of coastline.

Continuing west on Lower Granton Road note a break in the railway embankment (which was lower at this end) leading down onto the **Eastern Breakwater** of Granton Harbour constructed 1852-63. It is well worth walking out on the breakwater to get some indication of the large area of water enclosed by this harbour. This gap also gives access to the small sandy beach of Wardie Bay.

Beyond the breakwater, continue along the coast and past a block of flats, to reach the first buildings associated with the original development of the harbour, a row of terraced houses with bay windows. These date from the 1840s and are built of sandstone from Granton quarries with brick gable ends; it is assumed they were shops. Next is the entrance to some stables now used as a garage and then a (currently) blue-fronted building that was the Granton Tap Bar of the same date as the houses.

16 After passing the Tap, turn left into **Granton Square** and past an imposing late Georgian building of 1838, complete with a stone balcony from where the bustle of the harbour could be observed. This was built as the Granton Hotel to cater for travellers (sources attribute the design to William Burn or John Henderson), but since WWII it has been in military ownership. Formerly the navy's HMS Claverhouse it is now an Army Reserve Centre.

Continue ahead, cross over Granton Road and turn right. Pause to look north beyond the modern flats to the pier and take in the formal planning of Granton Square. The hotel is balanced by a large tenement building

69

Section 2 HARBOUR TO HARBOUR

Looking over the small Wardie Bay beach to the Eastern Breakwater and the new flat developments that occupy reclaimed areas of the former Granton Harbour

opposite (architect John Henderson also c1838) part of which was used as the harbourmaster's house and offices which, along with a range of warehouses beyond (not visible from this point), were all part of the original plan for Granton. If the square has the feel of a place built as part of a grander scheme that never came to pass, it is because the Duke of Buccleuch intended to build a small township. In early 1860 he advertised an architectural competition for houses (for three classes of tenant), church, manse, custom house, market and school.

Nothing really came of this scheme beyond a church and a custom house. However, the square has proved to be a handy turning point for buses and trams over the decades. The small building in the centre was formerly public toilets erected in the 1930, but sadly closed in a cost-cutting measure in 2011.

Cross Granton Crescent (where steps lead up to Granton Park, a small community park created to serve the inter-war council housing which has few facilities beyond a children's play area). Continue round the square and cross over **West Granton Road**, to pass in front of the tenement facing the former hotel.

Now cross over West Harbour Road, heading north towards the sea, to reach **Lochinvar Drive**. Before WWII, West Harbour Road did not exist. It was constructed along the line of a former mineral railway owned by the duke, which served a timber yard, a haul-up slip and a boat building yard. It then crossed the rail line to the Western Pier and continued west to an iron works, to end at Granton Quarry.

17 Walk down Lochinvar Drive lined with industrial units and modern flats. The route is now on Granton Pier which has been referred to as Middle Pier since the coal-handling jetties were developed on the Western Breakwater and it, in turn, became known as the Western Pier (there was never an Eastern Pier just the Eastern Breakwater). Middle Pier had been completed to a length of 518m by 1844 when it could accommodate 10 steamers. Because there was deep water close in to the shore at Granton, the pier did not need to go as far out as the one at Leith to get good clearance at low water and lock gates were not required. The pier is built of sandstone from the duke's Granton Sea Quarry (see p84) and

Section 2 HARBOUR TO HARBOUR

is now catagory A listed.

Very quickly it was recognised that such a long pier was going to need protection from the storms which sweep up and down the Firth of Forth so the two long breakwaters were built, also of Granton stone – the western one was completed in 1849 and the eastern one rather later in 1863. The current road name Lochinvar Drive recalls the harbour's WWII role when it was requisitioned by the navy (as it had been in WWI) and renamed HMS Lochinvar.

The modern flats on the right occupy land formerly containing the railway line turning – on a very tight curve – and associated sidings. A gap, the site of a former station, offers a lovely view east over open water to the eastern breakwater, Wardie Bay and beyond to new developments at Western Harbour, Leith. Beyond, the old stone wall on the right divided the two separate commercial operations which took place on the pier. The east side of the wall was for the ferry which had been sold by the duke to the railway company at an early stage, while the west side was initially the focus of the duke's commercial harbour operations. After passing the yacht club building, walk to the water's edge for a view of Thomas Bouch's innovative roll-on / roll-off slipway and some of the old Granton Station buildings which remain. The eastern side of the harbour is now a marina shared between the Forth Corinthian Yacht Club and the Royal Forth Yacht Club.

The duke's operations on the western side of Middle Pier received invaluable early publicity when Queen Victoria and Prince Albert landed there on their first visit to Scotland in 1842. That side of the pier was subsequently known as the Victoria Jetty in commemoration. Continue up the pier past another big housing development on the left to reach **Heron Place**.

Ahead, on the other side of the fence, is a stone warehouse built around 1840 as part of the original scheme, and beyond that a

THE DEVELOPMENT OF GRANTON HARBOUR

In the 1830s there was great debate about the sandbar and the problems it caused at Leith Docks. One solution for a non-tidal harbour on the Duke of Buccleuch's land at Granton was put forward by R.W.Hamilton, manager of the General Steam Navigation Co. It so enamoured the duke that he proposed to undertake the whole scheme at his own expense. The duke's Granton lands contained stone that could be quarried to build the harbour with minimal cost of transporting materials. Robert Stevenson (see p76) acted as engineer on the project.

Building a harbour from scratch is an enormous, risky and expensive undertaking (Leith Docks had nearly bankrupted mighty Edinburgh) so how did the Duke of Buccleuch succeed in doing it? When he inherited his titles at 13 years of age, it was 1819 and the height of the industrial revolution. He was effectively dealt a winning hand in life. He owned the land, he owned the rights to the foreshore, he had a quarry (see p83 & 84) and he had money (from his many other large landholdings) to invest.

But he also played his hand well, using his vision not just to invest in the harbour here, but also in mines and railways and the harbour at Barrow-in-Furness in England. His entrepreneurial vision paid off handsomely for when he died in 1884 he left an estate estimated to be worth £7.866 million pounds (approximately £9 billion today) making him one of the richest men in Britain at that time.

The first section of the pier was opened on Queen Victoria's coronation day in 1838 but the duke could not attend the opening ceremony because as a peer of the realm he was required to be at the Queen's coronation in London.

Section 2 HARBOUR TO HARBOUR

modern round structure that is the base for the Association of Forth Pilots. This body currently consists of around 25 master mariners who take charge of all large vessels – from cruise liners to oil rigs – to bring them safely into the harbours in the firth. They have been based at Granton since 1920.

18 Turn left and walk along **Heron Place** at the back of the flats. Here the route leaves the pier and passes onto reclaimed land. The western harbour basin at 28 hectares was always slightly larger than the eastern (only 21 hectares). A small amount of land reclamation was done along the shoreline of the western basin in the 1920s, then in 1961 the decision was taken by the Granton Harbour Company (created in 1932 to run the harbour but with the Buccleuch family at the helm) to reclaim 10 more hectares; work that took a decade to complete. This created space for modern warehousing accessible by road.

Cleared railway and industrial land here offers the possibility of using 'brownfield' sites to accommodate the city's growing population without pressure on the greenbelt, but in practice this development has proved difficult. A masterplan was drawn up in 2003 and some house building did take place before the financial crash of 2008, but that and the axing of plans to bring the city's new tram system to Granton brought work to a halt. In 2020 legal planning disputes were resolved and development has been resumed to a new masterplan.

19 Follow Heron Place as it bends left to emerge onto **Hesperus Crossway** (named after Hesperus II, one of the Northern Lighthouse Board's vessels which operated from here between 1964 and 1974) and turn right. If development on the harbour does resume as detailed in the proposed plans, then the owners, Forth Ports, hope that all the land up to the right will be covered in flats and beyond them to the west will be a hotel and new marina.

GRANTON FERRY

On completion of Middle Pier, the Duke of Buccleuch introduced a ferry service to Burntisland in partnership with Sir John Gladstone (the Leith born father of future Prime Minister William Gladstone) to connect the railways north and south of the River Forth. Gladstone owned the land at Burntisland on the north side of the firth and paid for improvements to the harbour there; he too had deep pockets. On the abolition of slavery, he had been awarded a sum equivalent to over £12 million today by the Slave Compensation Commission in respect of the slaves he owned on his Caribbean plantations.

The Edinburgh and Northern Railway had ambitions to push its lines north from Burntisland, so in 1847 it bought the Granton-Burntisland ferry from the duke. The railway company sought the advice of engineer Thomas Bouch (responsible for Portobello Pier (see p165), but most notorious for the Tay Bridge which collapsed killing many in a storm of 1878) to streamline the ferry operation. Bouch's solution was the world's first roll-on / roll-off ferry but for railway wagons only. Rail freight wagons could be hauled by crane onto the deck of a specially adapted paddle steamer, the Leviathan (designed by Edinburgh engineer Thomas Grainer) and then hauled off again at Burntisland. A platform on rollers, which could be moved up and down the slipways, gave a level access no matter what state the tide and both platform and boat were fitted with rail track.

This ferry continued to connect the north-south railways on the east coast until the building of the Forth Rail Bridge in 1890, which put an end to the ferry as a rail-freight connection, but the passenger ferry continued until WWII when it was suspended. It was resumed after the war but never achieved profitability, ceasing after only a few years.

Section 2 HARBOUR TO HARBOUR

Modern flats on land reclaimed from Granton Harbour, at the corner of Hesperus Crossway and Broadway

At the crossroads with **Hesperus Broadway** turn left onto **Chestnut Street**. This point is almost the centre of the reclaimed land in the Western Basin and gives a sense of how large a harbour the duke built, and just how much land there is to be redeveloped. The plans for Chestnut Street are a new 'community hub' with retail units and a health clinic on the right and more residential units on the left.

At the junction with **West Harbour Road**,

THE DUKE'S HARBOUR OPERATIONS

Granton was a large harbour and it prospered for 130 years, its trade reflecting the local industries which flourished over the years. Printing and publishing were successful early on because rivers around Edinburgh provided water power for pulping the cotton and linen rags from which paper was then made. By the mid-19th century the supply of rags could not keep up with the demand and it was discovered that paper could be made from pulped esparto grass. This grass was a wild plant which grew on the hills of southern Spain and North Africa and was harvested by locals. Over the next decade, as this process was widely taken up by Edinburgh papermakers, esparto became the main import at Granton Harbour; at its peak one-third of all the UK's esparto imports came in here.

Coal was the main export. By 1870 both the Caledonian Railway Company and the North British Railway had lines to the harbour meaning it could handle coal from both the Lothian and the Lanarkshire coalfields. The Duke of Buccleuch built timber jetties on the Western Breakwater and created a sophisticated coal-handling facility.

Also important was a 'bunkering' service for boats and ships to fill up with coal to power their steam-driven engines; this service was especially popular with fishing vessels. From the 1880s steam trawlers began to use Granton as their base, encouraging the support industries of ice factories and net production and mending close to the harbour.

Section 2 HARBOUR TO HARBOUR

The former depot and testing facility for the Northern Lighthouse Board on West Harbour Road

GRANTON DURING THE WARS

Granton was at the peak of its profitability at the outbreak of WWI, when it was requisitioned by the navy as a port for protecting the navy base further up the River Forth at Rosyth from German warships. The trawler fleet was also requisitioned and converted into minesweepers.

The harbour was not returned to the Duke of Buccleuch until 1920 and every effort was made to return it to pre-war profitability – fishing was particularly successful reaching its peak of 80 vessels. Even the coal business recovered sufficiently for a new coal jetty and there was a large celebration of the harbour's centenary.

However, the harbour was requisitioned again in 1939 and not finally handed back to private ownership until 1946.

look left to see a brick building which looks like a stranded lighthouse. It is in fact the former depot for the Northern Lighthouse Board, the body charged with looking after Scotland's lighthouses. The mock lighthouse design was no folly as it was used for testing lamps before they were put into service. Now marooned inland, it originally sat at the shoreline (just behind the mineral railway) before land reclamation started.

20 Cross West Harbour Road to **Waterfront Avenue**. Keeping to the right-hand pavement, follow this for 50m, then turn right onto Cycle Route 12, signposted for Silverknowes Esplanade and Cramond. The route runs parallel to Waterfront Avenue, turning away from the shoreline to avoid a kilometre-long stretch of West Harbour Road which has yet to benefit from redevelopment and is still industrial, presenting a bleak prospect for the walker. However, the most recent incarnation of the development plan proposes a new public park and cycle route for the area to

Section 2 **HARBOUR TO HARBOUR**

POST WAR CONDITIONS

Coal output from the Lothian Coalfield declined after WWII as many of the pits were old and worked out, but Britain was still a coal economy so coal imports grew. Over the 20th century ships had been converting from steam to diesel power and so the port developed an oil storage and handling capacity and continued its refuelling service.

The Granton Harbour Company (still under Buccleuch control) fought hard against nationalisation in 1947 but had to give up their private ownership in 1967 when a government body called Forth Ports was created and took compulsory ownership of Granton Harbour, along with its nearby rival Leith.

At this date, it was still a busy and profitable harbour, but as containerisation changed the nature of shipping there was only so much non-container business to go around and Leith won the battle. Closure as a commercial harbour came in 1970, with use by trawlers continuing for another four years until over-fishing in the North Sea took its toll and even the trawler business ceased.

replace the industry.

Waterfront Avenue is part of the site owned by Edinburgh council and a new road built at the city's expense to open up potential building plots. Embedded in the road's design are cycle lanes either side separated by trees, hedges and grass verges (space for future tram extension), giving it an open, campus-like feel.

21 On the left, beyond Kingsburgh Crescent is the site of Scotland's (possibly Britain's) first purpose-built car factory. It was constructed by the Madelvic Motor Carriage Co Ltd in 1899 (the company was founded not by some entrepreneurial businessman but by Edinburgh's City Astronomer, William Peck) to built electric cars. The business was short-lived and the premises were taken over first by Kingsburgh Motor Construction

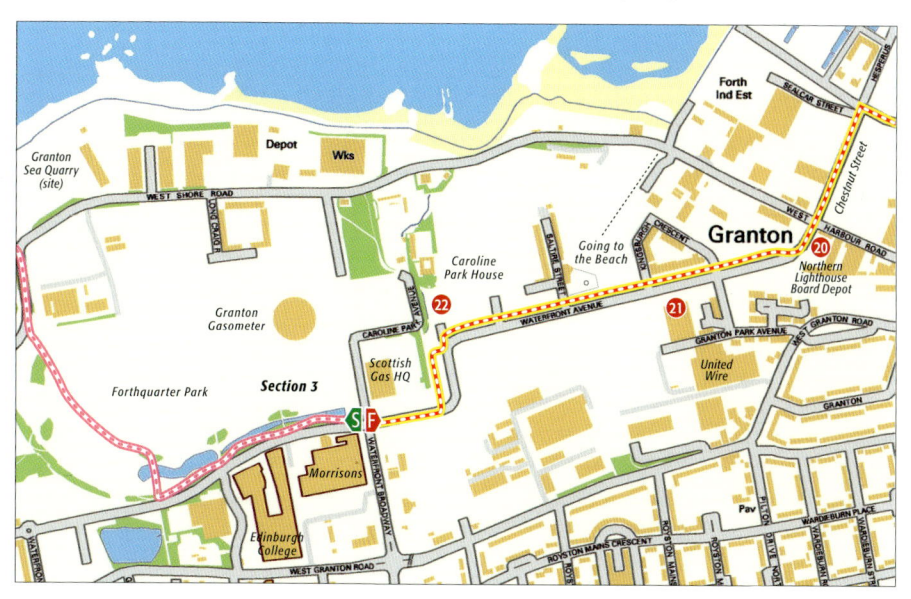

Section 2 HARBOUR TO HARBOUR

'Going to the Beach' sculpture beside modern flats on Saltire Street

Co, and then Stirling Motor Carriages Ltd. None could make the business profitable and the premises seem to have been unused for some years prior to 1925 when they were taken over by United Wire Ltd. This company produces fine wire mesh and continues to be an important employer in Granton, with modern new premises behind the old abandoned factory.

Despite the historic significance and listed status, the abandoned factory and the adjoining plot are scheduled for development to create a new National Collections Facility for the National Galleries of Scotland, adding to a similar facility which exists nearby for National Museums Scotland.

NORTHERN LIGHTHOUSE BOARD & THE STEVENSON FAMILY

Originally named the Commissioners for Northern Lighthouses, the Northern Lighthouse Board was formed in 1786 to build and maintain lighthouses around Scotland's coast. Its most famous engineers all came from one family, the Stevensons; father Robert and sons David, Alan and Thomas. Robert was born in Glasgow but was living in Edinburgh when, at the age of 19, he followed his stepfather into employment with the board. He mixed work with study, taking classes at both Edinburgh and Glasgow universities without gaining a degree, staying with the board for 50 years till 1842.

However, his work with the board did not prevent him taking on other work as a consultant engineer on projects including Granton Harbour and Regent Bridge (see Section 1 p29). In the spirit of the times, he contributed to scientific journals and from his work building the Bell Rock Lighthouse, he established that the waters of the North Sea were eroding the east coast of Britain and that great sandbanks were deposits of eroded material carried by the sea.

Two of Stevenson's sons produced children who became writers. Allan's daughter Katharine Elizabeth Alan de Mattos was a journalist, book reviewer and poet, while Thomas's son was the famous author Robert Louis Stevenson.

Section 2 HARBOUR TO HARBOUR

> ### WIRECLOTH & PAPERMAKING
>
> United Wire makes wirecloth – a fine woven wire mesh, which among other things is essential in the mechanised production of paper. Two men, William McMurray and brother-in-law Robert McFarlane were connected with a wire works in Leith in the mid-19th century. Their paths diverged but they both had a part in Edinburgh's industrial prosperity.
>
> McMurray bought Kinleith papermill near Colinton and (as well as mills on the River Wandle in London), acquired the rights to harvest the esparto then used for papermaking on several estates in Southern Spain and bought ships on which to import it. McFarlane continued in the wire business but specialised in wirecloth. Both sides of the business prospered, helped hugely by the tax on newsprint being abolished in 1855.
>
> In 1897 McFarlane oversaw the amalgamation of four Scottish wirecloth producers under the banner United Wire Ltd, relocating to Granton in 1925.

A little further on where the route crosses **Saltire Street** is roughly the junction where the duke's privately owned mineral lines connected with the Caledonian railway line from the pier, which is now used by a cycle route. The modern block of flats is an early phase of the area's redevelopment, anchored by a nostalgic statue entitled 'Going to the Beach' by Vincent Butler RSA. Keep walking straight ahead making for the skeletal form of the old Granton Gasometer.

㉒ Here, as the road bends sharply left, elaborate gateposts indicate the presence of something unexpected on former industrial land, a restored 17th century mansion called **Caroline Park House.** Beyond these gates, continue on the path to reach a T-junction, where the route turns left.

(To the right, but not on the route, is one of Edinburgh's most secret gardens. This walled

The restored 17th century mansion of Caroline Park House

77

Section 2 HARBOUR TO HARBOUR

Ancient and modern – the skeletal frame of the old Granton Gasometer from 1902, alongside the new stainless steel and glass of the 2003 Scottish Gas HQ

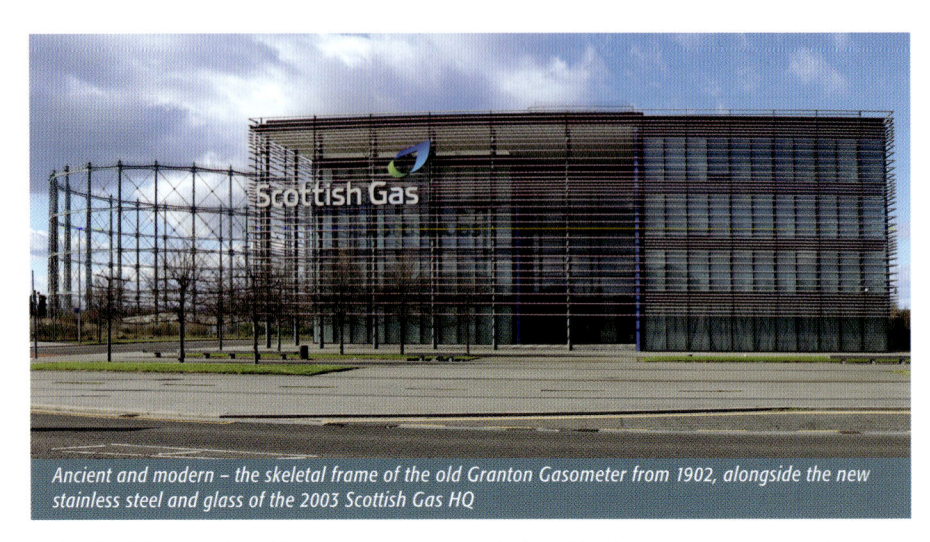

garden is all that remains of Royston Castle – sometimes called Granton Castle – substantial parts of which survived until demolition in the 1920s. Maintained by volunteers, the garden only opens for special events.

Turn left and follow the path to rejoin Waterfront Avenue, then right towards the new glass and steel HQ offices of **Scottish Gas**. The route is now crossing the final section of land covered by the Granton masterplan, which belonged to National Grid (who inherited the gas works site) and now belongs to Edinburgh council. This imposing office building was designed by Fosters + Partners who drew up the original plan for the gasworks site.

At the time of writing the area seems, as does Granton Harbour, like something of a frontier outpost. Very little of the old remains and most of what does can be seen from this spot. The **Granton Gasometer** dates from 1902 as does the red brick Granton Gas Works Train Station opposite the new offices (both by Walter Ralph Herring, chief engineer to the gasworks). Both have survived only because they are listed.

Of what was planned, little has yet been

CAROLINE PARK HOUSE

Caroline Park is named after Caroline Campbell, the great grandmother of the 5th Duke of Buccleuch, whose marriage to the Earl of Dalkeith in 1742 brought the Granton Estate into the Buccleuch family's possession. The design (dating from a circa 1690 remodelling of an older house) is very unusual for Scotland, both inside and out. Externally it looks quite French, while inside it contains state apartments even though there is no known connection to royalty. The gate posts are similarly idiosyncratic. Although the ones seen here are new, they are reproductions of originals on West Shore Road on the north side of the house.

The house ceased to be desirable as a residence when a private mineral railway line along the shore opened up the land between the harbour and the quarry to industry, and in 1872 it was let to the firm of A.B.Fleming & Co. They manufactured printing ink, had large chemical works in the grounds and used the house as their offices. It was only in 1987 that the Buccleuch estate sold it to private buyers who have since restored it to a family residence.

Section 2 HARBOUR TO HARBOUR

built. Diagonally across from the Scottish Gas offices on **Waterfront Broadway**, a modern development contains a gym and a Morrisons supermarket, with a building housing Edinburgh (formerly Telford) College.

All the new buildings date from the Fosters' masterplan of 2000 but, as at Granton Harbour, the financial crash of 2007-8 slowed development almost to a halt. However, Edinburgh council has been promised a contribution from the Scottish Government to re-energise development which will focus on low and middle-income housing.

Section 2 began in an area which had undergone regeneration in recent decades and ends here, in an area midway through an even larger regeneration project, the future of which still hangs in the balance. The two locations provide an interesting comparison. Leith's redevelopment benefits from a greater collection of old buildings to work with, and while it is arguable that by focusing on bringing visitors to the Shore the redevelopment has not always met the needs of ordinary Leithers, it has developed somewhere with a sense of a having a real centre.

Granton has even more challenges for redevelopment, not least the vast amounts of land for which new uses have to be found. It is more remote from the city centre, with poorer transport connections, and the established housing estates which bound it were already suffering from a degree of deprivation and a lack of amenities. As yet the planners have not created a 'centre' at Granton to act as a focus for visitors and locals alike, overlooking the obvious places to site this – either Granton Square or here at the crossroads by the new gas offices. Sadly, the potential of Granton's waterfront as an amenity for walkers and cyclists also remains unrealised.

The Morrisons supermarket on Waterfront Broadway has a cafe and toilets

Lothian buses 24 and 113 go to Princes Street, and the 47 goes to the West End (Charlotte Square and Lothian Road), all from the bus stop on Waterfront Broadway on the opposite side of the road from Morrisons

The 1902 red brick former Granton Gas Works Train Station is earmarked for redevelopment

Old Cramond Brig over the River Almond dates from the late 15th century

Section 3
WATER & WILDERNESS

Route: Granton to Maybury Road
Distance: 10km; 6.25 miles
Grade: Easy to Moderate on tarmac and earth paths, some long flights of steps
Access: Lothian bus 113 from Princes Street, 24 from Princes Street and 47 from Queensferry Street or Lothian Road. Buses stop outside Morrisons supermarket (*Waterfront Broadway bus stop*), Granton, from where it is a short walk north to the Scottish Gas HQ and Forthquarter Park

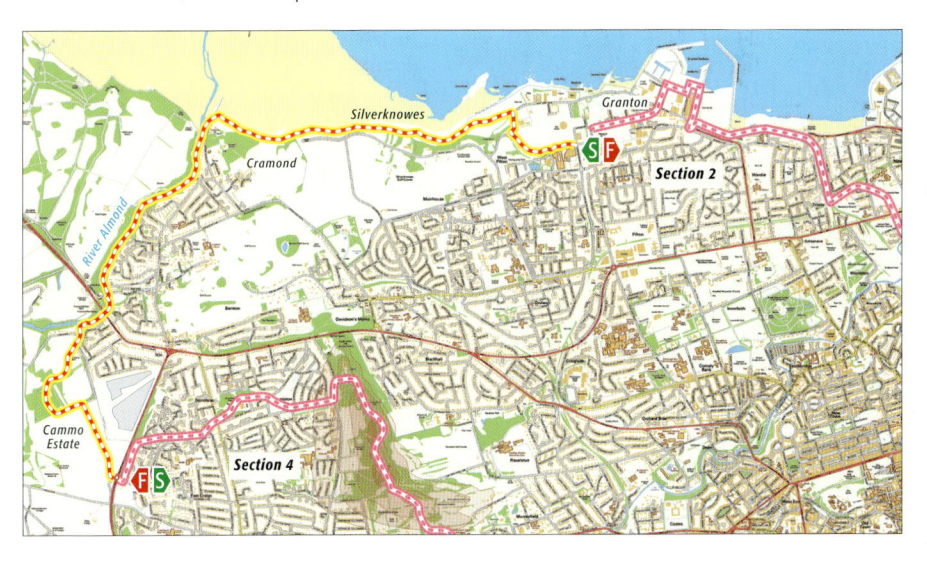

Edinburgh's western coastline comprises areas of land that have been reclaimed from industry and others that have passed directly from private estate to public open space. This section follows the coast, then turns inland beside the River Almond, where nature has reclaimed what once was industrial, to reach a man-made parkland turned to wilderness. Finally, it touches on greenbelt land which has succumbed to development

To continue or resume the route, turn west into the new **Forthquarter Park** opposite the Scottish Gas HQ building on Waterfront Broadway and follow a path which gently winds between the trees on the left-hand side of the Caroline Burn.

❶ This park has been developed as part of Waterfront Edinburgh, a plan to regenerate former industrial land in Granton and Leith. The masterplan was launched in 2003 and the park was completed before the financial crash of 2008 derailed the scheme. It occupies the middle section of the huge site of the former Granton Gasworks which dated from the start of the 20th century. The gasworks was a major employer in the area for the best

81

Section 3 WATER & WILDERNESS

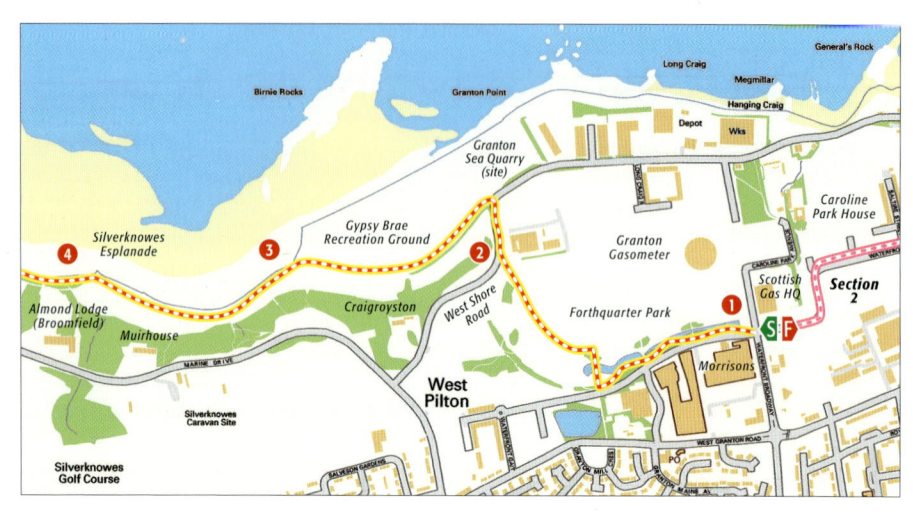

part of 90 years and closure left over 40 hectares of land unused, some of it contaminated.

Covering 20 hectares, Forthquarter is a significant new park for Edinburgh. It was designed by landscape architects Hyland Edgar Driver. The defining element of the park is a watercourse and ponds which have been created by uncovering the Caroline Burn, culverted for many decades, and creating a path to run alongside it on boardwalks. Some 800 trees and 43,000 shrubs have been planted along with wildflower-rich grassed areas, attracting deer, bats and butterflies. Another important element is a cycle route which connects to the shore.

Keep following the path beside the burn, ignoring the first two crossing paths. Ahead are dense developments of new flats (rebuilding of the Muirhouse and Pennywell council estates) and to the left, the new Edinburgh College campus occupies the southern section of the gasworks site. To the right, the currently undeveloped northern section is dominated by the disused **Granton Gasometer**.

At a third crossing path, look left to the other side of the road, where there is one of Granton's old quarries, Pennywell Parks, now flooded and forming another of the park's water features. This quarry ceased operating around 1900.

Turn right and cross the burn, then a pond on a new bridge to arrive at a T-junction with Cycle Route 12 and turn left onto this.

GRANTON GASWORKS

In 1896 the need for coal gas was growing along with the city. Production for Edinburgh, Leith and Portobello came under the control of joint commissioners who required a large new site for an up-to-date gasworks, away from residential areas and with rail links for the large amounts of coal required. At Granton the Buccleuch Estate had become so industrialised that the 6th Duke of Buccleuch was happy to sell the commissioners 43 hectares of land. The new works opened in 1902 complete with offices, gas producing plant, gasometer (two more were added later) and an internal network of narrow-gauge rail lines. The works had its own station on the Caledonian Railway's line from Princes Street Station, which was essential for its large workforce as the site was so remote.

Section 3 WATER & WILDERNESS

GRANTON GASOMETER

In 1965 natural gas was discovered under the North Sea, leading to a decade-long project to convert all of Britain's supply from coal gas to natural gas. Production ceased at Granton around 1976 but the three gasometres continued in use for some years, storing surplus natural gas. They formed a prominent feature of the city's skyline when viewed from the north but were scheduled for demolition under the redevelopment plans. With two demolished circa 2003, the original one was saved by the controversial decision to list it in 2010. Acknowledged in engineering terms, no one could think of a use for it and the site's owners considered it an impediment. However, recent schemes repurposing gasometres for flats at Kings Cross, London, Dublin and Vienna have shown what can be done with a bit of imagination.

The undeveloped site, to the left at the end of the park, latterly the location of the 1960s Gas Board office, was previously the site of Granton House, one of a string of mansions built along the high ground above the shore. Like so many of the mansions surrounding Edinburgh it came to a sad end – burning down in 1954 while being used as accommodation for families bombed-out during WW2.

❷ At the junction with **West Shore Road** turn right, cross over and walk downhill for approximately 150m. This spot now feels rural but it had an important industrial past. In the 1880s the land on the east side of the road was the site of A.B.Fleming's chemical works, at one time one of the largest plants manufacturing printing ink.

As the road bends right, turn left to enter open ground heading downhill on a wide grassy path. This is the **Gypsy Brae Recreation Ground**, which occupies land reclaimed to facilitate a planned, but never implemented, expansion of the gasworks between the wars. By modern standards this section of open space is something of a green grass desert. Before reclamation, the eastern section was the site of Granton Sea Quarry which played such an important role in the construction of Granton Harbour (see p71). Indeed, it is unlikely that the 5th Duke of Buccleuch could have afforded to build such a large harbour if he had not had so much good quality stone on his land.

One of Edinburgh's newest green spaces, Forthquarter Park occupies part of the old Granton Gasworks site

83

Section 3 WATER & WILDERNESS

Looking across Silverknowes Esplanade to Cramond Island and Fife

③ Follow this wide, grassy path west to the shore where it merges onto the tarmacked **Silverknowes Esplanade**, which is followed for 3km to Cramond. The route has now left the sandstone behind and is back on a shale formation known as the Muirhouse 'shrimp-bed'.

This was the site of a major geological discovery when a complete body of a conodont was found in the 1920s. These eel-like creatures have an important place in

> ### GRANTON SEA QUARRY
> *Quarrying at Granton is recorded as far back as the mid-16th century (including for use on Holyrood Palace). Although Granton Sea Quarry was specifically worked from 1835 to construct Granton Harbour, the stone was also used elsewhere. One famous use was for Nelson's statue atop his column in London's Trafalgar Square. Sourcing a large enough stone block proved difficult, but a particular attribute of Granton's rock was that it could be quarried in very large blocks, so the 5th Duke of Buccleuch gifted the required piece to the project.*
>
> *The rock hereabouts is a hard, cream coloured Craigleith Sandstone and part of a geological structure called the Granton Anticline – where layers of rock have bulged up in a dome. Subsequently, an ice sheet has scoured off the top, leaving a circular patten of outcropping rock, similar to slicing the side off an onion. These beds are known for their tree fossils.*
>
> *Production at the quarry ended swiftly in October 1855 when a section of the quarry face gave way in a storm allowing the sea to flood in, filling it in just 10 minutes. The quarry master and his family had a narrow escape when their house cracked open and fell into the quarry but no one was injured.*
>
> *When flooded, the quarry formed a natural harbour (although the entrance was narrow) but with Granton harbour so close it had no obvious use. In 1884 the oceanographer Sir John Murray (see p67) saw its potential and leased it from the duke to set up research facility with a moored ship acting as a floating laboratory. The institution moved to Millport on the Isle of Cumbrae in the Firth of Clyde in 1897.*

Section 3 WATER & WILDERNESS

> ### SHORELINE GEOMORPHOLOGY
>
> *A raised beach is a terrace-like platform or platforms, sometimes covered with round sea-washed rocks, between the foot of a cliff and the current high water shoreline. They indicate that, in a past time, the level of the sea was higher relative to the land. As the ice melted at the end of the last (and earlier) ice ages, a huge weight was lifted off the land and it rose, to some extent offset by the sea rising with the extra water.*
>
> *Raised beaches can be found all around Scotland's coastline. Detailed measurement of those on the shore of the Firth of Forth (by a team from the Geography Department of the University of Edinburgh led by Dr Brian Sissons in the 1960s and 70s) has enabled a good understanding of how the ice has advanced, depressing the land, and retreated – causing the land to rise – over the ages.*

evolution as the first creatures to have teeth, and previously only fossils of these teeth had been found. These little creatures may sound insignificant, but they are index fossils, one of a group used to date rocks.

As the trees thin out, note how the route is following a 'platform' beside the shore, backed to the south by a distinctive grassy escarpment. This is a geomorphological feature called a raised beach and occurs at many points along the shoreline.

Above the shoreline lie the remaining mansion houses that once stood along the higher ground. Set in small estates, mansions such as these came to ring the city in the late 18th and early 19th centuries; symbols of a peaceful and increasingly prosperous time.

From east to west were Granton House (already mentioned), Craigroyston, Muirhouse, Broomfield and Silverknowe. Before the construction of Marine Drive on the high ground, and the esplanade lower down, they were remote and private spots where the newly rich could enjoy the privileges of a small landed estate.

❹ The open land alongside the esplanade was once part of the estate surrounding Muirhouse mansion and was purchased by Edinburgh council after WWII. **Muirhouse** mansion can be glimpsed through the trees.

Cramond Beach below Silverknowes Esplanade

85

Section 3 WATER & WILDERNESS

The beach at Cramond can be popular in good weather. The large sculpture of a fish head is by Scottish sculptor Ronald Rae and was installed in 2009

The bulk of the estate, not visible from here, was used for council housing, firstly post-war as a site for the first of Edinburgh's many prefabs; then from 1960 a large permanent scheme was constructed housing many families decanted from the Leith slums. The land by the shore, however, was retained as public open space and integrated with the open lands on either side.

The next house visible through the trees is **Broomfield** (currently the Almond Lodge Hotel, no public bar). In 1881 this was bought by William Haig son of successful whisky distiller John Haig – John's other son was controversial WWI commander General Douglas Haig. In 1936 Edinburgh council bought this estate and laid out a nine-hole public pay and play golf course which was very unusual for its time. The course took its name from the neighbouring Silverknowe House. This mansion burnt down in 1960, but its estate added a further tranche of public open space by the shore. As you round the corner there is a low building on the left. This is the Broadwalk Beachclub and Cafe.

> The Broadwalk Beachclub and Cafe is a great place to stop for food, drinks and toilets. In good weather it can be very busy

This modern building replaced an old Victorian cottage from which a tearoom once operated, but restricted access to the shore during wartime caused its closure.

Beyond the cafe, the ground becomes flatter and the Esplanade continues through land that was part of **Lauriston Castle**, about 1km to the south. The castle, which is open to the public, was gifted to the city by the Reid family in 1926; another example of the public getting acces to the shore once a private estate came into the city's ownership. This area has remained open fields because, like the stretch of coastline just crossed, it was designated a (detached) portion of the Edinburgh Green Belt when that was created in 1957.

Passing a copse of trees, the route arrives at Cramond's sandy beach. Note the large stone sculpture of a fish head on the sand by Scottish sculptor Ronald Rae. A prolific artist, Rae

Section 3 WATER & WILDERNESS

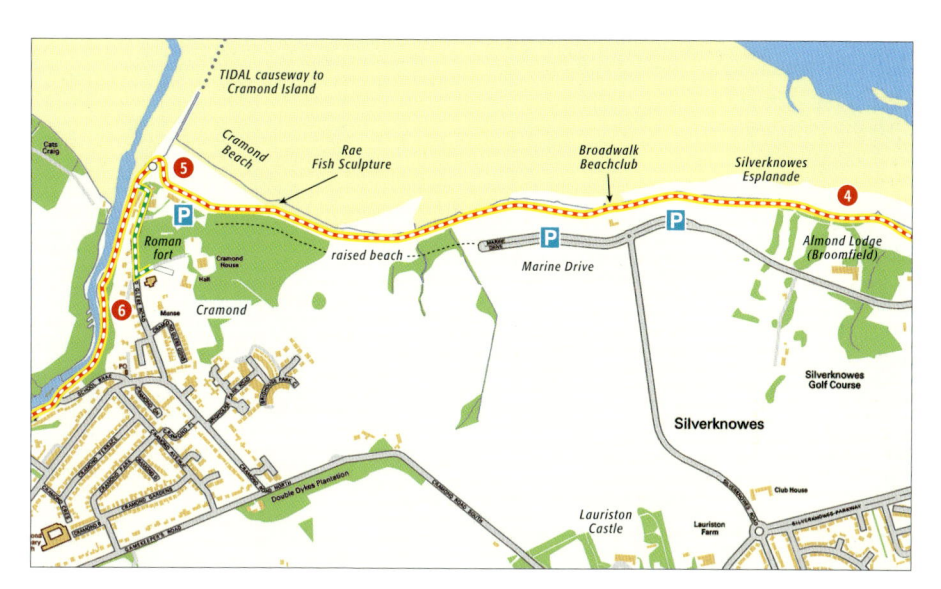

has carved many of his works in Cramond Kirkyard nearby and this particular one – carved from a piece of granite (not a local stone) – was purchased in 2009 with funds raised by the local community.

Keeping ahead, **Cramond Beach** widens on the right. It is an important location for sea birds and waders and there are several historic accounts of whales being stranded here; a pod of 25 whales are reported to have beached and died here in 1690.

When Cramond became part of Edinburgh in 1920, it was a remote and rather run-down village, but construction of the esplanade helped open it up to visitors, as well as giving access to the new golf course at Silverknowes.

❺ The esplanade comes to an end at a roundabout where a causeway on the right heads out to **Cramond Island**. It takes some time to walk out and back and explore the island, so save it for another day and be sure to check the tide times to avoid getting marooned.

> 👫 At the roundabout there are public toilets (open 10am to 6pm daily)

Turn left to leave the shore and follow the

CRAMOND ISLAND

Formed at a similar time to Arthur's Seat, Cramond Island is a volcanic feature called a dolerite sill, created by magma intruded between layers of sedimentary rocks. It became exposed during the last ice age when the ice sheet – which was over a kilometre thick – moved over the land eroding away the softer sedimentary rocks overlaying it. This hard rock was quarried in the past as it was particularly suitable for the floors of ovens.

The island was inhabited in the past and farmed as late as 1904. In World War II it was fortified and formed an important part of a chain of defence on the islands of the River Forth to protect the railway bridge and the dockyard at Rosyth. The concrete blocks lining the causeway are part of these wartime defences.

Section 3 WATER & WILDERNESS

Cramond Gallery Bistro on the quayside

old quayside by the River Almond. As you make the turn, a street called **Cramond Village** heads uphill to the left giving access to the Cramond Inn, Cramond Kirk and the adjacent Roman Fort.

> 🍴 *In the village there is the Cramond Inn (open for food and drink from 11am, 12.30 on Sundays, till evening) and on the quayside the Cramond Gallery Bistro (open 9.30am till 4.30pm or 5pm Saturdays)*

Follow the broad quayside road past the picturesque late 18th century workers' housing built when the village was booming (sympathetically restored c1960 by Lindsay & Partners for Edinburgh council and now Grade A listed). At the time of their construction, there were 343 people resident in the village, mainly iron workers, sailors and day labourers. Seven sailing vessels operated out of the harbour bringing in coal, iron (from Russia and Sweden) and lime, and exporting finished iron products and steel. A further five boats were working the local oyster beds, but even then, it was noted that they had been overfished.

The harbour has ancient origins and was used by the Romans who built a fort here as they pushed into Scotland and, for some decades, held territory as far as the Antonine Wall.

Note the steps on the quayside where the row-boat ferry used to take passengers across the river to Dalmeny Estate on the western bank. The service ceased in 2001 due to concerns about the spread of foot and mouth disease and never restarted. The road narrows as it passes the small quay leading into the boat yard, then becomes the path of the **River Almond Walkway** heading south beside the river.

To walk up the Almond Valley is to revisit the first phase of Scotland's industrial revolution when the power of water began to be harnessed, not just for processing grain, but also for manufacturing. It was this development of manufacturing industry, in the rural hinterland of Edinburgh, in the relatively peaceful decades

Section 3 WATER & WILDERNESS

ROMAN CRAMOND

Cramond's Roman connections were long known, but post-war archaeological surveys have revealed a sophisticated settlement with a fort covering 2.4 hectares and 4.5m high walls enclosing barracks, a commander's house, workshops, granaries, a bath house and workshops. Established to defend the eastern end of the Antonine Wall – the northernmost defence of Roman-occupied Britain and the Roman Empire – the fort is thought to have been occupied for about 30 years from 140 AD and is worth viewing if time allows.

In 1997 the man who operated the small row-boat ferry over the mouth of the River Almond detected something in the mud of the riverbed. When investigated, this turned out to be a large Roman sculpture depicting a lioness devouring a bound, male prisoner.

There has been talk of a new visitor centre and museum being built in the village to showcase its Roman remains, but nothing has come of this plan and, for now, this important sculpture is in the National Museum of Scotland in Edinburgh's Chambers Street.

after 1745, which generated the rising wealth of the city and made the New Town and the associated improvements possible.

6 As you leave the quay behind, look at the opposite bank and pick out the site of another landing place. Three 'bays' indicate the site of Craigie dock from where sandstone from the up river Craigiemill Quarry was shipped.

At a barrier, note an indent in the riverbank. This is an old dock at the highest tidal point on the river and, at high tide, sailing vessels were pulled here from Cramond by horses. Pass through the barrier into School Brae. The buildings on the left are the 18th century stores and offices of Cockle Mill.

Turn immediately right and follow the riverside path round a flat lawn which was the site of the **Cockle Mill** buildings before their final destruction by flooding in 1935. In medieval times, this was a water-powered grain mill when the Cramond Estate was owned by the Bishop of Durham. In 1752, it was taken over by the Smith & Wright Work Company of Leith and repurposed as Cramond Iron Works, coming into the ownership of the Cadell family and their business partners seven years later.

Yachts below Cramond Quay at the mouth of the River Almond

Section 3 **WATER & WILDERNESS**

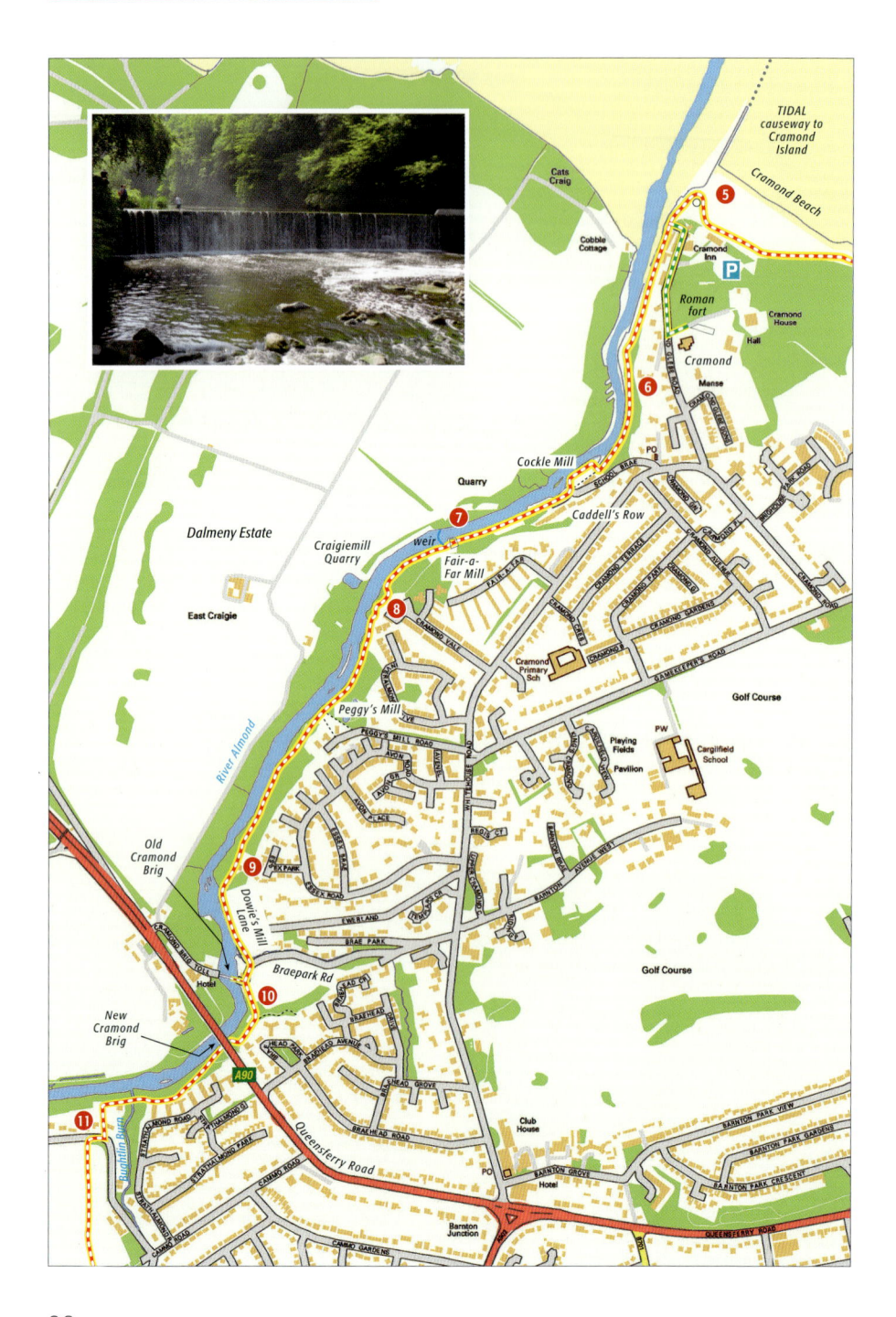

Section 3 WATER & WILDERNESS

River Almond Walkway at the site of the former Cockle Mill

It was then a slit mill where bars of raw iron were passed through rollers operated by the waterwheel (later steam engine) which 'slit' them into rods. These were used for making nails and products such as hoops for wine casks.

Following the path beside the river, note the white water; this is not natural. When the mill was water powered (the complex had three waterwheels) there was a large weir here to dam the flow and force the water into the mill

CRAMOND, THE CADELLS & THE SCOTTISH INDUSTRIAL REVOLUTION I

Between 1759 and 1868, one family, the Cadells, dominated the industry on the River Almond. The driving forces behind this industrial enterprise were William Senior and his son William Junior. Originally ship owners and builders in Cockenzie, East Lothian, the family imported raw iron bars from Russia and Sweden at a time when metal was worked in Scotland but locally occurring iron ores were not yet smelted.

In the 1750s the Cadells got together with English chemist Dr John Roebuck (he had studied medicine at the University of Edinburgh and settled in East Lothian) and English businessman Samuel Garbett and developed plans to start large scale iron production in Scotland exploiting the ironstone that was found alongside the coal seams. The site they chose – with water power, close to coal and ironstone deposits – was on the River Carron, near Falkirk.

This new works, which both smelted ore and made finished products, started in 1760 and under its later name, the Carron Iron Works, would become a powerhouse of the Scottish Industrial Revolution. At the same time, this partnership took over the two lower mills on the River Almond, which had been converted by Leith manufacturers Smith & Wright into slit mills for processing iron bars, and were collectively known as Cramond Iron Works.

By 1770 iron production at Carron was running smoothly and the partners reorganised how the businesses were run with the Cadells assuming full control of the Cramond Iron Works, bringing the two upper mills into the operation from the early 1780s, and continuing to innovate production methods and products over the years.

Section 3 WATER & WILDERNESS

The ruins of Fair-a-Far iron forge. The red walls exhibit oxide pollutants from the furnaces

lade. It is not known when it was destroyed but its remains cause the water turbulence. Iron working here ceased around 1868.

The path returns to the road (Caddell's Row). Here turn right to walk past the car park, where the housing to the left was built for the mill workers, and rejoin the Almond Walkway. In the early 19th century, a horse-drawn tramway ran along here connecting the next mill to the quayside at Cockle Mill.

After approximately 200m the ground broadens out and the path divides. Take the right branch which runs alongside the river and through the ruins of the iron forge at a spot known as **Fair-a-Far**.

7 This was the location for a corn mill, then a waulk mill (washing, stretching and beating of woven yarn), prior to Smith & Wright converting it to work iron in 1752. In 1772 the manager Thomas Edington (a major innovator in the Scottish metal industry in his own right) married Cadell's daughter and became joint owner of the works.

The surviving walls, which date from the 1750s, once contained two furnaces and a great forge-hammer. The buildings are constructed of locally quarried sandstone and the red tinge to the stone is a result of the iron rich pollutants given off when the foundry was in operation. More buildings remained before a severe flood on the river in 1935. The mill lade was also filled in at that date.

Walk to the barrier to enjoy the view of the spectacular weir which spans the river. This regulated the flow of water to the three water-wheels which once powered the iron works. Some fresher-looking stone at the far side of the weir is a 'fish pass', built in 2018. This allows salmon to avoid the weir and swim back upstream to spawn.

A line of square holes in the rock face above this, once contained supports for a timber constructed track along which wagons loaded with stone were hauled from Craigie quarry to the loading bays seen earlier.

Rejoin the main path up a short flight of stone steps and keep ahead for around 100m. The river is now in a narrow gorge as it passes through a bed of Hailes Sandstone which outcrops between two faults. The river cut the

Section 3 WATER & WILDERNESS

> ### CRAMOND, THE CADELLS & THE SCOTTISH INDUSTRIAL REVOLUTION II
> *The Cadell's ownership of Cramond Iron Works came to an end in 1868 after a banking crisis slowed the demand for iron and demonstrated that small operations like Cramond Iron Works had become uncompetitive. Newer plants in Lanarkshire were much closer to coal and ironstone sources and could produce cheaper products.*
>
> *However, the sale of Cramond Iron Works didn't seriously dent the Cadells. By the end of the 19th century, the family owned, or had owned, agricultural and mining interests on estates at Banton, Grange and Cockenzie, coal mines in Fife, the Clyde and Muirpark Iron Works, a pottery at Prestonpans, Saltpans at Ayr and Banton Brickworks at Kilsyth.*
>
> *The Cadells created quite a dynasty – one of William Junior's sons was a respected mathematician, while a grandson was in charge of the Duke of Buccleuch's coal mines before setting up the Bridgeness Iron Works. His son, in turn, was the eminent geologist Henry M.Cadell who worked with the Scottish Geological Survey. Robert Cadell, one of William Junior's nephews, was a partner in the firm which published Sir Walter Scott; a personal friend of Scott, Cadell ended up owning the copyright to his works after the author's death.*

gorge through the sandstone when the land rose relative to sea level after the ice age. With no room for a path under the cliff, a large flight of steps has been constructed.

8 These are known as the **Salvesen Steps**, after local landowner Captain Keith Salvesen (a descendant of Christian Salvesen who founded the Leith whaling business). In 1966 Salvesen solved the access problem by giving the council the strip of land over which the steps pass, as well as contributing to the cost of their construction.

At the time of writing, temporary metal steps have replaced the old rotted timber ones on

The wooden Salvesen Steps skirt a sandstone crag which blocks access to the riverbank

On the south side, the steps have rotted and been replaced by temporary metal ones

Section 3 WATER & WILDERNESS

Mill workers' cottages on Dowie's Mill Lane

the south side, and while there has been talk of a new permanent replacement suitable for wheelchairs and pushchairs, costs have, so far, proved prohibitive.

At the top of the steps, across the river and hidden in trees, are traces of Craigiemill

BRIDGING THE ALMOND ON THE ROUTE TO QUEENSFERRY

The City of Edinburgh Council is responsible for over 340 bridges and Old Cramond Brig is the most ancient. This stone bridge was built in the late 15th century to serve the pilgrim route from Edinburgh to St Andrews which crossed the Firth of Forth at its narrowest point via a ferry, named Queensferry after its founder Queen Margaret.

The number of pilgrims on the route dwindled after the Reformation and, with neglect, the bridge suffered a partial collapse and was unusable before being rebuilt in 1617. Subsequent repairs, including work by Robert Mylne, the master mason for Holyrood Palace, are recorded by dates inscribed on the parapets. It spans nearly 40m, using three arches (each slightly different in shape, reflecting age and repairs) constructed from local yellow sandstone.

By 1776, road traffic was increasing and there were two stagecoaches crossing the Cramond Brig on a regular service to the ferry. Thirty years later, military considerations persuaded the government to upgrade the harbour at South Queensferry and the road to it; the ferry crossing coming under the control of Parliamentary Trustees in 1810.

By 1823, increased vehicle traffic meant the narrow old brig was inadequate and a new bridge was built to an elegant design of eight, semi-circular stone arches by John Rennie (who designed the original Leith Docks and Waterloo Bridge in London). This bridge was replaced by the current utilitarian concrete road bridge in anticipation of increased road traffic when the Forth Road Bridge opened in 1964.

Section 3 WATER & WILDERNESS

Quarry. There was quarrying at several points along the river but this was the largest and produced good building stone. The path remains high for another 100m before another long flight of steps head back to the water.

Approximately 200m after the Salvesen Steps, where stairs come in from the left, is the site of **Peggy's Mill**. Not as ancient as Cockle Mill, there was a grain mill here for over a hundred years when the Cadells purchased it in 1782 and converted it to the production of spades for agricultural use as part of Cramond Iron Works.

The iron industry slumped after the Napoleonic Wars, so the mill was converted to papermaking, a business the Cadells already knew as William Jnr had inherited Auchendinny papermill near Penicuik, on his marriage. However, due to impurities in the water, the paper was never of great quality. After the Cadells sold up it was used for some time as a chemical manufactory and, in the early 20th century, for small scale furniture production before demolition in the 1960s. No traces now remain.

9 Keep on the riverside path for a further 250m, then walk right beside the river to see all that remains of the last of the old mills along this stretch of river – there are traces of the dam in the water and a sluice gate on the riverbank. Again, this was an older mill that was taken over by the Cadells in 1782, initially for iron working, but later converted to a sawmill for timber production.

Next, the path joins **Dowie's Mill Lane** where some of the cottages for the mill workers survive and the first glimpses of Cramond Old Brig can be enjoyed through the trees. At a T-junction with **Braepark Road**, turn right and follow the road past the gable end of a cottage and onto **Old Cramond Brig**. Don't cross over but admire the open views up and down the River Almond. Return to the cottage and rejoin the signposted River Almond Walkway, which starts by the wall behind the cottage.

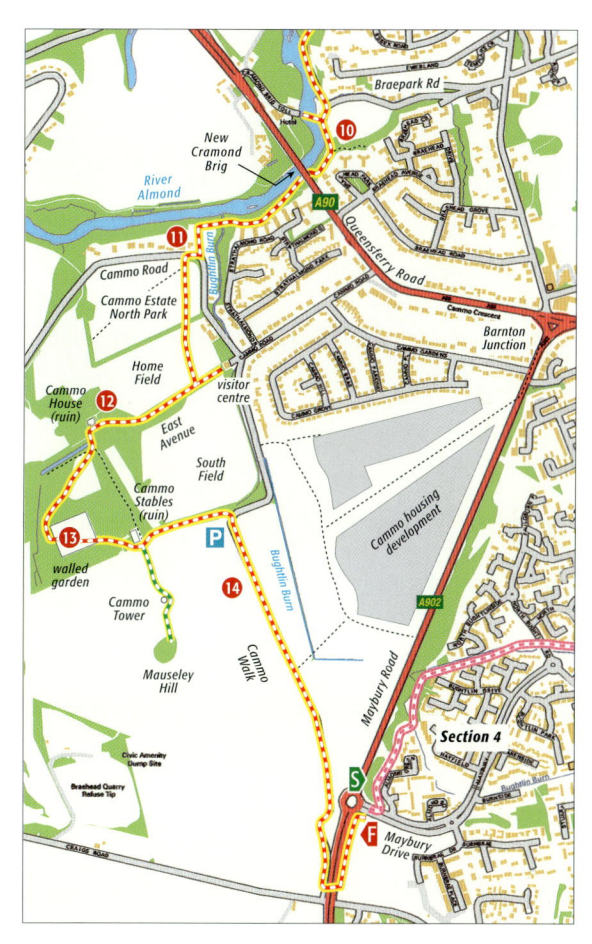

10 Keep to the main path (right fork) to reach an interpretation board on a stone plinth. This overlooks and explains some ruins known as Jock Howieson's Cottage. According to one of Walter Scott's tales, the land on which it stands was gifted to Jock by a grateful King James V in the 16th century after Jock saved him from an attack. In return for the gift, Howieson and his descendants were duty bound to wash the King or his descendants'

95

Section 3 WATER & WILDERNESS

Crossing the Home Field at Cammo Estate. With the nearby North Field, this was once Cramond Brig Golf Course, whose clubhouse was on the site of this modern white house

hands when they came this way. Regardless of whether the tale had any basis in reality, Scott had this hand-washing ceremony performed on George IV during his visit of 1822 as the King was on his way to depart for London from Port Edgar near South Queensferry. An old guidebook claims Queen Victoria, George V and George VI all partook of this handwashing ceremony here when they too visited Edinburgh.

Go down and up steps to the left of the cottage, then turn right onto the main walkway as it climbs with the river below to the right. Just before the path reaches a main road, turn right down a substantial flight of steps. At the bottom turn left and go under the modern **New Cramond Brig** carrying the A90 Queensferry Road. The steel structural supports were added in 1999 when the slim concrete design was found to have structural weaknesses.

With the river still on the right, ascend another stepped section, soon followed by a stepped descent to cross the Bughtlin Burn on a small wooden bridge. Beyond this, ascend another short set of steps and keep alongside a wooden fence before the path seems to come to an end. Turn left away from the river onto a narrow path between a wooden fence and a wire fence and hedge, to emerge on Cammo Road, leaving the riverside behind.

(11) Turn right, follow the road round for 20m, then cross over and go through a gate on the left into **Cammo Estate**. This 40 hectare public open space is a local nature reserve, but while it looks and feels rural, the landscape here is all man-made. Its specimen trees and buildings were added in the 18th century to enhance the vision of classical parkland. However, over the decades nature has softened the constructed landscape and produced a wildlife habitat that supports badgers, bats, roe deer and a diverse population of woodland and farmland birds.

Pick up a broad grassy path on the left and head roughly south across the meadow (called **North Park** on the map), aiming for a gap in the line of trees ahead. Go through and cross straight over a smaller meadow (**Home Field**), again heading for a gap in the line of trees.

Between 1907 and 1930, these two fields were leased by the estate's owners, the Maitland-Tennant Family, to the Cramond Brig

Section 3 WATER & WILDERNESS

Golf Club who laid it out as a golf course; it even hosted a professional tournament in 1912. The large modern house seen to the left as you cross Home Field was formerly the site of the Arts & Crafts style clubhouse.

Through the trees is a wide path, **East Avenue**, which once formed a grand entrance to the mansion house.

> 👫 *A small detour left down East Avenue leads to the lodge house with a small Visitor Centre and toilets. Unfortunately, opening hours are limited to just Thursday 1 to 3:30pm and Sunday 2 to 4pm*

Turn right and follow this avenue as it heads south-west then bends a little to the right to bring you to the ruins of **Cammo House**. Go left off the path to view the ruins, then take the first path on the left, heading south past the end of a 140m ornamental canal, which was part of the 18th century formal gardens.

🔴**12** Turn off right at the next junction, signposted to the Walled Garden, and follow an old tarmac path. Keep going through the trees in a south-westerly direction ignoring all other paths off left and right. After about 275m you come to the north-west corner of the walled garden where the path bends south with the wall on the left, to reach a gateway giving access to the garden.

CAMMO HOUSE

Cammo House was built in 1693 by John Menzies who acquired the estate by marriage. The house was noted to be in the style of Robert Mylne and contained elements which showed the transition between a baronial fortified house and a classical house.

In 1710 money troubles forced him to sell to John Clerk, who in turn owned the house till 1724 when he inherited his father's baronetcy and moved to the family seat at Penicuik. Clerk was an influential man in Edinburgh, a judge and a politician involved in the Act of Union between Scotland and England; he sat in the last of the Old Scottish Parliaments and in the first of the new British Parliaments.

Clerk sold the house to a relative, John Hog, who employed architect William Adam to remodel it but subsequently suffered money troubles and sold it to James Watson in 1741. Watson renamed it New Saughton and it stayed in the ownership of this family for three generations till 1873 when it was bought by Alexander Campbell.

Its final occupants, the eccentric Maitland-Tennant family, purchased it in 1898. Wealthy Mrs Margaret Clark had bought the house (with her own money) then in 1909 divorced her husband and adopted the name Maitland-Tennant. She continued to live at Cammo with one of her sons, Percival. The pair were reclusive and, as she dressed only in black, she was locally known as the Black Widow.

She died in 1955, when Percival abandoned the house to his 30 dogs and lived in the lodge house instead. Percival bequeathed the house and estate to the National Trust for Scotland on his death in 1975, but the trust struggled to know what to do with the rotting building. Vandals were more decisive and set it on fire – twice – so that by 1979 the decision was taken to demolish the house leaving the stabilised ruins which remain. Edinburgh council took over the estate in 1980.

Section 3 WATER & WILDERNESS

Despite their ruined state, Cammo Stables retain some of their classical beauty

13 This walled garden was another element of the Watson family's scheme for the gardens between 1778 and 1805. Although the walled garden had been allowed to become overgrown, it has been regenerated in recent years as part of the local development programme.

Cross the walled garden to exit at a gate in the south-east corner and continue east, following a sign to the stables, to reach the ruins of the classical **Cammo Stables** of 1811.

In the field on the right is **Cammo Tower** This is an early 19th century water tower which, when built, had wind-powered pumps and was originally topped with sails. The tower is worth the 10 minute there and back diversion to view it, with another 10 minutes to climb Mauseley Hill behind if desired. There is no access inside the tower.

From the stables, keep ahead taking the path downhill to the car park. Cross this and turn

---

CAMMO GARDENS

The first owner whose imprint can be detected on the gardens is Sir John Clerk, 2nd Baronet of Penicuik who took a great deal of interest in the gardens and garden design in general. His scheme was formal with straight avenues, parterres and enclosures containing roundels.

His successor Hog's main contribution to the garden was the canal (a scheduled monument), a formal feature but one which was left in place when the Watsons began remodelling in an open parkland style, ripping out the formal elements and thinning out the trees. The family enhanced this landscape by building a 'ha-ha' ditch to prevent animals straying into the formal gardens, without putting up a wall or fence, which would impede the view.

In the late 19th century Alexander Campbell planted the pinetum (not directly on the route), where fine specimen trees still remain. It could be argued that the Maitland-Tennants destroyed the gardens with their neglect, but looking at it another way, it was because the gift of the decaying estate to the National Trust for Scotland in 1975 was so problematic, that Edinburgh council acquired it in 1980 and reincarnated the estate as a Wilderness Park open to the public.

Section 3 WATER & WILDERNESS

right onto a narrow road, **Cammo Walk**.

14 Follow this south for a kilometre with views right to Mauseley Hill and left to a new housing development. The fields on which the houses have been built were once part of Edinburgh's greenbelt until 2016 when the council's Local Development Plan was approved. Among other things, the plan's stated aim was to address the city's need for new housing as, since the 1990s, it has experienced strong population growth. The 2011 census showed a city population of 477,000, which is estimated to have grown to 542,599 in 2021 with a further projected increase to 600,000 by 2035.

The plan allowed for some of the housing need this creates to be met by releasing land from greenbelt designation such as here at Cammo. 655 dwellings are being built while south of Mauseley Hill in the Maybury area, a further 1,700 dwellings are planned. The development incorporates two linear gardens to preserve views of Cammo Tower and Mauseley Hill, and the channel of the Bughtlin Burn is being deepened as a flood prevention measure.

Reaching a T-junction with Craigs Road, turn left and cross the A902 **Maybury Road** at the lights. From here, walk north for about 200 metres to the roundabout and turn right into Maybury Drive.

Section 3 has skirted the city's north-western extremity, offering history ranging from a harbour dating from Roman times, through early ironworking from the industrial revolution to gasworks and quarries. This is now bookended by contrasting modern housing developments – at Granton, development of the brownfield sites creeps on slowly, while at Cammo green fields are built over as soon as planning is granted. The difference being the much better road connectivity at Cammo. **F**

> 🚌 Lothian bus 31 back to the city centre from Almond Green – Maybury Drive, just east of the Maybury Road roundabout

Cammo Tower from the flanks of Mauseley Hill. In the background are the ruined Cammo Stables

99

Corstorphine Hill Tower – erected in 1871 by William Macfie of Clermiston

Section 4

WESTERN HEIGHTS

Route: Maybury Road to Balgreen tram stop
Distance: 7km; 4.25 miles
Grade: Moderate, some short steep ascents and descents, paths slippery when wet and waymarks in the woods need to be followed with care; limited toilets and refreshments
Access: Lothian bus 31 from Princes Street to Maybury Drive (*Almond Green bus stop*)

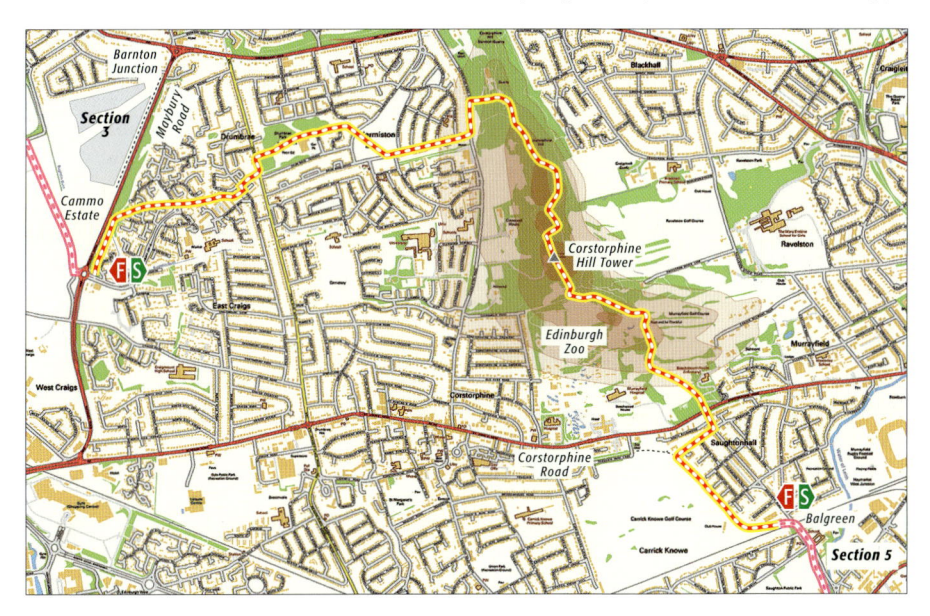

A long gentle climb through mixed post-war suburbs leads to Corstorphine Hill, the first of Edinburgh's outer hills. This is another volcanic feature which has been shaped by ice but with a different creation story to that of Castle Rock and Calton Hill. Once at the summit, this route joins part of the long-distance trail, the John Muir Way. This heavily wooded hill is not about panoramic vistas from the top but does reward with unusual views of the city on the ascent and descent

 From the Almond Green bus stop on **Maybury Drive**, east of the roundabout on Maybury Road, follow the tarmac pavement left into **Almond Green**, a low-density post-war housing development.

After a short distance the path goes off left and is followed downhill to cross over the Bughtlin Burn. This is the southern branch of the burn crossed on the approach to Cammo Estate in Section 3.

❶ Once across, turn left then approximately 150m further on turn right, before a second bridge. Here a large glacial boulder in the hedge is a reminder that this area was covered in

101

Section 4 WESTERN HEIGHTS

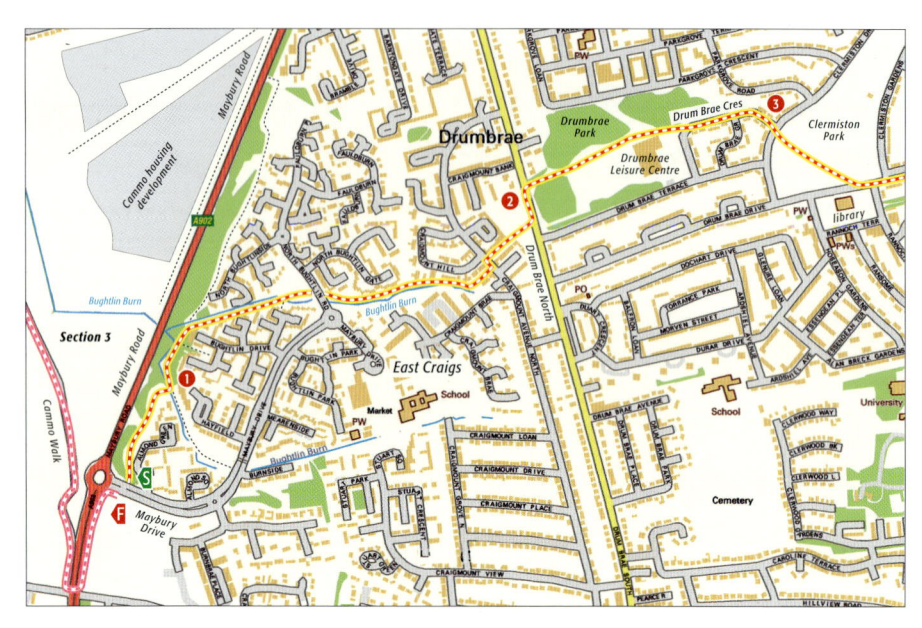

glacial debris when the last ice sheet retreated.

Follow the good tarmac path on the right side of the burn, heading gently uphill and now following the Bughtlin Burn's northern branch.

The underlying rocks here are undifferentiated shales from the Strathclyde Formation, so are still part of the geological feature called the Granton Dome, the upfolding of the rock contributing to the slope.

Where traditional suburban development would have culverted over the burn, happily here it has been kept and utilised for a pedestrian route through East Craigs. The straight path eventually recrosses the burn and then passes under **North Bughtlin Road**.

Keep to the burnside path and in approximately 150m stay right where it forks. Houses begin to front the path which soon turns away from the burn, narrowing as it passes between gardens, to exit onto **Craigmount Avenue North**.

Cross diagonally left over the road to a fenced alley, Drum Brae Walk, which quickly leads past houses to open green space and **Drum Brae North**. Walk a short distance downhill to cross this busy road via the island down on the right.

The northern branch of the burn goes under the road hereabouts, now in a culvert, and the southern branch does the same some 250m to the south. Between the two rise springs, which from at least the 1850s, supplied water for the nearby Corstorphine curling ponds. The ancient Scots winter sport of curling was formalised in 1838 by the formation of the Grand Caledonian Curling Club. Despite the building of indoor rinks in the 20th century, these ponds lasted till the housing was built.

Once across, turn left and walk up to the brow of the hill to enjoy the extensive views north over the Firth of Forth to Benarty Hill in Fife and south to the Pentland Hills

❷ At the brow, turn right onto the grass and cross **Drumbrae Park**, passing between clumps of trees and keeping to the left of the football pitches to reach Drumbrae Leisure Centre.

> *Drumbrae Leisure Centre has public toilets and there is also a small community cafe*

102

Section 4 WESTERN HEIGHTS

Beside the Bughtlin Burn at Craigmount Hill – an innovative style of suburban housing characterised by short terraces surrounding grassy courtyards, linked by footpaths utilising natural features

Only 4 hectares in size, this small park is very informal, with groups of low trees and shrubs surrounding the football pitches and a building housing the local leisure centre. It was designed to serve the needs of the large post-war council estate begun in 1954 and opened in 1961. At over 80m above sea level, it is a place of big skies and gusty winds.

Just before WWII, a survey by Edinburgh council had identified that there were 17,000 overcrowded houses within the city. War followed by post-war shortages of labour and materials meant this housing crisis could not be properly tackled till the mid-1950s. The post-war baby boom and an expectation of better standards added to the challenge. However, Edinburgh was fortunate to have this low-grade agricultural land on its fringe – the soil was stony, glacial till and dry due to its elevation above the lower springs. In the

EAST CRAIGS – A NEW APPROACH

The style of housing layout at East Craigs was innovative in its time and it arose out of a research project, the Housing Research Unit, within the School of Architecture at the University of Edinburgh. This was established under the university's first Professor of Architecture, Robert Matthew (Edinburgh born and educated but, in the immediate post-war years, Chief Architect and Planning Officer for London County Council where he designed the Royal Festival Hall).

This research put an emphasis on the needs of the people who were going to live in the houses and on the quality of the spaces around the properties. From this research, a style of courtyard housing within a network of paths was devised. It was adopted here at East Craigs on what was formerly Southfield and part of East Craigs Farms, with a great emphasis on preserving landscape features, trees and greenspace with pedestrian routes separated out from the traffic access.

Section 4 WESTERN HEIGHTS

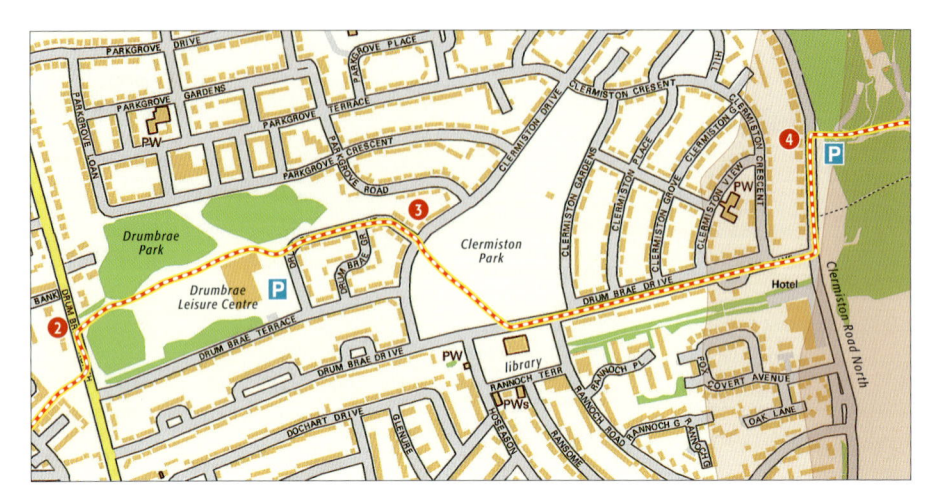

following decade, the city managed to complete an average of just over 1,300 houses a year.

After the leisure centre, join a tarmac path and follow it round past the car park to **Drum Brae Crescent**, and walk left along this elevated road. On a fine day, there are views north over the treetops and houses to the Firth of Forth, Benarty Hill and the prominent Lomond Hills.

❸ At the T-junction with **Clermiston Drive**, cross over to the playing fields of **Clermiston Park**. This little park – the highest in the city – is just over 5.5 hectares and was opened in 1956 when, again, it was designed to serve a new council housing scheme. Cross the park diagonally right aiming for a large white building, Drumbrae Library Hub, seen through a gap in the trees. The hub opened in 2012.

> *There are public toilets at Drum Brae Library Hub and there is a Scotmid Co-operative supermarket in Rannoch Terrace behind the building*

Turn left on **Drum Brae Drive** and walk uphill. A grass strip with trees suggests that when the estate was constructed a tram route was planned, but this would have been abandoned in 1956 when Edinburgh council decided to scrap its trams.

As already noted, the soil here is till, comprised of debris carried along by the ice sheet and deposited when it melted, and is not great for agriculture. Between the wars, an enterprising grocer by the name of Andrew Ewing purchased the land to the right (south) of the road, the site of Clermiston Mains Farm, and ran an impressively large poultry farm to supply his chain of 250 shops across central Scotland and northern England with eggs.

The shops went by the name Buttercup Dairies and had a logo of a small girl in a bonnet holding a buttercup under the chin of a cow and asking, "Do you like butter?" A devout Baptist, Ewing believed all the eggs laid on Sunday should be given away and the wealth he amassed in his lifetime should be given away before his death.

Drumbrae Leisure Centre

104

Section 4 WESTERN HEIGHTS

Cold War relics at Barnton Quarry – site of a one-time government bunker in the event of nuclear attack

At the T-junction with **Clermiston Road North** the open spaces of Corstorphine Hill can be seen directly ahead. Turn left here, cross over the road and walk downhill. Ignoring the pedestrian entrance through the wall on the right after about 40m, continue down for another 150m to the walled car park for **Corstorphine Hill**.

❹ Turn in here and follow a rough vehicle track past the car park and through a metal barrier, to where it ends at a turning circle. Left of the track is the disused **Barnton Quarry**, containing a Cold War era bunker that is slowly being restored for public access. Old maps show that quarrying took place at several sites on Corstorphine Hill. Barnton Quarry, which was already in use by 1850 and worked till around 1930, was the largest with the dolerite

THE COLD WAR BUNKER – A NEW USE FOR AN OLD QUARRY

During WWII the disused Barnton Quarry housed an RAF Fighter Command Centre. Then, in 1952 as the Cold War intensified, a deep underground bunker was constructed to house a Radar Command Centre. Eight years later, it was further developed to become a Regional Seat of Government in the event of a nuclear strike.

Now a substantial complex, it had room to house more than 400 people over three floors, with the whole range of facilities to allow government to be maintained by ministers, military personnel and the emergency services. It had to contain suitable accommodation to house the Queen should she be in Scotland when nuclear war began and it even had a fully equipped BBC studio so government could communicate with the population.

The bunker is protected by 10-foot-thick concrete walls and blast-proof doors. At the surface, a small concrete building gives no clue to the huge underground complex. The bunker is slowly being restored so that it can be opened to the public as a museum.

Section 4 WESTERN HEIGHTS

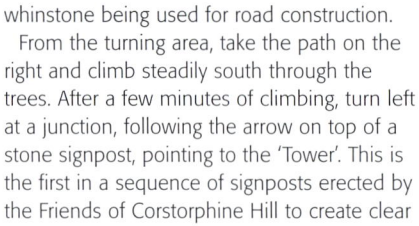

Approaching Corstorphine Hill Tower

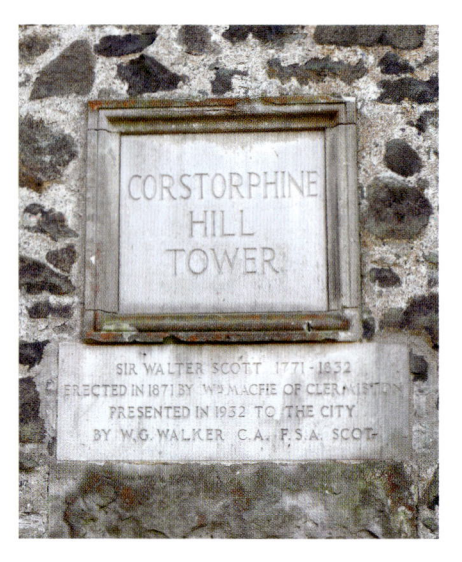

whinstone being used for road construction.

From the turning area, take the path on the right and climb steadily south through the trees. After a few minutes of climbing, turn left at a junction, following the arrow on top of a stone signpost, pointing to the 'Tower'. This is the first in a sequence of signposts erected by the Friends of Corstorphine Hill to create clear routes, as the paths up here can be confusing. Pass through a wooden barrier then as the path forks, ignore a second barrier up on the right and take the left fork heading slightly downhill on a well-defined path. In a few minutes there is a second signpost. Keep ahead here, again following the arrow to the 'Tower', and descend the undulating path to

GEOLOGY OF CORSTORPHINE HILL

Corstorphine Hill is a volcanic feature called a sill. It was formed at the same time as the volcano of Calton Hill, climbed in Section 1, but here the magma did not breach the surface, instead spreading horizontally between layers of sand and silt which had already been deposited on the seabed. In time, pressure turned the sand and silt into soft flagstone and sandstone rocks, while the magma cooled to form hard dolerite rock – essentially becoming a hard rock filling in a soft rock sandwich.

In more recent geological times, the surrounding landscape experienced severe forces which caused all the rock layers to be lifted and tilted so that they were no longer horizontal but dipping down to the west. During the last ice age, as the ice sheet moved across the landscape from west to east, its sheer force scraped away the soft flagstone and sandstone rocks of the top layer, exposing the harder dolerite below.

This exposed top face of the dolerite layer forms the western, gentle 'dip' slope of Corstorphine Hill, while at the top of the steeper eastern 'scarp' slope, the dolerite presents a jagged edge. This edge acquired its profile as the ice exploited cracks in the rock and plucked off large areas as it passed over. Below the dolerite is an outcrop of softer flagstone and sandstone, protected by the dolerite from erosion by the ice above.

Section 4 WESTERN HEIGHTS

CORSTORPHINE HILL TOWER

The builder of this tower was Clermiston Estate owner William Macfie, the son of a successful sugar refiner. The Macfie family was representative of a segment of Edinburgh society who made their money during the early industrial revolution and then purchased small country estates immediately beyond the city.

Macfie was a passionate fan of Sir Walter Scott, and in 1871, he built this tower to commemorate the centenary of the writer's birth. The tower is constructed of local dolerite with sandstone dressings. It rises up through four storeys to a viewing gallery where a panoramic view of central Scotland can be enjoyed over the treetops.

In 1932, on the centenary of Scott's death, Edinburgh council was asked to purchase it but considered the asking price of £350 too high. In response, a wealthy gentleman called W.G.Walker bought it and gifted it to the city. In times past it was open daily with a park attendant dispensing tickets, but now it is only open to the public on Sunday afternoons in summer and autumn and is staffed by volunteers.

reach metal railings. The slope to the left is very steep and has been quarried in places.

A further signpost is reached in a few minutes, this time at the top of steps on the left which come up from Hillpark Grove to the east. Ignore the steps and keep ahead on the main path still following 'Tower' signs. Below here at Craigrook were more quarries – long since filled in – and Craigrook Castle, which remains, but now surrounded by suburban housing.

The path makes a bend to the left and begins to climb again, passing through another wooden barrier. Many detached boulders litter this side of the hill; plucked by the ice but not carried far. Passing a bench, views of the northern suburbs can be seen to the left through the trees.

5 At the next signpost turn sharp right following the arrow to the 'Tower' and ascend an earth path up a steep slope. As the route flattens, a further signpost points left to the 'Tower'. Follow this up a flight of steps to finally reach **Corstorphine Hill Tower**, sometimes known as Clermiston Tower. Corstorphine Hill is only 162m high but offers fine views in all directions, if and where you can find a gap in the trees.

This public park came into the ownership of Edinburgh council in 1924 and forms a

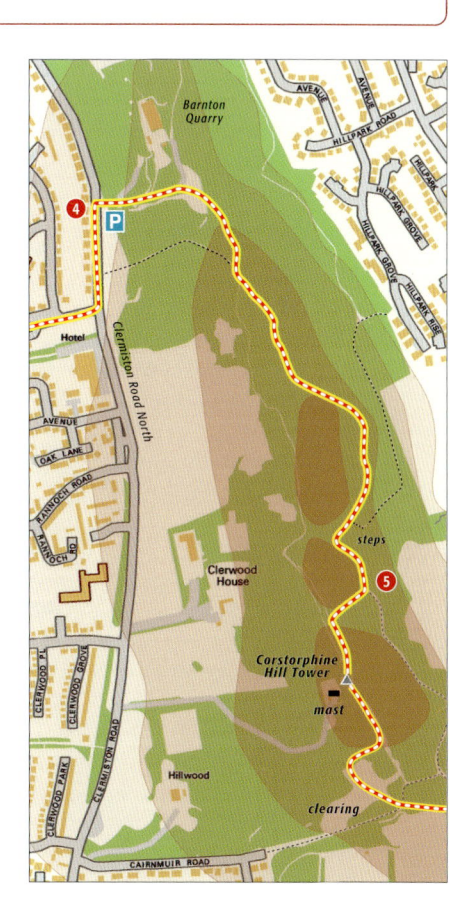

107

Section 4 WESTERN HEIGHTS

This slab of glaciated dolerite lies on the west side of Corstorphine Hill. Vertical 'striae' grooves gouged by the glacier indicate its west to east direction of travel. In this case from bottom to top

Corstorphine Hill woodland

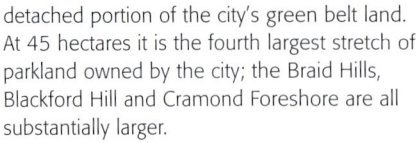

detached portion of the city's green belt land. At 45 hectares it is the fourth largest stretch of parkland owned by the city; the Braid Hills, Blackford Hill and Cramond Foreshore are all substantially larger.

Leave the tower in a southerly direction with the communications mast to the right and the ruins and the rocky highpoint of the hill on the left. The route is now on a section of the John Muir Trail with its wooden posts and distinctive trail markers (some with a picture of John Muir's face) and follows those markers and the 'Rest & Be Thankful' arrows on the stone signposts.

As the route swings to the right and descends, notice the smooth rock underfoot. Here, the dolerite was worn smooth by the ice sheet into a feature known as a glacial pavement. In places distinct grooves or 'striae' can also be seen. These were gouged by boulders embedded in the ice sheet as it passed over and help to indicate the direction of travel. The striae here were important. In the 1850s the geologist Robert Chambers became convinced

JOHN MUIR WAY

This 134-mile coast to coast walking and cycle route from Dunbar to Helensburgh was opened in 2014 and commemorates the life and work of Victorian naturalist John Muir. Born in Dunbar in 1838, Muir and his family emigrated to the USA when he was 11. Muir was instrumental in the preservation of areas of wilderness in the mountains of California and Nevada and is known as the 'father' of national parks. In the USA, the 211-mile John Muir Trail is seen as the premier long-distance trail.

Scotland's John Muir Way ends at Helensburgh on the Firth of Clyde where it connects to Loch Lomond and the Trossachs National Park, created in 2002 and Scotland's first national park. Muir never lost his connection to his Scottish roots and carried a volume of Robert Burns poetry with him on all his travels through the American wilderness.

Section 4 WESTERN HEIGHTS

> **EDINBURGH ZOO**
>
> *The location of the Zoo here is no accident. An earlier menagerie in the city in the mid-19th century had not been a success because the conditions were not suitable for non-native animals, so when the Zoological Society of Scotland (ZSS) was founded in 1909, it sought enough space for large open enclosures and a sheltered south-facing site.*
>
> *Corstorphine Hill is aligned generally north-south, but at the south end it has an easterly projecting spur like the foot of a boot. Below the spur's sheltered south face was the 30 hectare estate of Corstorphine Hill House. When the estate came on the market in 1913 the society had not yet raised the funds required but Edinburgh council stepped in, bought the estate and effectively leased it to the society.*
>
> *The ZSS commissioned Patrick Geddes and Frank Mears to produce the layout for the lower section (the upper section was under lease to Corstorphine Golf Club till 1928). In 1913 the Zoo was gifted three King Penguins brought back on a Christian Salvesen whaling ship. The penguins bred and produced chicks, the first penguin chicks born outside their natural habitat in the South Atlantic, a measure of the ZSS's success in finding a suitable site.*

of the emerging theory of glaciation as an alternative to earlier theories that landscapes such as these had been shaped by the Biblical flood. Chambers (he was a partner in publishers W&R Chambers and a friend and biographer of Sir Walter Scott), was known to bring fellow scientists up Corstorphine Hill to view these examples.

At a T-junction turn left, still following 'Rest & Be Thankful' signposts. The path now emerges into a small clearing with a picnic table to the left and two masts ahead.

Descend through the clearing and re-enter the trees, to reach a four-way junction. Cross straight over and climb a flight of steps with a stout metal fence on the right. The fence is

The clearing on the summit ridge, before the two masts and the Rest and Be Thankful

109

Section 4 WESTERN HEIGHTS

Looking north to Granton Gasometer, the Firth of Forth and Fife

the perimeter of Edinburgh Zoo, and although the animals cannot be seen, they can often be heard.

Along this part of the route, more glacial debris – boulders and rocks – line the path. Where the path forks, keep left away from the fence and follow a gentle descent before curving back to rejoin it. From here there are views over the northern suburbs, with the Granton Gasometer, a prominent feature on Sections 2 & 3 of the route, clearly visible.

6 Keep beside the fence to reach a bench and the **Rest and Be Thankful**, a fine viewpoint east across **Murrayfield Golf Course** towards Edinburgh Castle and Arthur's Seat. Continue descending beside the fence, south towards Corstorphine. Go through a stone archway and follow a rough path ahead, down the south side of the hill beside a mesh fence, with fine views south to the Pentland Hills. The descent is steep and rocky in places and will be slippery when wet. The ground can also be quite muddy after rain. Cross open hillside, veering to the left and sticking to the worn earth path, to pass through gorse, re-enter woodland and reach a wall. Descend the tarmac path beside the wall to exit through the park gates onto **Corstorphine Road**.

> ## THE REST AND BE THANKFUL & ROBERT LOUIS STEVENSON
>
> *This spot was immortalised by Edinburgh writer Robert Louis Stevenson (grandson of engineer Robert Stevenson, see p76) as the location where David Balfour and Alan Breck Stewart, the two principal characters in his 1886 novel Kidnapped, part company. "We came the by-way over the hill from Corstorphine; and when we got near to the place called Rest-and-be-Thankful, and looked down on Corstorphine bogs and over to the city and the castle on the hill, we both stopped, for we both knew without a word said that we had come to where our ways parted."*
>
> *The bogs Stevenson refers to have since been drained and turned into golf courses, with mature trees now punctuating the landscape, but the view, which encompasses Edinburgh Castle, Calton Hill and Arthur's Seat, is still magnificent.*

Section 4 WESTERN HEIGHTS

Arthur's Seat and Murrayfield Golf Course from the Rest and Be Thankful

111

Section 4 WESTERN HEIGHTS

Blackford Hill, centre, and The Braids, right, from the southern end of Corstorphine Hill

Cross over at the lights, turn right, then left down **Balgreen Road**, still on the route of the John Muir Way. Just before the second turning on the right, Balgreen Avenue, note a low stone wall on either side of the road.

This was a bridge over a man-made river called The Stank which is now enclosed in pipes. The river was all that was left of Corstorphine Loch, a large natural loch which was drained in stages from the 1670s.

Turn right into **Balgreen Avenue**, signposted Cycle Route 9. At the end of this cul-de-sac ascend a flight of steps onto the bed of the disused Corstorphine branch railway line and follow it left.

❼ This line was a short 5km suburban spur built by the North British Railway which operated from 1902 to serve the village of Corstorphine. The line enabled the village to grow as a commuter suburb and by the 1930s suburban development had spread out to meet the growing village. Intermediate stations were built here at Balgreen and at Pinkhill. It closed in 1968 reflecting the switch of

---

CORSTORPHINE LOCH

Corstorphine was one of seven lochs within the vicinity of Edinburgh which the great Edinburgh Victorian geologist Henry M.Cadell (grandson of William Cadell who owned the Cramond Iron Works described in Section 3) called the 'seven eyes of old Dun Edin'. The others were Gogar, Craigrook, The Burgh Loch (site of The Meadows) and Holyrood, now all drained, and Lochend and Duddingston which remain but much reduced in size.

Corstorphine, the largest stretching 5km along the south side of Corstorphine Hill from Roseburn in the east to Broomhouse in the west, was drained between 1670 and 1763 by cutting drainage ditches like The Stank. At its eastern edge, the Water of Leith flowed into and drained out of it, and the river still meanders across the bed of the drained loch.

Draining left a great swathe of flat land suitable for development. Later, two of the city's major sporting venues were built on this 'lake flat' – Murrayfield Stadium, home of Scottish Rugby and Tynecastle Park, home of Heart of Midlothian Football Club (they take their name from the Walter Scott novel).

Section 4 WESTERN HEIGHTS

commuter traffic from rail to road.

Carrick Knowe Golf Course is below on the right. There are a lot of golf courses in Edinburgh. One count puts the number within the city boundary at over 20, six of them council owned, and they add a considerable amount to the total green space within the city boundary. Not all the golf clubs are thriving though. In November 2018 Carrick Knowe Golf Club announced that, because its membership was down to just 20, it was closing after a century at the site. However, the course is still home to Carrickvale Golf Club.

> *Carrick Knowe Golf Course is an Edinburgh Leisure venue and toilets in the clubhouse are open to the public. The clubhouse can be accessed by descending the stairs on the bridge over Glendevon Park road*

After approximately 650m, Section 4 comes to an end at **Balgreen tram stop**, roughly the point where the Corstorphine branch line came off the main Glasgow to Edinburgh line. The railways, like the sports clubs, made effective use of the drained loch bed.

John Muir Way signpost above Balgreen Avenue

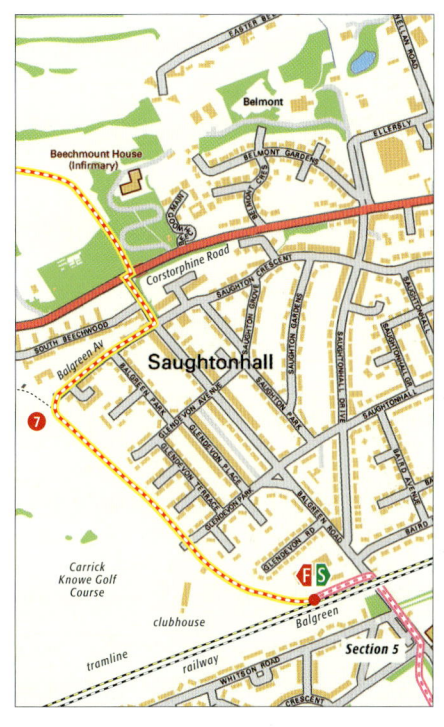

The railway lines have now been joined by the new Edinburgh tramline. Edinburgh removed its Victorian tram network in 1956, but the idea of a tram network to help relieve traffic pressure resurfaced in the 1990s as other cities successfully brought back trams. The whole scheme has been fraught with financial and political difficulties. Only part of the original scheme has been completed and at many times the original cost. However, as has been seen at Leith in Section 2, the system has proved successful and continues to expand.

This part of the line from the city centre to Edinburgh Airport has been operational since 2013 and utilises redundant railway track bed from here to Haymarket. An extension is underway with a completion date of 2023.

> *The best option for returning to the city centre is to take the tram from Balgreen*

Balgreen tram stop and the Jenners depository building

Section 5
HEALTHY SUBURBS

Route: Balgreen tram stop to Greenbank
Distance: 8km; 5 miles
Grade: Moderate – steps, steep climb plus gentle descent, muddy in places
Access: The quickest and most direct way to Balgreen tram stop is by tram from Princes Street. Lothian buses 1 and 22 from Princes Street stop in Stevenson Drive on the north edge of Saughton Park (*Balgreen Primary School bus stop*)

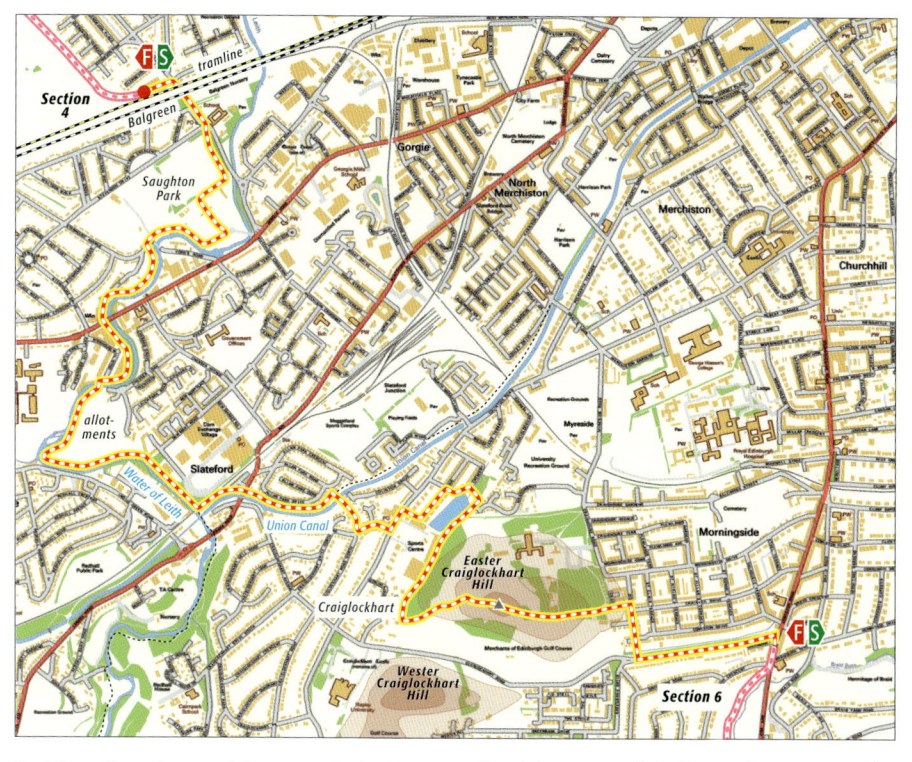

In Victorian times this part of the Water of Leith was still industrial, surrounded by open countryside crossed by railways. In the 20th century this flat land was used by the city for subsidised housing aimed at raising the health and well-being of the working classes who had largely been left behind in the Old Town when the wealthy abandoned it for the New Town over 100 years earlier. The route then climbs onto Easter Craiglockhart Hill, another of Edinburgh's seven hills, and one which became colonised by late Victorian ideas of health – outdoor pursuits, asylums and hydropathic hotels

Section 5 HEALTHY SUBURBS

Approaching the entrance gates in the walled garden of Saughton Park, which reopened in 2019 after a seven-year restoration costing £8 million

S From Balgreen tram stop, cross over the tramlines to a path beside the large Jenners Depository building, and follow it rightwards, downhill to **Balgreen Road**. The Jenners building has been a landmark for rail travellers since it was built in 1926 (now listed, architect James Bow Dunn). Jenners, the iconic Princes Street department store which closed in 2021, originally used the building to store the furniture of Edinburgh people working abroad, many in the Colonial Service.

More recently it acted as a warehouse for their retail stock, but became redundant in the modern retail environment. The building continues to be used as a storage facility. Cross Balgreen Road at the lights and turn right to go through a pedestrian tunnel under the tramline and the main Glasgow and Fife railway.

1 Continue a short distance to Balgreen Primary School and Balgreen Library on the left. They were designed by city architect Ebenezer James MacRae in 1932 as part of the new subsidised working class housing scheme which occupies a large site off **Stevenson Drive**, on the other side of the road. Here, MacRae needed to design a scheme at higher densities than the earlier garden suburb ideal but, rejecting tenements, he produced a humanely scaled development incorporating a distinctly European influenced crescent of terraced housing.

At the lights in front of the school, cross back over Balgreen Road, then Stevenson Drive and enter **Saughton Park**. Follow the path along the edge of the park to the left of the sports pitches and past the skateboard park to reach the access road and car park for the Balgreen Road entrance to Saughton Park's rose gardens. Turn right onto a path beside a wall and follow it to gates on the left, which access the walled garden.

> 🍽 🚻 *Saughton Park rose gardens have toilets in the Winter Garden and Conservatory at the eastern Balgreen Road entrance, and a cafe and toilets near the west gate entrance*

Saughton Park reopened in 2019 after a seven-year refurbishment and restoration project costing £8 million, and represents a major re-envisioning of the Edwardian concept of a public park.

Section 5 HEALTHY SUBURBS

The original Saughton Park predated the surrounding council housing but certainly aided MacRae's vision of creating a healthy environment to rehouse Old Town slum dwellers, where they would be able to better their lives.

The 17.4 hectare park came into being in 1900 when the grounds of Saughton Hall were purchased from Sir William Baird by Edinburgh council for £53,000. At that date the house was leased to the eminent psychiatrist Sir John Batty Tuke who ran a private asylum for the insane, but it too was purchased in 1907.

In its first few years the park was primarily used for sport with a nine-hole golf course and playing fields. Then, in 1908, it was used for the Scottish National Exhibition. Following the removal of the temporary exhibition buildings (they were sold and re-erected at Edinburgh Marine Gardens, Portobello), the park was laid out with formal flower beds including a Rosary, American Garden, Rock Garden and Sweet Pea garden, and a new cast iron bandstand was installed. It reopened in 1910.

Post WWII, the park had its ups and downs. It was renowned for its extensive rose garden and paddling pool, but in 1954, after it was found to be full of dry rot, the house was demolished in a controlled fire. The Winter Garden was renewed in 1984 and a skate park built in 2010. However, some of the older elements were decaying and in 1987 the rusting and unsafe bandstand was dismantled

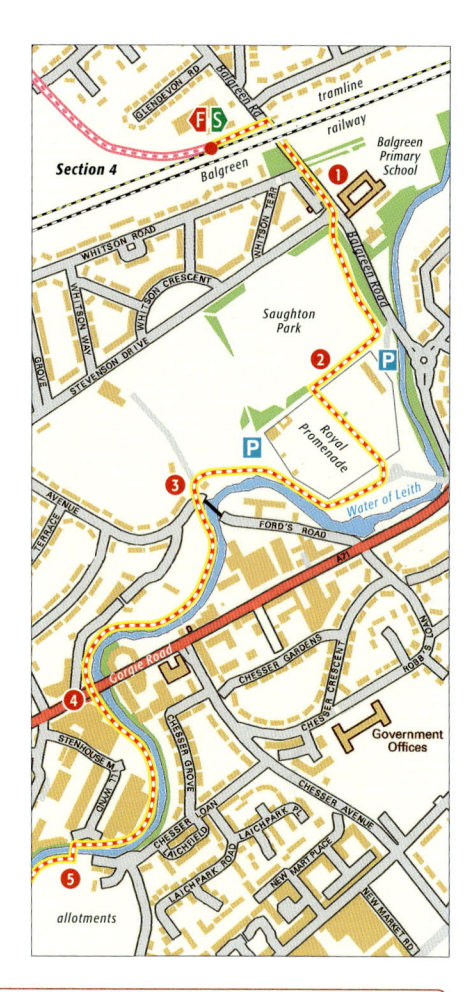

SIR JOHN BATTY TUKE

John Tuke graduated in medicine from the University of Edinburgh in 1856. After time abroad he returned to Scotland, specialising in mental health. First working in Fife, he then took up a post at Saughton Hall Private Asylum in 1868. This institution had been created in the 1790s to cater for mentally ill patients of 'higher rank' and Tuke soon made it a base for implementing his new ideas about psychiatry.

Tuke's revolutionary idea was that insanity was not a moral deficiency but had a physiological basis, so it was not harsh regimes of incarceration but care and cure that were needed. He was prominent within the Royal College of Physicians, giving lectures (particularly on the madness associated with the early weeks after childbirth) and was for some years its president. As his professional renown grew, he was given many honours including honorary degrees and a knighthood.

Section 5 HEALTHY SUBURBS

Spring blossom and topiary in Saughton Park's walled garden

and put into storage. By the early 2000s the park was run down and neglected.

Edinburgh council's project has been a mix of restoration and repurposing of buildings and structures from all points of its history, together with some 21st century concepts. The bandstand has been reinstated, although not at its original position, and the sundial restored, as has the Exhibition Bridge over the Water of Leith at the junction of Balgreen Road and Gorgie Road. Other developments have been the installation of outdoor gym equipment, the creation of a playpark, and conversion of the old stable block into a cafe and toilets. The footprint of the old house has been delineated as a new piazza.

Replanting has been done with an eye to biodiversity and the park is officially carbon neutral thanks to a ground source heat pump. In a nice twist, the old Gorgie Weir on the Water of Leith has been converted into a mini hydroelectric scheme. The completed project

1908 SCOTTISH NATIONAL EXHIBITION

The Scottish National Exhibition was opened in May 1908 by Queen Victoria's son Prince Arthur of Connaught and closed six months later. During these months, and undeterred by some strange weather – snow in the first week of May and summer warmth in October – 3.5 million visitors came to enjoy the exhibition. Attractions included the Palace of Industries, the Machinery Hall, the Fine Art Galleries, ornamental flower beds, firework displays and even a vegetarian restaurant.

It wasn't all educational as there was also a funfair with a water chute and a Cakewalk, a Figure of Eight Railway, House of Troubles, Spiders Web Maze and Moulin Rouge. While most attractions were apparently a success, the Venetian gondolas on the Water of Leith apparently were not! A most unusual exhibit was a Senegalese village complete with 100 men, women and children from Senegal. A baby born during the occupants' stay was allegedly christened 'Scotia Reekie'.

Section 5 HEALTHY SUBURBS

> ### SAUGHTON PARK BANDSTAND
>
> Cast iron bandstands such as that in Saughton Park were once common in public parks but are now quite rare. Within its modern boundaries, Edinburgh used to have six (Saughton, West Princes Street Gardens, The Meadows, Victoria Park, Leith Links and Portobello Promenade) but now only this one remains.
>
> It was made by the Lion Foundry in Kirkintilloch (which also made red letter boxes and telephone kiosks) and was one of their standard models – no 23. The Meadows Bandstand was purchased by the city at the same time, the bandstand in Princes Street Gardens was older and a gift to the city, while the Leith and Portobello bandstands were purchased by their respective local authorities. The modern repair and reinstatement of the ironwork was carried out by Charles Laing & Son.

was reopened by HRH Princess Anne in her capacity as the Patron of the Royal Caledonian Horticultural Society.

❷ At the gates, turn left onto the **Royal Promenade** which bisects the walled garden. Note that the gates are locked from 6pm to 9am. If they are closed, return to the car park to walk around the southern wall and enjoy an extra stretch of the Water of Leith.

Continue ahead on Royal Promenade, with the winter gardens and conservatory on the left and the rose garden and bandstand on the right, to pass out of the walled garden through the restored ornamental gates. Turn right after the gates (the path ahead leads to the Exhibition Bridge) and follow the **Water of Leith Walkway** round to a car park, cafe and the Ford's Road entrance at the west gate.

❸ At the gateway, turn right onto **Ford's Road**, ignoring the footbridge straight ahead, then back left onto the Water of Leith Walkway at the end of a low stone wall. The route has now rejoined the John Muir Way, left at Balgreen tram station at the end of Section 4. The path keeps close to the river as it loops round a small open green (shown on old

Saughton's relocated cast iron bandstand – last of its kind in the city

Section 5 HEALTHY SUBURBS

Alongside the green waterway of the Water of Leith

maps as a football pitch), which likely acts as a small flood plain and was once part of Saughtonhall Mains Farm; some old farm buildings can still be seen. The riverside feels more enclosed as it makes another loop under a metal bridge to emerge on busy **Gorgie Road**.

❹ Cross over at the lights to rejoin the walkway between the car showroom and the road bridge over the Water of Leith, signposted Slateford and Balerno. The path swings round the back of what is now a modern industrial and retail park, previously the site of the hamlet of Stenhouse Mills (of which Stenhouse Mansion remains on the other side of the sheds). More recently the area was the site of Stenhouse Stadium, one of Edinburgh's four greyhound racing tracks.

❺ Next, cross a wooden bridge over the Water of Leith by the site of the Saughton Corn Mill and pass the allotments. Allotments sprang up all round Edinburgh before and during WWII but many sites were lost when mass house building resumed after the war. This site survived because it was bought by Edinburgh council in 1957. It is the largest allotment site within the city.

WATER OF LEITH WALKWAY

Creating a public footpath to run the whole length of the Water of Leith within the urban area of Edinburgh seems a natural thing in this day and age, but must have seemed an impossible dream when first suggested in 1949.

Back then, the banks of the river were in private ownership and at 20km long there were many owners, most of them industrial or commercial concerns. It was only as deindustrialisation took hold in the 1970s that the opportunity arose to start making the plan a reality. The first section of the path opened in 1973 and now walkers and cyclists can enjoy it from Balerno on the western side of the Pentland Hills, to the shore at Leith.

Section 5 HEALTHY SUBURBS

> ## STENHOUSE STADIUM
>
> *Stenhouse Stadium was built to host greyhound racing. It opened in 1932 on a site previously used as a football ground for the Civil Service Strollers team. Despite this being the depths of the Great Depression, the opening meeting was attended by 10,000 spectators. The large council scheme at Stenhouse had just been completed to the design of city architect Ebenezer James MacRae, part of the 6,400 houses Edinburgh council built with subsidy under the 1924 Housing Act in a drive to improve living conditions.*
>
> *These were occupied by working class families employed in industries based around Gorgie which were not as badly affected by the Great Depression as the heavy industries of Leith. They enjoyed a hugely improved standard of living in the suburbs in new houses with gardens, low cost public transport and new mass pastimes such as speedway, greyhound racing and the cinema. Greyhound racing stopped around 1950 but trotting races and show-jumping continued for a short while before closure and demolition.*

Just before WWI there were radical plans for an early garden suburb on either side of the Water of Leith at this point. But these came to nothing. The western part of the site was bought by the Government for **HM Saughton Prison** (visible on the far bank) which opened in 1920 to take inmates from the old Calton Prison when it closed.

The river and the Water of Leith Walkway now make a sharp bend round the southern end of the allotments and past **Saughton Cemetery**. Up on the higher ground to the left, is a large retail and industrial site which, from 1909, housed the corn and cattle markets, displaced from their central sites by the expanding Waverley Station.

The slaughterhouses were relocated from Fountainbridge after a long campaign, firstly by

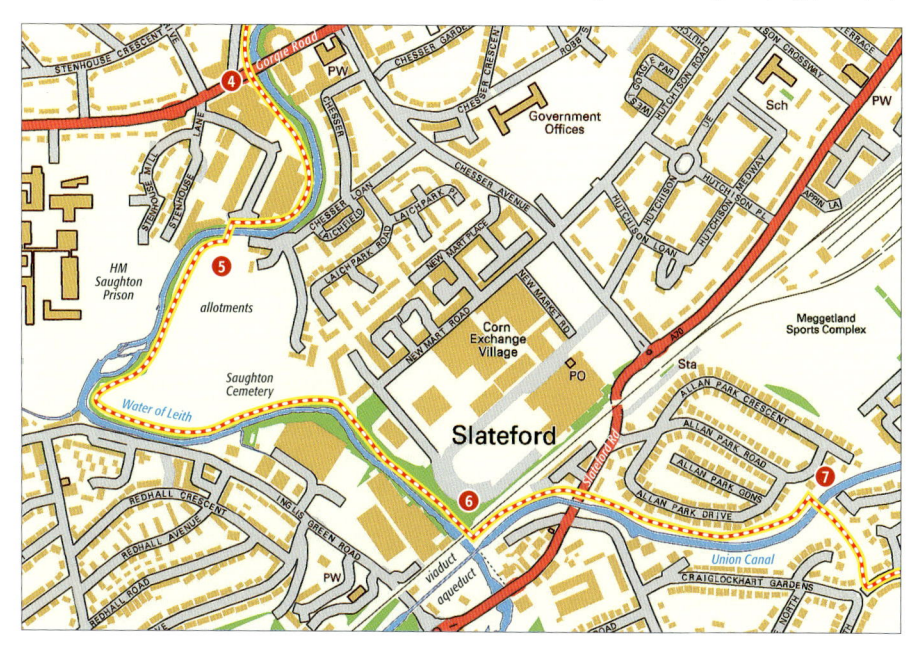

Section 5 HEALTHY SUBURBS

Slateford canal aqueduct, front, Slateford rail viaduct, behind, and the Water of Leith Visitor Centre

Edinburgh's public health pioneer Henry Littlejohn and continued by Councillor (later Lord Provost) John W.Chesser. Littlejohn was also a pioneer in forensic science and is cited as an inspiration for the character Sherlock Holmes, whose creator Arthur Conan Doyle studied medicine under him at Edinburgh University.

6 Keeping ahead on the riverside path, two impressive stone bridges soon come into view. The first one is Slateford Viaduct carrying the railway, the second is Slateford Aqueduct carrying the **Union Canal**. The next section of the Water of Leith Walkway passes below these bridges and required stretches of cantilevered timber boardwalk to be built. It was the final section completed in 2002, with funding from the Millennium Project.

These long bridges – both around 150m in length – were required to span the flat river valley between the sides of the Hailes Syncline, a geological structure where beds of sedimentary rock have been bent into a U-shaped fold. Among these is a bed of Hailes Sandstone which was quarried nearby.

The broad, flat valley floor on the south side of the river is currently occupied by retail and industrial units but was previously the location of the large cleaning and dying premises of A.J.Macnab, complete with workers' cottages and a prominent chimney.

> 🍽 👥 *On the left, beyond Slateford Aqueduct and before Lanark Road, is the Water of Leith Conservation Trust Visitor Centre which has a small cafe. The toilets can be used for a small donation*

Walk under the railway viaduct and then, before the aqueduct and the Water of Leith Visitor Centre, ascend the flight of timber steps on the left to the canal towpath. The canal is carried over the aqueduct in an iron trough and the same design can also be seen on the aqueducts over the River Almond and River Avon further west on the Union Canal.

Turn left on the towpath and head east beside the canal towards the city centre. As the canal starts to bend to the right away from the railway, it passes over **Slateford Road** via a

Section 5 HEALTHY SUBURBS

SLATEFORD AQUEDUCT & VIADUCT

Completed in 1822, the aqueduct is the older of these two structures. It carries the Union Canal which linked the Forth & Clyde Canal to Edinburgh at Falkirk (where the Falkirk Wheel is now), providing a shorter route for coal to be brought to the growing city from the Lanarkshire coalfield. It was the last canal built in Scotland and took many years to come to fruition having first been suggested shortly after the Forth & Clyde was opened in 1790.

The canal was designed by the engineer Hugh Baird with input from Thomas Telford. Baird solved several technical difficulties by following the 240 foot contour line, cutting out the need for locks between Falkirk and Edinburgh, but requiring three long aqueducts, over the rivers Avon and Almond, and here at the Water of Leith. This aqueduct crosses the 150m wide river valley in only eight arches and its 23m height creates pleasing proportions. It is the second longest aqueduct in Scotland (Baird's own Avon Aqueduct is longer) and has hollow spandrels in the arches to reduce the amount of stone required. While originally intended to carry coal, the canal also carried some passengers to and from Glasgow in its early days; taking seven hours but smoother than by road.

The canal's advantage was lost in the early 1840s when the railway line was constructed – not the adjoining line, but the Edinburgh-Glasgow line a little to the north. The line here is the Caledonian Railway's 1848 line from Carstairs, which was competing with the North British Railway to complete the first Edinburgh to London line. It also had the obstacle of the valley to contend with and this 14 arch stone viaduct was designed by the Caledonian's engineer Joseph Locke, one of the titans of the early railways.

smaller concrete aqueduct dating from 1937 and known as the Prince Charlie Aqueduct due to its proximity to the site of Bonnie Prince Charlie's 1745 headquarters.

❼ In another 300m, ascend a ramp on the left to the bridge over the canal and turn right. Cross over the canal to join the route of the John Muir Way. The path here is particularly

Approaching the Prince Charlie Aqueduct on the Union Canal towpath

Section 5 HEALTHY SUBURBS

Entrance gate to Easter Craiglockhart Hill Nature Reserve, still known as Happy Valley

wide because for a few years between 1909 and 1914, well before the construction of the inter-war bungalows, it was the site of a stretch of light railway operated by building contractors Colin MacAndrew Ltd.

More than 1km long, the railway ran from Slateford Station across the canal and up the hill towards the vast construction site for the new Redford Barracks near Colinton (to where the British Army Garrison at Edinburgh Castle relocated in 1923).

In a short distance, the grass-lined path

CRAIGLOCKHART – FROM HAPPY VALLEY TO NATURE RESERVE

Happy Valley originated in the 1870s when businessman John Cox, whose family had an old-established glue and gelatine manufactory at Gorgie Mills, bought the landed estate here and set out a pleasure ground. The estate had previously been in the hands of the Monro family, three generations of which, all called Alexander, had famously held the Chair of Anatomy at Edinburgh University – one had taught Darwin.

The land on the north side of the hill was marshy, so Cox built a dam across the valley of the Megget Burn to create several ponds which were used for boating, skating and curling. The complex thrived as the suburban railway made it more accessible in the 1880s. Outdoor skating declined when covered rinks opened and, by the 1920s, two ponds were filled in and a dance hall and amusement park had been built.

After WWII the amusement park did not reopen and tennis became the dominant sport on the site. The facility was taken over by Edinburgh council in 1959 and is now the home of Scottish Tennis. It has frequently hosted the Scottish Championships.

The largest boating pond remains and the rest of the site is managed to provide wildlife habitats and maintain the variety of tree species originally planted by Alexander Monro II.

Section 5 HEALTHY SUBURBS

emerges onto **Craiglockhart Road North**. Turn left and continue to a T-junction with **Colinton Road** opposite Craiglockhart Leisure & Tennis Centre. Cross at the lights, walk to the left, then turn right into **Lockharton Avenue**. Follow it as it bends left and then turn right into **Lockharton Crescent** to reach railings overlooking a pond.

❽ A short distance down, go through the opening in the railings and cross a small area of parkland with a very rural feel. This is **Easter Craiglockhart Hill Nature Reserve** which many still know as Happy Valley.

Follow the path round the wooded (east) side of the pond, ignoring a stepped path to the left, and at the far end take the path straight ahead to pass behind the **Craiglockhart Leisure & Tennis Centre** buildings.

> 🚻 *Craiglockhart Leisure & Tennis Centre is an Edinburgh Leisure venue and has public toilets. The lane between the warehouse-like buildings and the indoor tennis courts gives access to the main entrance*

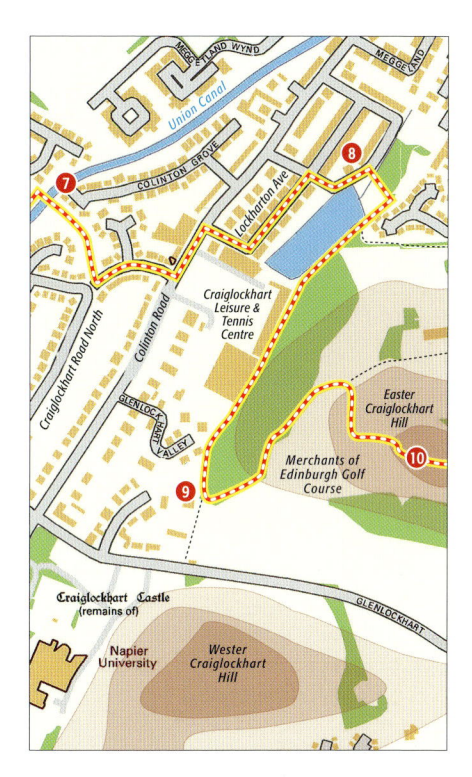

The largest of a number of ponds that once filled Happy Valley is now a local nature park

125

Section 5 HEALTHY SUBURBS

Corstorphine Hill from the top of Easter Craiglockhart Hill

To the left of the path is a heavily wooded and very steep cliff of basalt. This is the 'crag' part of the classic 'crag and tail' created here at **Easter Craiglockhart Hill** by the passing ice sheet – a feature already familiar from Castle Rock and Calton Hill.

The woodland path skirts the western flank of this volcanic hill following the line of another geological feature, the Colinton Fault. This major geological fault, which runs south-west to the north-east across the city to Leith, has displaced the sequence of rocks so the route leaves the layers of younger Hailes Sandstones, and moves to the older sandstones from the Kinneswood Formation, through which the volcano erupted..

❾ Past the sports buildings, take a path on the left to start the climb up Easter Craiglockhart Hill. This broad stepped path, initially with a fence to its right, leads to a junction. Turn left, signposted Hill Top, and follow the path beside a stone wall, the boundary of **Merchants of Edinburgh Golf Course** on the right.

Where the path dips, follow steps by a gap in the wall to ascend over more open ground. At a four-way signpost, follow the sign to Hill Top up the right-hand stepped path to reach the summit. This is fairly flat and there is no trig

---

WESTER CRAIGLOCKHART HILL & EASTER CRAIGLOCKHART HILL

Both Craiglockhart hills are volcanic features from the lower carboniferous period and so of the same age as Calton Hill, but the underlying rocks here are reddish pink sandstones from the Kinneswood Formation.

On Easter Craiglockhart Hill most of the rock was formed from ash (called tuff) with some basalt. In contrast, basalt dominates Wester Craiglockhart Hill, with the Kinneswood sandstone more visible on the east side of the hill where there was a small quarry in the 19th century.

The valley between the two peaks was cut by the torrents of meltwater which flowed as the ice sheet began to melt; it could not flow down the valley of the Water of Leith as that was blocked by an ice dam. The hill has been designated a Regionally Important Geological Site.

Section 5 HEALTHY SUBURBS

CRAIGLOCKHART HYDROPATHIC HOTEL

Nestled under Wester Craiglockhart Hill is the Napier University Campus (taking its name from the Edinburgh inventor of logarithms, John Napier). The large Victorian building was built in 1880 as a hydropathic hotel. These institutions were a popular mid-Victorian reincarnation of the spa (Scotland had 22) but with more emphasis on cold-water treatments and fresh air rather than the social life. But, as with spas, hydros needed a water supply and, like John Cox's Happy Valley, this hydro exploited the springs which rise here along the Colinton Fault.

The designers Peddie & Kinnear were prolific Edinburgh architects, most notable for their Old Scots style buildings lining Cockburn Street. As well as designing several hydros, Peddie was an investor in the company that built this one, which sadly went bust in 1884. A buyout enabled the hydro to continue till WWI when it was requisitioned as a military hospital. From 1916 it specialised in the treatment of shell-shocked officers under the regime of Dr W.H.R.Rivers. The story of the time spent there by two of its most famous patients, the poets Siegfried Sassoon and Wilfred Owen, has been told both in Sassoon's own writing and in the Pat Barker novel 'Regeneration'.

From 1920 the building was a convent and teacher training college. In 1986 it was acquired by Napier and the 'space age', titanium-roofed lecture theatre by architects DBP was added in 2004.

point to mark the highest point but there is a well-placed bench to sit on and enjoy the panoramic view.

From here it is evident that Easter Craiglockhart Hill and **Wester Craiglockhart Hill** to the south, are two distinct hills. At 176m, Wester Craiglockhart Hill is the higher of the two by 19m and is crowned by a trig point. However,

Hydropathic hotel, military psychiatric hospital, seat of learning – Napier University's Craiglockhart Campus

127

Section 5 HEALTHY SUBURBS

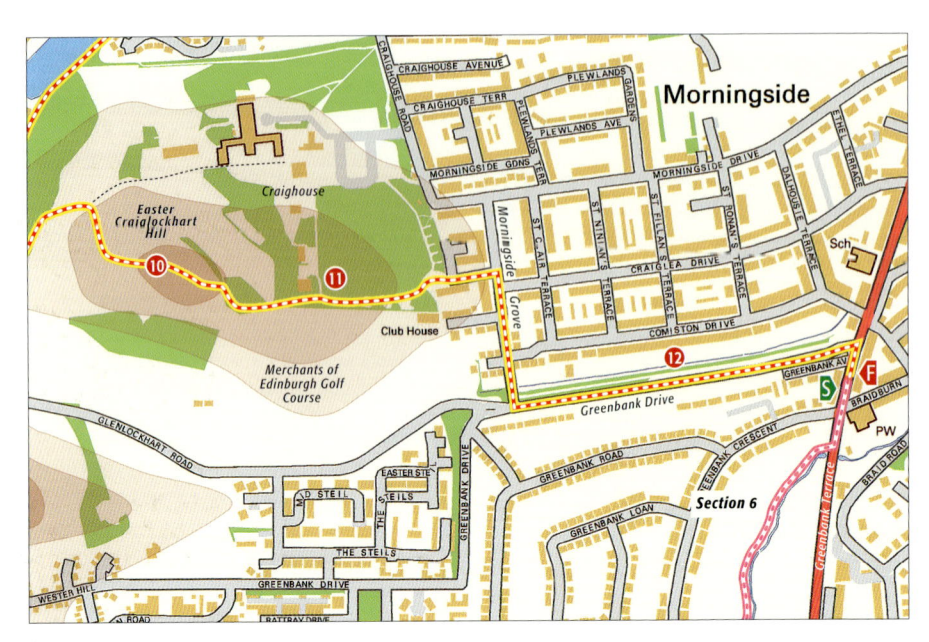

despite the steep and narrow, dry valley that separates them and the drop in height between them, the two hills are often bundled together and counted as just one of Edinburgh's seven hills (see p138).

At Easter Craiglockhart Hill there are 35.5 hectares of council owned land over which the public has access, continuing the policy of previous owner Alexander Monro II, who allowed the public to wander on his estate

> **CRAIGHOUSE**
>
> *Craighouse Asylum was created under the guidance of Dr Thomas Clouston and opened in 1894. Clouston, another physician trained at the University of Edinburgh, was then the Superintendent of the Royal Edinburgh Asylum in Morningside, a lecturer on mental diseases at the university and a doctor of international renown.*
>
> *Clouston oversaw the purchase of this estate including a 16th century house (Old Craig House) and construction of the new facility. The large main block, called New Craig House, and several outlying pavilions were designed by Sydney Mitchell (one of the architects of Ramsay Garden overlooking Princes Street Gardens) in a free renaissance style, deliberately looking like a large country house familiar to the wealthy paying patients.*
>
> *The full drama of Mitchell's free renaissance asymmetric composition is not obvious from this angle, but from the north these buildings form a very romantic skyline as the various towers and turrets protrude through the trees. As a hospital it is unrivalled in its scale and sumptuous design.*
>
> *Changes in the treatment of mental health conditions meant the institution was redundant by the 1990s and was sold to Napier University. In 2014 planning permission was granted to convert the grade A listed buildings into flats and to build some new houses in the grounds.*

Section 5 **HEALTHY SUBURBS**

THE LOST HYDRO

Morningside Hydropathic Hotel was built on the eastern slopes of Easter Craiglockhart Hill on land that was part of Plewlands Farm, the elevated position being considered beneficial to health. Completed in 1879 to the designs of architect William Hamilton Beattie, the hotel was a large turreted building, fitted out with baths and a swimming pool. Beattie was much in demand for large buildings and helped shape the look of Edinburgh, being responsible for Jenners Department Store in Princes Street and the North British Hotel, above Waverley Station.

The hydro failed to prosper, closing in just three years. For a short time, the building was occupied by Morningside College, a boy's school but, as with the hydro, it suffered from poor transport services. It was temporarily occupied by patients from the Edinburgh Hospital for Sick Children during an outbreak of typhoid fever in the city. When no permanent profitable use could be found, it was sold for demolition in 1900, by which time the adjoining streets were a well-established residential suburb.

over 200 years ago. The site is designated as a Local Nature Reserve and an Area of Great Landscape Value. The open meadow, ringed by woods and gorse, supports a variety of plant and bird life, including sparrow hawks, buzzards and kestrels.

10 At the top, walk south to the fence to view the thick slab of basalt which forms the side of Wester Craiglockhart Hill and, to its right, the architecture of the Napier Campus. Note the audacity of the early golf professional Ben Sayers who, in 1907, designed the Merchants of Edinburgh golf course which straddles the hills and valley.

When ready to leave this spot, take the path running roughly east, continuing in the same direction as the final stage of the ascent. Keeping the golf course to the right, the route

Looking south over the Merchants of Edinburgh golf course to the Pentlands

129

Section 5 HEALTHY SUBURBS

South Craig – part of the former Craighouse hospital complex, and now private residences

soon heads through a gap in a wall and back into the trees. At a T-junction of paths, turn right and keep gently descending.

⓫ On the way down, watch out on the left for a large building with a dramatic silhouette. This is not a mansion but South Craig, part of the Victorian Craighouse psychiatric asylum.

Keep to the right beside the golf course wall to where the path flattens out, then drop gently to a gate and an exit onto **Craiglea Place**.

On the right-hand side is a terrace of solid Morningside villas, but note the curious stone arch in the wall that divides the gardens of two of the houses. This is likely to be the remains

CITY POORHOUSE & CITY INFECTIOUS DISEASES HOSPITAL

The new Edinburgh City Poorhouse was built from 1865 on open farmland beyond the city's boundary. It replaced the Georgian workhouse more centrally located in Forrest Road, which was displaced by slum clearance work under the city's 1867 Improvement Act. The new poorhouse was designed by George Beattie and his son William (who designed the Morningside Hydropathic Hotel, see panel p129).

New ideas on provision for the increasing number of poor to be catered for as the city's population rapidly expanded, meant the new institution needed an expansive site, impossible to find within the city's then boundaries. Over 1,500 could be housed and, if able-bodied, they would be set to work, the men breaking stone and bundling firewood, and the women doing laundry and sewing.

To the south of the poorhouse was the City Infectious Diseases Hospital which also needed a remote site. Both institutions have long since closed and the sites have been extensively redeveloped for flats, including the retention and conversion of some original buildings.

Section 5 **HEALTHY SUBURBS**

of the garden wall of a short-lived Victorian building, the Morningside Hydropathic Hotel (see p129), that occupied this site before the houses were built.

At the end of Craiglea Place, turn right and walk down **Morningside Grove** past a terrace of houses numbered 28 to 38 on the right, which were built on the site of the Morningside Hydropathic Hotel. At the T-junction with **Greenbank Drive** turn left.

⓬ This long straight, tree-lined avenue is now a public road but, when constructed, it was the private drive giving access to another of the medical institutions which sprang up in the south of the city in late Victorian times, the Edinburgh City Poorhouse. The site of the poorhouse was further west and has since been redeveloped with some of the old buildings converted and new flats built.

In recent decades, the closure of many of the large Victorian institutions (including Craighouse, the Infectious Diseases Hospital, Princess Margaret Rose Hospital at Fairmilehead, Leith General Hospital and the Royal Infirmary beside the Meadows), which were built on the outskirts of the city, has provided opportunities for new housing.

Walk to the end of Greenbank Drive to reach the T-junction with **Greenbank Terrace**, where Section 5 ends.

Note the red sandstone lodge house on the right, which stood at the entrance to the Edinburgh City Poorhouse and hospital complex (see panel opposite). Contemporaneous with the building of the Infectious Diseases Hospital, it was designed by City Architect, Robert Morham.

There was another lodge on the opposite side of the road, but that has been replaced by modern flats and only a wall and gateposts remain. **F**

> 🍽️ 🚻 *Cafes and shops can be found in Comiston Road, about 200m to the left on Greenbank Terrace. Alternatively, there is take-out coffee at a petrol station 200m to the right on Greenbank Terrace*

> 🚌 *Lothian bus 11, 15 and 16 back to the city centre. Lothian bus 5 takes a less direct route to North Bridge. The bus stop is on Greenbank Terrace, some 40m to the right*

Arthur's Seat from the east end of Easter Craiglockhart Hill

The Royal Observatory on Blackford Hill. The unusual copper drum tops to the towers were designed to withstand the fierce winds which can be experienced on Edinburgh's hills

Section 6
SOUTHERN HILLS

Route: Greenbank to Nether Liberton
Distance: 8.5km; 5.25 miles
Grade: Moderate to strenuous, gentle and steep climbs and descents, paths can be muddy
Access: Lothian bus 11 (*Braid Burn bus stop*), 16 (*Greenbank Loan*) and 15 (*Braid Hills Hotel*) from Princes Street

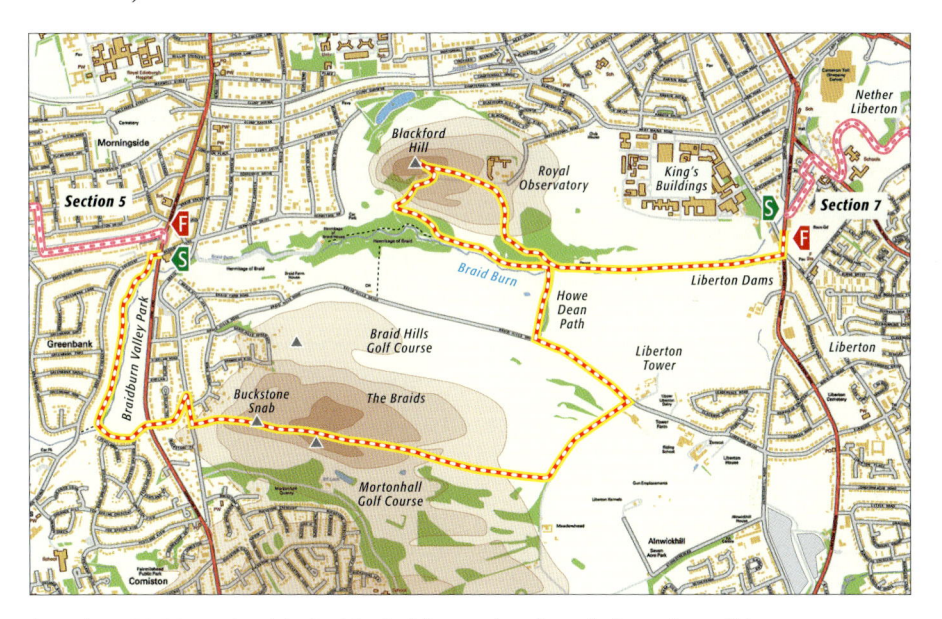

Leaving 1930s suburbia behind, this section heads into the wilder scenery of the open and windswept expanses of the Braid Hills and Blackford Hill. The landscape remains shaped by volcanoes and the ice ages but the features are different, the rocks are older and it is the melting ice sheet which has left its mark on the landscape. Moor and rough grassland predominate, offering city dwellers the opportunity for leisure and observing the heavens

Walk south on **Greenbank Terrace** to the traffic lights at the crossroads by **Greenbank Parish Church**. Turn right into **Greenbank Crescent**, cross over and go through the large ornamental gates with stone pillars into **Braidburn Valley Park**.

After a short distance, a path on the right is signposted Fly Walk. This historic route leads back to Greenbank Crescent and was taken many times by the writer Robert Louis Stevenson, walking between his home in Edinburgh and relatives in the village of Swanston at the foot of the Pentland Hills.

Ignore this turn and continue following the main path along the valley floor right of the Braid Burn. The park occupies a broad valley

133

Section 6 SOUTHERN HILLS

Looking north from Braidburn Valley Park to the distant monolithic New Barracks of the castle, on the right

aligned north-south through which the burn runs – seeming too small for its valley – and up which there are superb views of the Pentland Hills.

This 11 hectare park dates from 1933 when bungalow sprawl was at its height and a large wedge of land between here and the Infectious Diseases Hospital was developed with

> ### BRAID BURN
>
> *Edinburgh's third most significant watercourse, the Braid Burn flows some 14km across the city's suburbs and is the amalgamation of a number of burns that have their source in the northern end of the Pentland Hills. At Duddingston its name changes to the Figgate Burn (followed for a while in Section 8), before it discharges into the Firth of Forth at Portobello. Its course is roughly parallel to the water courses of both the River Almond and the Water of Leith.*
>
> *Although it looks like a small burn, it drains a large basin covering just over 30 square kilometres and its hillside feeder burns swell greatly after heavy rain and during snowmelt. There were several episodes of severe flooding in the 1980s and 1990s leading to Edinburgh council undertaking a £43 million flood defence scheme.*
>
> *The burn did not carve the valley – that was done by glacial meltwater approximately 15,000 years ago. The burn generally flows south-west to north-east but the hard rocks of Craiglockhart Hill and the Braid Hills forced the meltwater to take a south-north route between them, cutting the Braid Burn valley through softer rocks.*
>
> *The burn has a brief literary mention in Edinburgh writer Muriel Spark's 'The Prime of Miss Jean Brodie' when, in 1946, Miss Brodie sits in the Braid Hills Hotel discussing the great love of her 'prime' with one of her former pupils and they "looked out of the wide windows at the little Braid Burn trickling through the fields and at the hills beyond, so austere from everlasting that they had never been capable of losing anything by the war".*

Section 6 SOUTHERN HILLS

The Pentland Hills from Braidburn Valley Park

hundreds of detached, stone-faced, slate-roofed bungalows; many by builders Hepburn & Sons who advertised four apartment bungalows for sale at £650 (£47,000 today).

Most of the streets here take their name from Greenbank Farm on whose land they, and the park, were built. The farm was part of the larger Mortonhall Estate which included Blackford Hill, visited later in this section. The entrance gates are older than the park, relocated here from Comiston House, a Georgian mansion a little to the south on Camus Avenue.

The slope up to the left was given over to allotments during WWII, which remained in use until the 1960s. There is not a lot of formal planting in this park but in spring and summer large swathes of daffodils and blossom add colour. Sections of the park are now being cultivated as wildflower meadows.

135

Section 6 SOUTHERN HILLS

Interpretation board and viewpoint above the Braid Burn in Braidburn Valley Park. In the background is Easter Craiglockhart Hill, ascended in Section 5

❶ About 750m from the entrance gates, as the path and burn turn right to exit the park, cross the Braid Burn on a small bridge. Turn right, wind uphill beside trees to reach a three-way path junction and go left to an interpretation board and viewpoint.

Return to the main path and go straight over to exit onto **Comiston Springs Avenue**. Turn left to the junction with Comiston Road and cross at the island. Walk up **Riselaw Crescent**

> ### COMISTON SPRINGS
>
> *By the start of the 17th century Edinburgh was experiencing a crisis with its water supply which hitherto had come from wells, lochs and springs close to the Old Town but were now inadequate. Parliament granted the city an act for a novel scheme to bring water through lead pipes from springs here at Comiston.*
>
> *The spring heads were named after birds and animals; peewit (old Scots for lapwing) hare, fox and swan – reflected in the local street names – and were marked by carved figurines which are now in the Museum of Edinburgh. The engineer of this scheme was Peter Brauss of Holland to the designs of the architect William Bruce and Robert Mylne, King's Master Mason, (who did the Tower at Leith). A small wellhead building can still be seen in the small park between Oxgangs Avenue and Swan Springs Avenue, one of seven originally built.*
>
> *The water flowed, by the force of gravity, to the large Castlehill cistern near the top of the Royal Mile and in turn this cistern supplied the five public wells within the city. With the addition of an extra source from a spring at Swanston this served as the city's water supply until the building of the New Town.*
>
> *The springs and the pipes only ceased to function in 1949 and the spring water is now discharged into the Braid Burn.*

Section 6 SOUTHERN HILLS

> ## BRAID HILLS GOLF COURSE
>
> Golf dominates the Braid Hills and was central to the park's creation. Early forms of the game had been played on Bruntsfield Links south of the Meadows since the 15th century. Links are more usually associated with coastal areas but at Bruntsfield the land had been 'muir' – common woodland on the shore of the Burgh Loch.
>
> Over time the timber had been cut for building and, from around 1508, James IV had sanctioned quarrying. This left a lumpy terrain with small quarry holes which the locals made use of for golf. However, by the end of the 19th century the building of tenements on neighbouring land meant the area was densely populated. Bruntsfield Links began to fulfil the need of a public park and the golfers became a hazard.
>
> The city made noises about banning golf on the links to howls of protest from the golfers who suggested they should have a replacement course on the Braid Hills, which were now accessible by the tram route to Morningside which stopped just a 15 minute walk away.
>
> The council were convinced and duly acquired a significant part of the Braid Hills from the Cluny Trust for £11,000 (£1.4 million today) and extended the boundary of the municipality under the Edinburgh and Police Extension Act, to include it. The new course which opened in 1889 was something of a revolution because hitherto golf in Edinburgh was played exclusively on links and this was not a links course.
>
> Its creation can be credited with reinvigorating the game in the city. Links courses such as Leith had suffered from encroaching industrial use and the club that played there, the Hon. Company of Edinburgh Golfers, had moved to Musselburgh in 1836. After the Braids opened a further 16 courses were opened in Edinburgh over the next 20 years – none of them true links courses. The first of these was the private Mortonhall Club on the south side of the hill, which was formed in 1892.

as it bends left to reach Braid Road.

❷ Turn right along **Braid Road**, keeping to the right-hand side. After 130m there is a gap in the stone wall on the other side of the road, signposted Braid Hills. Turn in here and follow the main path uphill, keeping right when it forks.

Edinburgh council owns a total of 94 hectares of land on the Braid Hills, including the Hermitage of Braid, most of which was purchased in 1890 to be "used in all time coming for the purpose of a public park and pleasure and recreation ground for the use of the inhabitants of Edinburgh".

The views open out as the path clears the trees nearing the summit, first passing a viewpoint indicator which was designed and funded in 1995 by local residents George Russell and John Bartholomew (a cartographer from a famous family of Edinburgh cartographers). It is an excellent

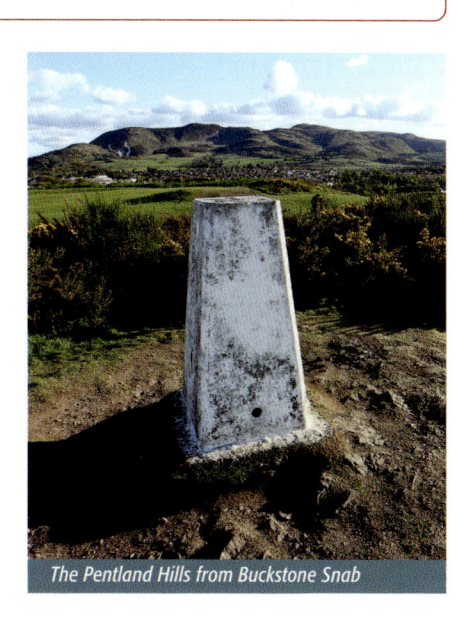

The Pentland Hills from Buckstone Snab

Section 6 SOUTHERN HILLS

Viewpoint indicator on Buckstone Snab. In the middle distance are Blackford Hill and the Royal Observatory, while Salisbury Crags and Arthur's Seat dominate the view north, with the Firth of Forth and Fife beyond

point to view Edinburgh's six other hills.

❸ Keep ahead, aiming between two communications masts, as the path passes a trig point which marks the 208m high point

EDINBURGH'S SEVEN HILLS

The Braids are the fifth of seven Edinburgh hills climbed on this route – Castle Rock, Calton Hill, Corstorphine Hill, Easter Craiglockhart Hill, The Braids, Blackford Hill and Arthur's Seat. It is often stated that Edinburgh is 'built on seven hills' and it is generally understood that the saying refers to these hills, albeit that Easter Craiglockhart Hill and Wester Craiglockhart Hill are often bundled together as 'Craiglockhart Hills', to create the seven when, in reality, there are eight.

However, historically, these were not the original 'seven' hills. When the phrase was first used, the city of Edinburgh was more compact and Corstorphine Hill, both Craiglockhart hills, The Braids and Blackford Hill stood some distance outwith its boundaries.

The original seven hills are thought to have been Castle, Calton, Abbey, Multrees, St John's, St Leonards and Sciennes. Of these, St John's, St Leonards and Sciennes are now so well and truly built upon that they no longer stand out in the city landscape but their identity survives in the names of city districts, and Multrees has recently been revived for a new shopping centre.

The idea of a city being built on seven hills is often linked with Edinburgh's identification of itself with Ancient Athens, which it expressed in its many early 19th century buildings in the Greek Revival style. However, while modern Athens can claim seven hills, ancient Athens could not. The 'seven hills' claim (made by many other cities around the globe) is to identify the city with Ancient Rome, the Eternal City, which was famously built on seven hills. But both these self-identified connections say much about how Edinburgh saw itself in the early 19th century as an international intellectual powerhouse and a city that would endure.

By a happy coincidence, Edinburgh's boundaries have extended throughout the intervening years to the extent that they do now include the seven distinct hills climbed on this route.

Section 6 SOUTHERN HILLS

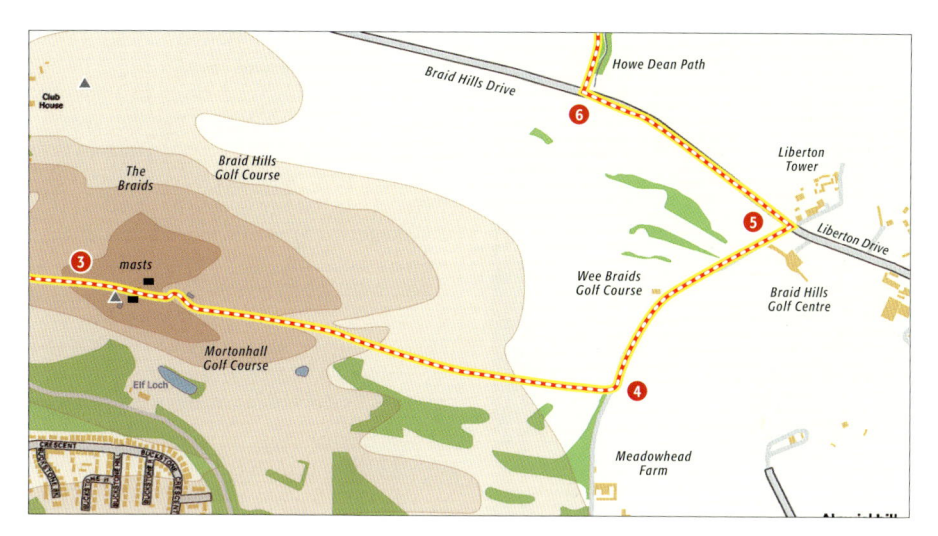

known as **Buckstone Snab**. The Braids has more than one summit which is why it is generally referred to in the plural. The 213m highest point, which curiously seems never to have been named, lies on the other side of the boundary wall with Mortonhall Golf Course. It can be gained by continuing along the path to a point beyond the two masts and going through a gate in the wall on the right. A lower 178m point lies about 400m to the north in the middle of the public Braid Hills golf course.

The path makes a zigzag through a gorse-lined former quarry, before following a straight course through trees and shrubs heading east. This path is known as **The Ride** because it is a

Beyond Buckstone Snab, a track leads through the gorse and between the two communications masts

139

Section 6 SOUTHERN HILLS

bridleway shared by horses, mountain bikers, joggers and walkers. It is the only Edinburgh council owned park in which riding is permitted.

The Braids, like the city's other hills, is a volcanic feature but older, being formed in the Lower Devonian period (roughly 410 million years ago) during the same period as the Pentland Hills. Unlike Arthur's Seat and Castle Rock, these hills are not plugs of cooled magma but are composed of ash and lava, which have been uplifted by immense earth movements and subsequently scoured by an ice sheet. The landscape here seems so broad and open and the climb so undramatic that it is not immediately obvious that this is also a crag and tail feature, but it is.

Various parts of the hill have been designated as an area of urban forest, a local biodiversity site and an Area of Great Landscape Value. The wild and windswept nature of the terrain makes for a unique city landscape.

Remain on the main path as it makes a slight kink with golf courses on both sides, to reach a T-junction with the access road to **Meadowhead Farm**.

❹ Turn left and follow the footpath to the left of the road, past the Wee Braids Golf Course kiosk to emerge onto **Braid Hills Drive** where it changes from Liberton Drive, opposite Liberton Tower Lane

Liberton Tower is a four-storey plain tower house dating back to at least the 15th century and was originally owned by the Dalmahoy family. By 1610, while in the ownership of William Little, sometime Lord Provost of Edinburgh, it was abandoned in favour of a more commodious and up-to-date fortified dwelling called Liberton House, which still exists about 500m to the east along Liberton Drive. The tower was restored in the 1990s by the Castles of Scotland Preservation Trust and can be hired for holiday accommodation.

> About 100m to the right on Liberton Drive is the Braid Hills Golf Centre which has good cafe and toilet facilities open to the public. Worth taking advantage of, as the next stretch has no facilities

❺ Cross Braid Hills Drive onto a pavement and follow this west, with views over metal railings to farmland (more greenbelt land), Edinburgh University's King's Buildings Campus and Arthur's Seat beyond. Between

Descending the Howe Dean Path to the Braid Burn

Section 6 SOUTHERN HILLS

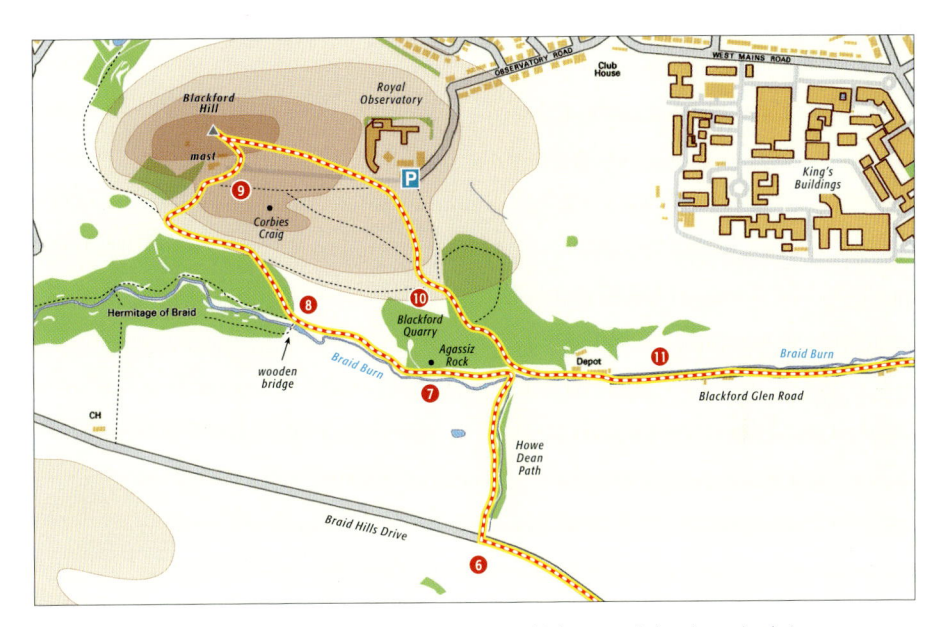

the trees are glimpses back to Liberton Tower. In 500m, a set of handsome red sandstone gateposts with arts and crafts nameplates are reached. These form the entrance to **Howe Dean Path** and are probably by City Architect Robert Morham.

❻ This steep, and in places stepped path, descends beside the small Howe Dean Burn and requires care after rain, when the burn can overflow onto the path. Alternatively, there is a higher parallel path to the left.

Descending, both the height of the Braid Hills behind and the size of the Braid Burn's valley ahead, become apparent. As with Braidburn Valley Park, this valley was not carved by the burn but by more voluminous glacial meltwaters.

Old quarries top and tail the Howe Dean Path. The top ones were worked out early but those at the bottom, beside the Braid Burn,

AGASSIZ, EDINBURGH & THE ICE AGES

It was Louis Agassiz, a Swiss born American geologist, who first put forward in print the alternative theory that landscape features in Northern Europe, previously attributed to the Biblical flood, had been created by the vast glaciers of an ice age in the geologic past.

In 1840 he was brought to an outcrop near the entrance to Blackford Quarry on the south side of Blackford Hill in the company of Charles Maclaren (see panel p143), the then editor of the Scotsman newspaper and himself a keen geologist who is reported to have claimed that striae – gouged grooves – on the surface of the rock were the work of ice.

The striae on what is now known as Agassiz Rock are now less visible due to weathering, while modern geologists do not always agree that they were created by ice – water from the melting ice sheet seems more probable. However, the spot has been designated a nationally important site in recognition of the part it played in the advancement of understanding landscape processes, following Agassiz's visit. (See also Section 4, p108-9).

Section 6 SOUTHERN HILLS

Agassiz Rock at the foot of Blackford Hill

were far larger and worked for whinstone (a quarrying term for any hard, dark rock, rather than a geological term) between 1826 and 1953, largely for road building. At the valley bottom cross the Braid Burn, go left, then after approximately 125m turn right into the quarry.

7 Known as **Agassiz Rock**, the rockface straight ahead is where geologist Louis Agassiz noted gouged grooves in the rock, which supported the theory that glacial ice ages had sculpted the landscape. Return to the main path and continue on the right side of the burn to reach a junction of paths and signposts at a substantial **wooden bridge**. Don't be tempted by any of the rougher paths up on your right before this point. They lead to the top of Blackford Hill, but involve a rough ascent over more difficult terrain.

The land here forms part of the Hermitage of Braid and Blackford Hill Local Nature Reserve. While the route takes the right fork here, anyone wishing to make a detour to see more of the **Hermitage of Braid** and its historic house can continue ahead for 650m. The access path from the western entrance on Braid Road makes a lovely walk in its own right, so the Hermitage of Braid is worth saving for another day to do it justice.

> Hermitage of Braid House has public toilets, but they close at 4pm and may not be open on Saturdays

8 From the junction at the wooden bridge, turn right and follow the sign pointing uphill towards Blackford Hill and Blackford Pond. Follow this stepped path as it winds gently uphill, curving left through trees.

Eventually the path begins to emerge from the trees with a field on the left. Pass an information board on the right and a few paces further on, turn right onto an earth track across a clearing. The track leads to a flight of broad timber stairs heading up towards a phone mast. Follow these uphill and then turn left across a grassy slope keeping the mast on the left-hand side.

9 Cross the access road to the communications mast and curve left on a grassy path round the fence. Walk straight ahead to the higher (more northerly) point and the trig pillar on 164m high **Blackford Hill**; another glacial 'crag and tail'. The route has climbed the edge of the crag and will descend the tail. There is evidence of a prehistoric hill fort on the summit and Blackford Hill is a

142

Section 6 SOUTHERN HILLS

THE LAVA FLOWS THAT CREATED THE SOUTHERN HILLS

Blackford Hill and the Braid Hills were formed some 70 million years before the volcanic eruptions that created Castle Rock and Calton Hill to the north. When these southern hills were created, three land masses were colliding to create a new continent called Laurussia which, at that time, lay south of the equator. This process triggered volcanic activity and mountain-building in an event known as the Caledonian Orogeny.

Here, the volcanoes were in a desert landscape and the eruptions were thought to have been brief and violent, but occurring over centuries. Each episode of eruptions produced slightly different types of rock; on the Braid Hills, trachytic and andesitic lavas over basaltic – andesitic tuff and on Blackford Hill, basalt and andesite lavas (the youngest in the sequence) over trachytic tuff. The layers of tuff indicate explosive eruptions before the lavas flowed.

An early investigator of these lava flows was Charles Maclaren (see panel p141) who noted the striae on Blackford Hill. No location of a main volcanic vent has been identified, so the assumption is that, in the vicinity of The Braids, Blackford Hill and the Pentlands, there were many small volcanoes.

scheduled ancient monument.

These 43 hectares of public land were purchased from Lt Col. Henry Trotter, the owner of the Mortonhall Estate, in 1884 for £8,000 (£1m today). Although on the very fringe of the city (once again the municipal boundary was moved to incorporate a new park) it was accessible, as a new railway line, the Edinburgh Suburban & Southside Junction Railway Line, opened the same year with a station just to the north-east. A path led directly from the station to the park's north-east gate, where a monumental arch constructed from red sandstone was erected to the designs of Sydney Mitchell to commemorate Lord Provost George Harrison who had overseen the land purchase.

Edinburgh council now owns 63 hectares on Blackford Hill with the house and estate of Hermitage of Braid being gifted to the city by

North-east to Salisbury Crags and Arthur's Seat from the trig point on Blackford Hill

Section 6 SOUTHERN HILLS

Blackford Quarry, the Higgs Centre for Innovation, left, and the Royal Observatory from the Howe Dean path

ROYAL OBSERVATORY

The first Royal Observatory was on Calton Hill, as visited in Section 1. The Blackford Hill buildings opened in 1896 and remain a working observatory and scientific research facility. They were supplemented by the opening in 2018 of the Higgs Centre for Innovation, named after Nobel Prize winner and Edinburgh University Professor Peter Higgs of the 'Higgs boson' theory. The observatory complex is not open to the public, but organised visits can be booked via its website.

The Royal Observatory is considered an "outstanding and unique nationally important group of buildings…[of] detailed bespoke design for a scientific facility". The design is Italianate and the construction uses a Northumbrian sandstone; the copper drum tops to the towers are unusual, but the shape (a dome is more usual) was chosen to withstand the fierce winds which can be experienced on Edinburgh's hills.

The architect of the original sections of the building was W.W.Robertson of HM Office of Works Scotland. The two drums are of different sizes as they contain telescopes of different dimensions – one a reflector, the other a refractor – but both are part of the original design. Many ornamental panels adorn the original part of the building.

The buildings were constructed after the Earl of Crawford gifted his personal astronomical instruments and library to the Scottish nation, on the proviso that a suitable building be provided to house them. As well as observing the heavens, this new observatory continued to provide a time signal via telegraph to Calton Hill (see p32) and the One o'clock Gun at Edinburgh Castle, then later to a time signal at Dundee and the clock at HM Rosyth Dockyard on the Forth.

Section 6 SOUTHERN HILLS

KING'S BUILDINGS CAMPUS

The University of Edinburgh has a distinguished reputation in the sciences, and geology in particular. Till the 18th century, science was not a formal discipline but this changed in 1770 when the University set up a Chair of Natural History. The first scientific discipline to split off from that was geology when the Scottish geologist Robert Murchison endowed a Chair in Geology at the university one hundred years later. Even though science degrees were awarded from 1868, they were issued by the Faculty of Arts until a science faculty finally came into being in 1893.

By WWI the science faculty had outgrown the space available at New College, so the university purchased West Mains Farm here on the city's southern boundary to create a modern science campus. King George V laid the foundation stone in 1920, expressing in his speech the hope that the "progressive application of science" could be put to "the service of man". Providing the new buildings took time and money, and at first the Department of Geology occupied wooden huts purchased from the military, which were originally on St Andrew Square to billet American soldiers.

On campus there are buildings and roads named to commemorate many distinguished scientists associated with the city and the university; geologist James Hutton, James Clerk Maxwell (the father of modern physics who was born and educated in Edinburgh), Daniel Rutherford (an Edinburgh physician and the first to isolate nitrogen), Charles Darwin and two Scots who made their reputations in America, conservationist John Muir and inventor Alexander Graham Bell. Distinguished women with a connection to the university, have been remembered too; chemist Christina Millar, the astronomer Mary Bruck and physicist Marion Ross.

its owner John McDougal in 1938. Hermitage of Braid and Blackford Hill are also designated as local nature reserves.

To leave the summit, turn east and follow the well-trodden path descending the hill's 'tail' with views of Arthur's Seat with the Firth of Forth beyond. As the green copper domes of the **Royal Observatory** come into view, look right to see a distinct mini 'crag and tail' feature called **Corbies Craig**.

Keep walking downhill, heading to the right of the observatory building. Cross the access road again and continue on a grassy path heading south-east away from the observatory towards two metal benches. Pass to the right of the benches, heading for a gap in the gorse bushes ahead. Go past another bench on the left, then swing round left before the fenced-off top of **Blackford Quarry**, heading for a wall.

⑩ From the wall, follow the path diagonally downhill to reach the top of a stepped path. Turn right down this to arrive back on the valley floor opposite the footbridge over the Braid Burn and the Howe Dean Path. Turn left and follow the Braid Burn downstream on a gravel path which bends across a bridge to pass a council depot (in another section of former whinstone quarry) and join Blackford Glen Road.

⑪ Continue along **Blackford Glen Road**, passing the buildings of a former dairy farm, beyond which Edinburgh University's King's Buildings Campus can be seen through the trees and above the hedge on the left.

At the hamlet of **Liberton Dams**, just before the junction with Liberton Road, Liberton Brae and Kirk Brae, there is a distinct hump in the road as it passes over a large grass-covered structure, clearly seen beyond the wall on the left. This isn't a dam across the Braid Burn, which it crosses, but the housing for water pipes from springs and reservoirs in the Pentland Hills. The hamlet predates this structure and derives its name from a small

Section 6 SOUTHERN HILLS

LIBERTON DAMS & EDINBURGH'S WATER SUPPLY

Edinburgh experienced one of its periodic crises with its water supply in the wake of the Napoleonic Wars. In an attempt to solve the problem, a new joint stock company – the Edinburgh Water Company – was formed in 1819 to implement bold plans to bring water from the Pentland Hills. Crawley Spring near Flotterstone on the south-east side of the range, was selected to provide the water supply and it came into the city in the pipe which crosses the Braid Burn here in a conduit. James Jardine engineered the 13.7 km pipeline which delivered 6.8 million litres of water a day.

This scheme worked well for several years but, by the early 1840s, when Edinburgh and Leith were experiencing rapid population growth and there was a run of very dry summers, the city found itself once again chronically short of water. The next three decades were to see various battles over the city's water supply, only partly resolved by constructing more Pentland reservoirs and a much bigger cistern on Castlehill at the top of the Royal Mile.

In 1871 the Edinburgh & District Water Trust was formed to supply Leith and Portobello as well as Edinburgh. Under the new trust, water was piped from Portmore Loch and the newly built Gladhouse Reservoir in the Moorfoot Hills to a large waterworks between Alnwickhill Road and Liberton Gardens 1.5km south of the Braid Burn, and a point already on the pipeline from Crawley Springs.

Here, from its opening in 1879, water was stored in reservoirs and passed through a series of filter-beds before entering pipes to the city. Two new pipes were laid alongside the older one from Crawley Springs and all three cross the Braid Burn at Liberton Dams. The waterworks have since been developed for residential housing called Liberton Grange.

Looking north over farmland beside Braid Hills Drive, to Edinburgh University's King's Buildings

Section 6 SOUTHERN HILLS

Approaching Liberton Dams on Blackford Glen Road

mill dam on the lade (now filled in) which controlled water for the mill at Nether Liberton to the north.

12 Continue on the road to the junction. The village of Liberton is up on the hill to the right. Before the suburbs of Edinburgh crept out and covered the farmland, there were four small hamlets in the vicinity; Liberton Dams, Nether Liberton, Over Liberton, and Kirk Liberton. As well as the collection of cottages and villas, Liberton Dams had a school, a mission hall and even a dairy.

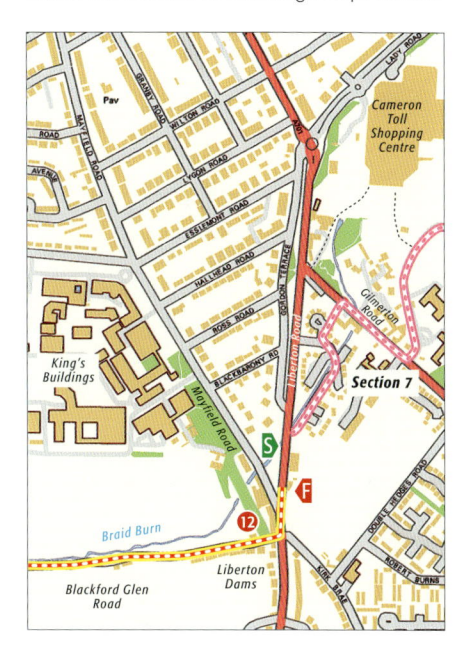

Nether Liberton lies to the north and has retained its name. Over Liberton was the housing around Liberton Tower at the foot of the Braid Hills, while Kirk Liberton up on the the brae became the centre of modern Liberton. It wasn't until the early 20th century that Liberton became part of Edinburgh.

Turn left and walk past Braefoot Terrace to **Mayfield Road**. Cross over to **Liberton Road** and follow that for about 50m to a bus stop on the left, where Section 6 ends. **F**

Cameron Toll Shopping Centre is about 650m north on Liberton Road, accessed via Nether Liberton Lane at the start of Gilmerton Road. It has refreshments and toilets

Lothian bus 31 and 37 to Princes Street, 7 to North Bridge, 47 to Lothian Road and Queensferry St

147

The ruined 15th century tower house and later fortifications of Craigmillar Castle

Section 7
COAL & CANDYFLOSS

Route: Nether Liberton to Portobello
Distance: 11 km; 6.75 miles
Grade: Easy – mostly flat but one gentle climb and descent – through parks and short stretches of road walking. There are few cafes or toilets in the central part of this section
Access: Lothian bus 7 from North Bridge, 31 and 37 from Princes Street, 47 from Queensferry St and Lothian Road (*Gordon Terrace bus stop*)

From the floodplain of the Braid Burn, this section rises to a low sandstone ridge, which is topped by Craigmillar Castle. Beyond this, a major geological fault is crossed and the route moves onto younger sedimentary rocks. Among these rocks are seams of coal which once brought prosperity and employment locally. Following the edge of the coal seam the route reaches the shore at Portobello, where mineral springs were important in the development of Scotland's only planned Regency spa town

The Braid Burn passes below **Liberton Road** and is easily accessed via a gap in a low sandstone wall on the east side of the road, between the southbound **Gordon Terrace** bus stop and a row of modern flats. Go through the gap and descend a tarmacked

149

Section 7 COAL & CANDYFLOSS

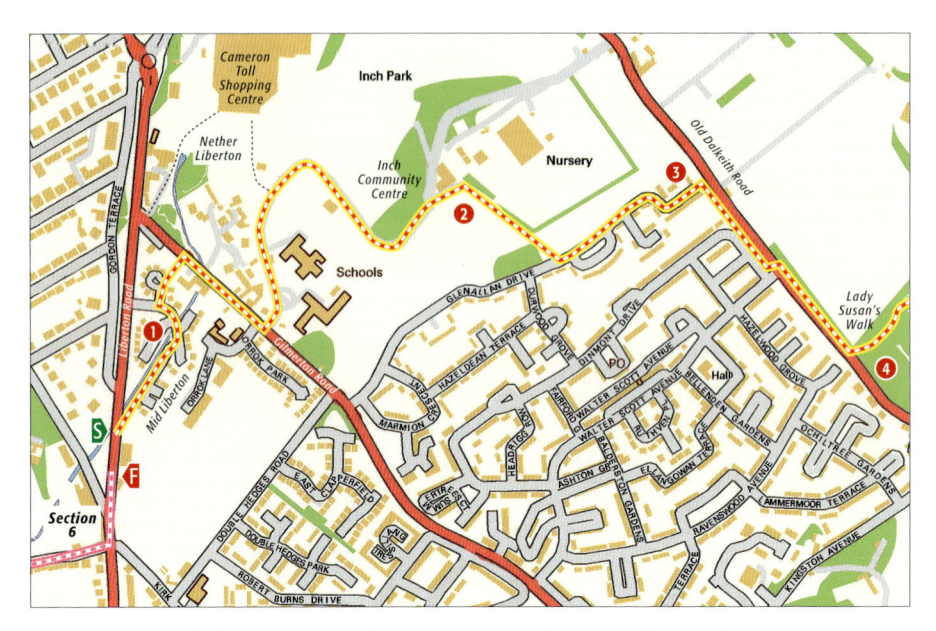

path to a road, **Mid Liberton**, in a small modern housing estate, with the Braid Burn on the left. The walled flood defences between the burn and the road are testimony to the capacity of water the burn can carry after heavy rain or snowmelt in the Pentland Hills. Traditionally flood plains such as these were not built upon, but the need for housing within the city prompted development, which was then affected by severe flooding in the 1980s and '90s. These walls are part of Edinburgh council's £43 million flood defence scheme.

❶ Go left on the road bridge over the burn and follow the road round to the right, keeping right where it forks, heading towards a turning area at the end of the cul-de-sac. Just before the turning area, turn right onto a hedge-lined path and follow it between the houses to emerge onto **Gilmerton Road**.

Cross Gilmerton Road and turn right, now walking south-east with a low stone wall to the left. Cross the entrance to Old Mill Lane –

INCH HOUSE

The oldest section of Inch House dates from 1617 and was built for George Winram and later altered by his son (also known as Lord Liberton). During the Civil War, Winram was on the Royalist side and, when he died at the Battle of Dunbar in 1650, the house was seized by Cromwell. It was acquired by the politician Sir John Gilmour in 1660.

In 1792 the estate passed to a cousin, William Little of Liberton House, who added Gilmour to his name. He and his son, who inherited five years later, were responsible for the Georgian additions. In 1887 the estate passed to a cousin, Sir Robert Gordon, who again added Gilmour to his name. He commissioned architects MacGibbon & Ross to remodel part of the house in their signature Scots Baronial style, adding turrets, attics, bay windows and a door surround.

The name Inch derives from the Gaelic for island as the house sits on a small mound. The Braid Burn flooded regularly in the past and the house was surrounded by water at times.

Section 7 COAL & CANDYFLOSS

Extended and refashioned over the years, the oldest section of Inch House dates from the 17th century

down which can be glimpsed older buildings which testify to past mills on the Braid Burn. On the right-hand side of the main road, before the corner with **Orrok Park** road, the slanted roof of an early 17th century doocot (dovecot in English) can be seen above the hedge. This is the largest surviving doocot in Edinburgh and is Grade A listed. Like the doocot seen in Lochend Park in Section 1, the pigeons which nested in it were used as food in winter and their droppings provided manure.

Take the next turning left between stone gateposts – signposted **Inch Community Centre** – which gives access to **Inch Park** and Liberton Primary School. Stay on the pavement on the left-hand side of the road.

> *About 250m from the stone gateposts, a signposted path on the left leads to Cameron Toll Shopping Centre which has refreshments and toilets*

Continue round the drive past the sports club to reach Inch House. Edinburgh council purchased this 25 hectare estate of Inch with its mansion house in 1946 with a view to building housing on its southern portion. The grounds are now primarily laid out as sports pitches. The house was first used by the council as a school and since 1986 as a community centre.

> *There are public toilets in Inch Community Centre, but opening times are generally limited to mornings and early afternoon*

2 From the far end of the car park at the front of the house, turn right to follow a path with a fence on the left and a playground on the right. The other side of the fence was once a formal garden but it is now Inch Nursery, the council's plant nursery and training centre, where all the plants are propagated for parks and gardens across the city. When the path eventually reaches a junction with **Glenallan Drive**, turn left.

The housing here was one of the first council schemes planned after WWII. At the time of planning, the long-serving City Architect Ebenezer James MacRae had just retired which may have been a factor in the decision

Section 7 COAL & CANDYFLOSS

Craigmillar Castle across the open meadows of Craigmillar Castle Park

to put the design out for open competition. It was won by a young English architect David Stratton Davis; MacRae and Lady Gilmour (who had lived in Inch House prior to the sale) were among the judges. The design was extremely conservative – low-rise, with few flats and the streets laid out on garden city principles, with names from the novels of Sir Walter Scott. As built, the houses had delicate copper porch hoods, some of which can still be seen.

❸ Follow Glenallan Drive to where it ends at metal barriers, go through these and follow a footpath which bends to the right. After a second set of barriers the path emerges from behind a wall to run parallel to **Old Dalkeith Road**. Keep ahead here, first on the path, then the pavement and go over the entrance to a road (Walter Scott Avenue) to reach a pedestrian crossing.

Cross the main road, turn right and follow the high wall for about 125m to a stone-linteled doorway in the wall, with a plaque indicating **Lady Susan's Walk**.

❹ Go through the doorway to enter **Craigmillar Castle Park**. This large park covers 62 hectares and was purchased from the Gilmour family by Edinburgh council in 1965. Follow the path, ahead, to the left of the information board, walking roughly east-north-east through woodland. At a junction of paths in a clearing, turn right to exit the woodland into a meadow and follow a grassy path uphill. At the top, views open up over the outer

LADY SUSAN

From the 17th century, both Craigmillar Castle and Inch House were in the ownership of the Gilmour family with the Inch becoming their main residence in the 1790s. Paths connected the two properties. Lady Susan, after whom this part of the path is named, was the wife of Sir Robert Gordon Gilmour and she regularly enjoyed the walk from her home to the picturesque castle ruins. In 1936 she was made a Dame in recognition of her voluntary work in support of district nursing services. The doorway was bricked-up for many years and only opened for access in 2009-10.

Section 7 COAL & CANDYFLOSS

suburbs and the new Royal Infirmary of Edinburgh. In 1997 the park was enhanced by the planting of 40,000 new trees as part of the Millennium Forest Scotland project.

Curving left round the trees, continue uphill past a bench to pass between two stands of trees. Over to the right are the first views of the extensive remains of **Craigmillar Castle**.

The castle was built here because an outcrop of Kinnesswood Sandstone provided both a good defensible site and a suitable building stone. Stone here is known to have been quarried from as far back as the 14th century for the earliest parts of this castle.

In the early 20th century, the quarry in the woodland immediately north-west of the

EDINBURGH SANDSTONES

Sandstone has literally made Edinburgh. The volcanic rocks may have defined the terrain but it is the sandstone which gives the buildings their look. The sandstones from various sites across the city have different characteristics which have met the differing needs or fashions of the city's designers and builders from the 15th century, when James I outlawed building in timber, till the start of the 20th century, when brick and concrete began to take over. In consequence, quarrying and stone dressing were important industries to the local economy and a great wealth of knowledge of stone was built up locally.

The sandstone from the quarries surrounding Craigmillar Castle is part of the Kinnesswood Formation and is a little older than the Craigleith Sandstones from the Gullane Formation. Both were laid down during the early Carboniferous period but the Kinnesswood stone formed under drier conditions than the Gullane stone, the landmass drifting north in the intervening time. The different appearance and structural qualities of the two sandstones influenced the buildings they were used for.

Prior to the start of Edinburgh's love affair with classical architecture, it was stone from the Kinnesswood Formation (and another sequence, the Ballagan Formation from long worked-out quarries closer in to the Old Town), which were the pre-eminent building stones. The properties of Kinnesswood stone made it suitable for 'rubble' work. To the layperson's eye this is more artisanal – the blocks can vary in size, they are rough faced and may or may not be arranged in regular courses. As the joints are not generally tight, a lot of mortar shows.

This is the style of stonework at Craigmillar Castle, where aesthetics were of much less concern to the builders than strength. Kinnesswood stone can have quite pink colouring, ranging through red, brown, yellow and buff, while the Gullane stones are grey. Kinnesswood stone was also used for parts of the Palace of Holyroodhouse in the 16th century (for corbel, flagstones and gateposts), and in the 17th century for parts of Edinburgh Castle and Parliament House, the interior courtyard of George Heriot's Hospital and Duddingston Kirk.

The fashion for the more refined designs of classical architecture called for a stone which could be worked in the style of 'ashlar' (regular shaped blocks, precisely cut with very thin, almost invisible joints) which could also be quarried in massive blocks for columns. Gullane Formation sandstone fitted perfectly with the architects' vision to create such classical gems as Charlotte Square in the New Town and University of Edinburgh Old College on South Bridge.

But while the preference for Gullane stone reduced the demand for Kinnesswood stone, even the classicists needed its properties in some circumstances. It was selected for the arch of Regent Bridge (see p29) and its water resistant qualities came in handy in the late 19th century when it was used for a new retaining seawall at Leith Docks.

Section 7 COAL & CANDYFLOSS

castle was the site of a fireworks factory, making use of its relative remoteness. Because of the importance of the quarrying here, this hill is another of Edinburgh's designated Regionally Important Geological Sites.

Keep ahead towards a gap in the wall and follow the path as it swings right round the north end of the castle. Craigmillar Castle is of national historic significance and is owned and run by Historic Scotland, so while access to the park is free, there is an entry charge to the castle. Continue ahead downhill to join a tarmac path and reach **Craigmillar Castle Road**.

5 Cross the road at the traffic lights and continue ahead on a tarmac path. Keep left where it forks and pass through Hawkhill Wood, site of yet another quarry. Stay on the main cycle route ignoring paths to the left and head gently downhill into **Little France Park**, were the route crosses the Pentland Fault and onto a geological structure called the Midlothian Syncline (see panel opposite).

CRAIGMILLAR CASTLE & PARK

The castle began as a 14th century tower house constructed by the Preston family. It has many royal connections. During the 'Rough Wooing' when King Henry VIII of England sought to use military force to bring about the marriage of his son Edward to the young Mary Queen of Scots (Mary I of Scotland), the English troops under the Earl of Hertford attempted to burn it down. See also Section 1, p43 on the seizing of Leith.

Mary was twice a guest at the castle, in 1563 and 1566, and it has gained historic notoriety for a conspiracy known as the Craigmillar Bond in which some of Mary's advisors and supporters agreed (without Mary's knowledge), to murder her unpopular husband Lord Darnley. After Mary's flight from Scotland, the castle was used by the Earl of Mar (Regent to the infant James VI, later James I of England and Ireland), as his base when he besieged Edinburgh Castle.

In 1660 it was bought by the Gilmour family (also owners of Inch House). They ceased to live in it around 1790 and it quickly became an attraction as a picturesque ruin. Even Queen Victoria came to visit it in 1886. The Gilmours continued to own the castle until they gifted it to the nation in 1946. Craigmillar is one of the best examples of a surviving medieval castle in Scotland.

Section 7 COAL & CANDYFLOSS

> **MIDLOTHIAN SYNCLINE**
> East of the Pentland Fault, layers of rock have been folded into a U-shape along an axis running roughly through Musselburgh/Dalkeith/Rosewell, creating a feature called a syncline. Later erosion has exposed older rocks at its outer edges. The rocks in the syncline, which were formed in the Carboniferous Period (350 to 300 million years ago) when the land lay further south, contain several seams of coal which were created when the swampy forests were periodically covered as sea levels rose. Here on the west side of the syncline, the layers of rock dip very steeply which made the coal difficult to work.

One of Edinburgh's newest, this 45-hectare park is part of the regeneration of the wider area. It provides a green corridor through which travel on foot and by bike is encouraged between residential and employment areas and a diverse range of habitats for plants and animals have been created. The park stretches south-east for 2km across this former mining area, to a ridge on the other side of the valley and incorporates the estate of Edmonstone House, which was derelict for half a century.

The council purchased that estate as part of the park's creation for something in the region of £20 million. This land is right on the edge of the city boundary and in 2013 was incorporated into the greenbelt. The park's name Little France harks back to the time of Mary Queen of Scots' residence at Craigmillar Castle when she brought many French courtiers and servants with her.

The land flattens out at a junction of paths. Keep roughly ahead (slightly right) crossing a minor channel of the **Niddrie Burn,** with a large car park to the right and to the left a new area of wetland meadow. Then in approximately 200m reach a chunky metal bridge and cross the main channel of the burn onto **Little France Drive**. In keeping with the philosophy of the park, this road is closed to private vehicles. To the south the parkland continues, but here the route turns left.

❻ Follow the pavement for approximately 150m with a view to the left over the new lochan. This lochan and the wetland meadow are designed to absorb and manage flood water as necessary, as well as creating new wildlife habitats.

New landscaping, integrating flood prevention and habitat diversification, has been created by Julie Waldron a landscape architect at Edinburgh council. The funding has been a partnership between the council, Scottish Enterprise and the developers of nearby housing. The concept of the new park is part of the much wider £20 million Craigmillar Redevelopment Plan.

It is fitting to have a lochan created here as, in prehistoric times, the whole of this broad, flat valley was covered in a loch, now only traceable by the alluvial deposits it left behind.

Just beyond the lochan the road opens again to all vehicles and becomes **Pringle Drive**. Turn left into **Sandilands Drive** and where this

Little France Park wetlands

155

Section 7 COAL & CANDYFLOSS

Alongside the Niddrie Burn in Hunter's Hall Park, with the Jack Kane Sports Centre ahead

bends right keep ahead onto a path which then turns right to pass along the backs of the new flats and continues to rejoin **Pringle Drive**. Turn left then, just before a bridge over the Niddrie Burn, cross the road and pick up the burnside path once again.

❼ Follow the path down a flight of stairs into **Hunter's Hall Park** and continue in the same direction on a rough path heading north-east, Once again, new housing is to the right but left

NIDDRIE, COAL & EMPIRE

The house of Niddrie Marischal belonged to the Wauchope family. Originally a medieval tower house, it was rebuilt in the 17th century and greatly added to in 1823. Hunter's Hall Park takes up the southern and eastern part of the landscaped grounds of the house which had been in the family's ownership (almost) constantly for 600 years. Another branch of the family owned nearby Edmonstone Estate.

Much of the family money came from mining; there were three coal mines within 800m of the big house and a small network of private rail lines to take away the coal. As at Cammo, visited in Section 3, the final occupant of the mansion house was an heirless woman, Jean Muir, second wife of General Andrew Gilbert Wauchope.

The general had been a hero of the 1898 Anglo-Egyptian Sudan Campaign and it was reported that when he arrived home his carriage was pulled up to the gates of the house by hundreds of willing miners. In his speech to the assembled crowds – which included a brass band, a pipe band and school children, as well as the estate's tenants and miners – he said he hoped Niddrie coal would soon be used to power the locomotives on the Khartoum Railway.

On Jean Muir's death in 1943, Edinburgh council purchased the house and land. The house suffered a serious fire in 1959, which left it derelict and it was demolished in the following decade. All that remains of this once wealthy estate is the Wauchope family's mausoleum, behind a block of flats on Niddrie House Drive, opposite Great Carleton Square.

Section 7 COAL & CANDYFLOSS

> ## SCOTLAND'S ENSLAVED MINERS
>
> *Early mining was so tough and skilled miners so hard to keep hold of, that an Act was passed by the Scottish Parliament in 1606 which bound miners to a mine or owner in perpetuity, effectively making the miner a slave. Mine workers at this date were not just men but also women and children.*
>
> *Nearly 70 years later, another act allowed mine owners to abduct beggars and vagrants and forcibly add them to their workforce, where they had to toil for no wages. Miners had a monetary value and could be bought and sold with the mines.*
>
> *The bondage of miners was revoked in Acts of 1775 and 1799 but, as Hugh Millar (see Section 8) noted a quarter of a century later, the living and working conditions of miners at Niddrie were still hardly any better than their bonded forebears.*

across the burn are two mid-1960s 15-storey tower blocks, Wauchope House and Greendykes House. Beyond them was Greendykes, a post-war low-rise council housing estate which suffered many problems and became unpopular when the area lost its employment base. It was demolished around 2010. Planned regeneration was slow initially, but the new park seems to have been a spur to new house building.

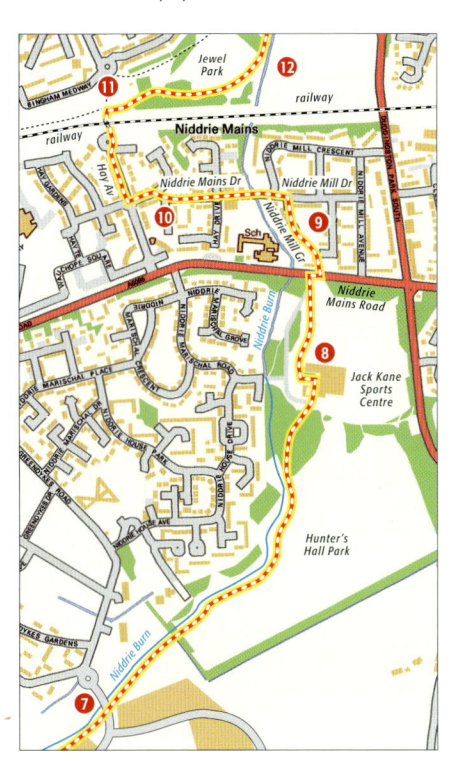

This section of the Niddrie Burn was only restored as a surface channel in 2013 after being culverted for some decades under land used for more public authority housing. The burn originally flowed north-east of its current channel, through a lush parkland landscape that surrounded a mansion house called Niddrie Marischal, which included a pond and a waterfall and was heavily planted with trees. The only remains of this private idyll are the trees on the south edge of the park which formed its boundary, and a mausoleum left of the burn which is now surrounded by housing. Part of the wealth on which this estate was created came from the rocks below – coal.

Hunter's Hall is a substantial community park of 28 hectares, which sits above the coalfield. It opened in 1955 as the surrounding area was being developed for council housing. It is mostly used for sports pitches and plans have been floated to build a new velodrome – to replace the one recently demolished at Meadowbank stadium – and a BMX track.

Continue along a new path through the park beside the Niddrie Burn towards a forbidding looking concrete building. This is the **Jack Kane Sports Centre** designed by Brian Annable of the city architects' department in

157

Section 7 COAL & CANDYFLOSS

The Jack Kane Sports Centre and Hunter's Hall Park from the northern entrance

the mid-1970s and named after a popular former Lord Provost of Edinburgh. Before the sports centre, swing right then left to reach the car park and cross straight over the access road to reach the front entrance.

> 🚻 *The Jack Kane Sports Centre has public toilets, along with food and drink from a vending machine*

❽ From the entrance, walk out towards the access road, but before reaching it, turn right and follow a short section of road to a footpath. This leads north across the park and past a play area to reach the entrance on **Niddrie Mains Road**.

To the east of the park the landscape was markedly different. Beyond the road called The Wisp were the pitheads for three of the Niddrie Pits, and the private mineral railway which ran north-south connecting the various other pitheads – all now gone. Prior to 1884 there was a fourth pithead here, No7, but that was closed following a fatal fire (see panel opposite).

> 🚻 🍽 *About 700m (8 mins) to the right along Niddrie Mains Road and Newcraighall Road is the very large Fort Kinnaird Retail Park which has cafes and restaurants*

Cross over Niddrie Mains Road and walk through metal barriers into a small, paved open space. This is a little post-war, low-density housing scheme called Niddrie Mill. Its name goes back to a small hamlet which in the mid-19th century, had a threshing mill on the banks of the Niddrie Burn. By the end of that century it had gone and the community was dependent on the local industries of coal, brickmaking and quarrying – which in turn have also gone.

❾ Keep to the left-hand side of the square, then take a hidden path by a hedge and go diagonally left into a second square and **Niddrie Mill Grove**. Walk up this to a T-junction and turn left down **Niddrie Mill Drive**. Cross over the Niddrie Burn and go through a set of metal barriers into the Hay Estate which has been substantially redeveloped and

JACK KANE

Although not born in Edinburgh, Jack Kane grew up in a mining family on the Niddrie Mains council estate. He became a local councillor just before WWII and eventually rose to be the first Labour Lord Provost of Edinburgh, serving in that post from 1972 to 1975.

Instrumental in the initiation of the Craigmillar Festival in the 1960s (with Helen Crummy), he was awarded an OBE for services to the local community but declined the conventional honour of a knighthood on completion of his term as Lord Provost.

A champion of the cause of bringing services to the deprived peripheral scheme at Craigmillar, the local public voted to name the new sports centre after him when it opened in the mid-1970s.

Section 7 COAL & CANDYFLOSS

NIDDRIE MINING TRAGEDY

The 24th of May 1884 was a sad day for the local mining community. Just as the men were arriving for the 6am shift (one of three eight-hour shifts which worked the mine day and night) a fire broke out in the shaft of pit No7. Around 40 men were still underground at the time and efforts were immediately made to rescue them and extinguish the fire using water from the Niddrie Burn. Many managed to get themselves out through shafts connected to another of the pits but 16 were known to be trapped.

After several hours, the fire was extinguished, and when the rescuers could get in they found the men huddled together, most of them unconscious but seven already dead through lack of oxygen.

Boys began working underground around age 14 and often started their mining life assisting their father. One such father and son team was caught up in the tragedy; 51 year old William Hamilton was found dead and was noted to be clutching his 16 year old son in his arms, unconscious but still alive.

reconditioned in recent decades. Keep ahead, now on **Niddrie Mains Drive**, passing the small Hays Park on the right to reach a T-junction.

10 Go left, still on Niddrie Mains Drive, to a mini-roundabout and turn right into **Hay Avenue**. At its end keep ahead on a footpath and pass under the bridge carrying the south suburban railway line. When built this was part of the Innocent Railway (see p160).

11 On the other side, take the right-hand path through **Jewel Park** (signposted to The Jewel, Brunstane and Queen Margaret's University) and rejoin the John Muir Way, last followed beside the Water of Leith and the Union Canal at Craiglockhart in Section 5.

At just 2.5 hectares, this small community park opened in 1959 to serve more council housing schemes. The one to the left is Bingham – first used as a site for prefabs and concrete 'Orlit' houses in the immediate post-war period and rebuilt over the years with more traditional housing. The park takes its name from a coal seam which was prized for its low sulphur content and thus well-suited for use in domestic fires. This seam was worked from Newcraighall Pit and known locally as the Klondyke because, when sunk in 1897, there was talk of it producing coal for 300 years. Sadly it closed in 1968 and the Fort Kinnaird Retail Park is now built over it.

12 The path swings round to rejoin the Niddrie Burn and continues beside it ignoring turnings off to the right and left. Before the path emerges onto **Duddingston Park South**, the pitched-roof building to the right, on the other side of the burn, is the Jewel Miners Welfare Society and Social Club of 1930, another sign that the walk route is still following the Midlothian coal seam. Up to the beginning of the 20th century there was a small mining settlement amid the fields here called Jewel Cottages. Where the path meets the main road, the office and warehouse units behind the railings were on the site of the Portobello Fever Hospital, located here when this was a more remote and undeveloped area.

13 Cross the road at the lights and go left then right onto a path into **Magdalene Glen**, with the Niddrie Burn still down on the right. The glen takes its name from a chapel dedicated to St Magdalene which once stood 1.5km to the east, close to where the burn – by then called the Brunstane Burn – discharges into the Firth of Forth. In recent years the council has installed new play areas in this small burnside park as part of the compensation for the loss of land at Portobello Park for building a new school.

Stay on the main path (signposted to Superstore, Brunstane, Queen Margaret

159

Section 7 COAL & CANDYFLOSS

INNOCENT RAILWAY

This follows the route of the first railway to arrive into Edinburgh, built by the Edinburgh & Dalkeith Railway Company from 1831. The line started in the city's St Leonards district and ran to Dalhousie on the River South Esk, with a branch line off to Leith. A small section of that route, between Duddingston Junction to the west and Niddrie Junction to the east, was also used for the Edinburgh Southern & Southside Suburban line of 1884 – which was important in the development of the suburbs and the brewing industry at Craigmillar.

The Edinburgh & Dalkeith's original line did not use locomotives to pull its wagons but horses, where the gradients permitted, and cables pulled by stationary engines where the gradients were too steep. The lack of steam locomotives gave rise to a myth that it was less danger to the public and so it acquired the name the Innocent Railway.

The line was conceived as a way of transporting coal from the Midlothian coalfield to Edinburgh to sell to the domestic market and to Leith for the export market; it was mine-owners who formed and financed the company and who were the primary investors in it. Initially there was no thought of running passenger services, but early on an enterprising coach owner began to run passenger services on the lines – also horse-drawn – to Fisherrow on the coast. When this proved a surprise hit with the public, the railway company began to run its own passenger services.

The railway crossed Wauchope land and a legal agreement was drawn up under which Mr Wauchope received a payment for every ton of freight transported on this section. By 1835 he realised he was missing out on payment for passengers because such a service had not been thought of when the agreement was made. The railway company disputed his claim and the matter ended up in court in 1842 where the judge decided Mr Wauchope was due half a penny per ton of passengers.

This payment did not last for long. The larger North British Railway Company bought out the Edinburgh & Dalkeith in 1845 and ceased to run passenger services on this section of the line, but it continued to be used for coal, only stopping in 1968. The tracks between Duddingston Junction and St Leonards have gone and the route of the line – including the spectacular 217m long tunnel engineered by James Jardine – is part of National Cycle Route 1.

University, Musselburgh). When the path forks, stay on the upper path (left fork) and in about 300m, an underpass leads below the four lane **A1** road leading south to Berwick-upon-Tweed. This is roughly the site of another of the Niddrie pits (No9). Come out of the underpass and keep left between the road and a retail warehouse, until another underpass on the left can be taken back under the road.

> 🍽️ *The retail warehouse is The Range home store, which has a cafe*

14 Follow the path up a slope to the four lane main road. Turn left, walk to the traffic lights, cross over and turn left again, walking west – with Arthur's Seat visible in the distance – to reach **Hope Lane**. Beyond is the new **Portobello High School**, controversially built on the only part of Portobello Public Park not covered by the golf course.

The park was created by Edinburgh Corporation following the merger of the two burghs in 1897, its provision being one of the conditions of the merger as Portobello Corporation had been unable to find land within the burgh to permanently provide such an amenity. The park was ploughed up for agriculture during WWII, being restored only in 1953.

160

Section 7 COAL & CANDYFLOSS

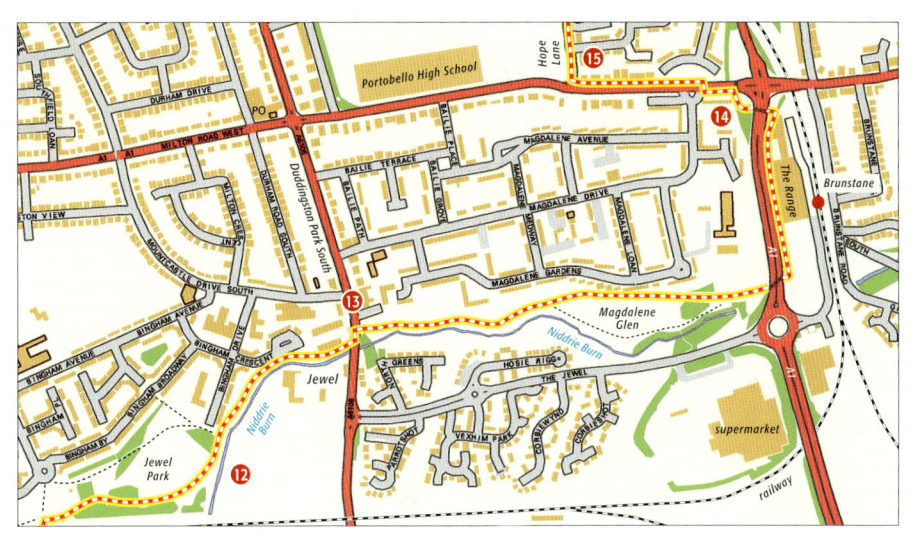

When a site was being sought for the rebuilding of Portobello High School in the early 2000s, the issue of the lack of land in the Portobello area was once again highlighted and the park was chosen as the site. Opponents of this scheme claimed the land was "inalienable common good land" and the issue went through the courts which upheld this view. In order for the scheme to proceed, the council had to obtain a Private Parliamentary Act. Originally the park covered just over 22 hectares, much of it taken up with the golf course, but is now a lot smaller following the building of the school.

15 Turn right into **Hope Lane** and as the road turns left, keep straight ahead onto the footpath. The route now follows an impressive elevated footbridge, first over the main East Coast railway

PEAK OF THE COAL INDUSTRY

By 1860 the Wauchopes' mines at Niddrie were leased to J&C Grieve trading as The Niddrie Coal Co. In 1874 Benhar Coal Co. bought part of the First Duke of Abercorn's Duddingston land with a view to reopening long flooded mines. The two companies soon merged and, despite losses from ongoing water problems preventing the Duddingston mines restarting, this new company had the capital to sink mines at Newcraighall and Woolmet in 1897.

The Niddrie & Benhar was only one of half a dozen large colliery owners in the Midlothian coalfield. At their peak in 1923 this company employed 2,565 people at their three mines. Niddrie was the oldest and was a multi-pit mine with 15 pits and it was worked out and closed by 1933.

The coal from the various seams was suitable across the spectrum of uses – household, gas production, bunkering coal for ships and steam coal for locomotives. It was taken directly to Granton Harbour by rail and approximately half of their production was exported. The Niddrie & Benhar's coal mining operation was taken over by the National Coal Board in 1947 when the whole industry was nationalised. Woolmet, like Newcraighall, continued to be productive into the 1960s.

Section 7 COAL & CANDYFLOSS

on the mainline, mostly caused by coal trains going up to Leith docks; this crossed Hope Lane on a bridge. It closed in 1967 and a new bypass road for Portobello was cut which opened in 1986. The road was named after the comedian and music hall star Sir Harry Lauder who had been born in the town. The building of the bypass necessitated elevating Hope Lane on this 300m span bridge as it heads into Portobello, and the bridge comes to an end on the Lothian Lines embankment.

🔟 When the bridge ends, descend steps to the junction of Hope Lane North and **St Mark's Place** and follow the latter north to a T-junction facing a row of shops.

> 🍽️ *Turning left leads to a bakery, cafes and takeaway on Portobello High Street*

Cross over to the shops and walk right to cross over **Pittville Street** to the entrance into the small but very pleasant **Abercorn Park**. This little park is the remnants of Portobello Links, although strictly speaking this is Joppa, a suburb of Portobello, as this was the Duke of Abercorn's land. Development around the park dates from a layout plan of 1801 but, as the variety of late Georgian, early Victorian styles around the square attest, development was slow.

The park is associated with two characters. Thomas Ord staged open air circuses on this spot in the early 19th century, prior to the start of house-building when it was still part of the then much more extensive links, and Hugh Dewar was a doctor whose career in this area spanned late Victorian and Edwardian times. There is a memorial to Dewar in the park.

Follow the left side of the park down to exit back onto Pittville Street, then turn right and follow the road to the sea at Portobello Promenade. The street layout here expresses one aspect of Portobello's character – that of a planned Regency Spa town. And indeed it is that, but Portobello is a town with a split personality – it was also an industrial centre, but that is described in more detail in Section 8.

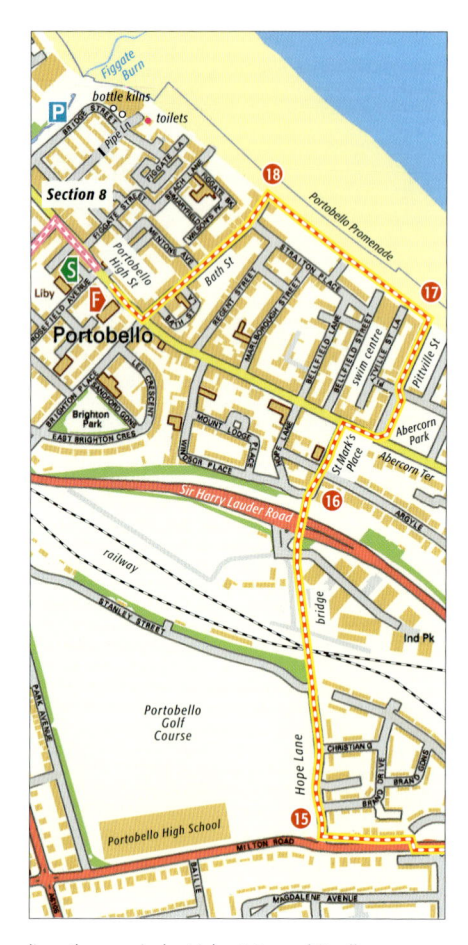

line, then an industrial estate and finally over **Sir Harry Lauder Road**. The bridge is still called Hope Lane and as a thoroughfare it predates the railway. After the North British's main line was built, Hope Lane crossed it on a bridge and then descended to ground level, crossing then undeveloped land on which the council laid out a short-lived public park at the end of the 19th century on land leased from the Duke of Abercorn. This was quickly displaced by the development of the Portobello Goods and Mineral Depot for the North British Railway – a use maintained at least till WWII.

In 1915 another railway line was built here called the Lothian Lines to relieve congestion

Section 7 COAL & CANDYFLOSS

Hugh Dewar's memorial, left, in Abercorn Park. The chimney is part of the 1898 Swim Centre on the Promenade

Portobello takes its name from a cottage on the main road from Leith to Musselburgh. It was built in the 1740s (demolished 1851) by a retired sailor who had taken part in the battle of Puerto Bello, Panama in 1739. There was known to have been sea bathing here in Georgian times with bathing machines on the beach being advertised in 1795. Portobello's development as a spa town took off around 1805 when two mineral springs were discovered and the Edinburgh gentry began to take houses for the summer. This drove the development of several streets of small but attractive houses. One of these springs was noted to be "in the vicinity of Joppa".

The kilometre-long straight beach which runs north-west from the outcrops of the rocks of the Midlothian Syncline at Joppa to the mouth of the Figgate Burn (which was the Braid Burn higher up its course) is quite a feature in itself. Before the development of the town, this large, relatively flat, open space was made use of by the military as a parade ground when large numbers of troops had to be gathered.

17 Having reached the sea, turn left and walk along the **Portobello Promenade** for approximately 200m. This is the oldest section of the promenade and, while providing public access to the beach, it has its origins in a very practical scheme to conceal a sewage pipe. The

PORTOBELLO BEACH AS MILITARY PARADE GROUND

Bonnie Prince Charlie found the large beach at Portobello a suitable site to review his Jacobite troops in 1745 after their victory at the battle of Prestonpans.

In 1822, another of the events choreographed by Sir Walter Scott for the visit of George IV took place on the beach when the King reviewed the Scottish Lowland Cavalry regiment in front of a crowd estimated at 50,000 people.

This military association continued into the 20th century as cavalrymen from nearby Piershill Barracks continued to exercise their horses on the beach up till 1934 when the barracks closed and the troops moved out to Redford Barracks on the south side of Edinburgh.

Section 7 COAL & CANDYFLOSS

Portobello Promenade and beach

arrival of a piped water supply in the town in 1850 led to the widespread adoption of the flushing toilet.

However, the waste had nowhere to go except into the town's Figgate Burn and ultimately the Firth of Forth. The beach and particularly the old (very small) harbour at the mouth of the Figgate were despoiled. When there was a cholera epidemic through 1853-4 the council realised the town's reputation as a healthy place was in jeopardy and a plan for a sewage system was initiated. As with all such schemes the implementation was not smooth, but it was largely complete by 1860.

As part of the scheme, an intercepting sewer ran along the shore and the first version of the promenade was constructed – a stone-faced earth bank – to hide it from view and protect it from storm tides between Bellfield Street to Bath Street. It proved too insubstantial, being swept away in a storm of 1867. Rebuilt and extended, it was all swept away again in another storm in 1877.

The fine red brick Portobello Swim Centre between Pittville Street and Bellfield Street was built in 1898 to the designs of City Architect Robert Morham. It was another facility which Portobello councillors got Edinburgh to provide on the merger of the two burghs.

> *Portobello Promenade has a variety of cafes and there are shops and supermarkets in the town. There are toilets at Portobello Swim Centre, at the north end of the Promenade at Pipe Lane, at the High Street end of Bath Street and in Portobello Library on Rosefield Avenue opposite Portobello High Street police station*

Beyond the Swim Centre, the small Straiton Place Park is reached, opposite a fountain on the seaward side of the promenade. This fountain was gifted to the town by long-serving Town Clerk Alex Paterson on his retirement in 1874 – it survived the 1877 storm.

The park, just a children's play area, was created in the 1960s by demolishing several houses and shops. At that time there were plans to widen the promenade, but this coincided with the start of mass tourism to the Mediterranean and several decades of decline for the town as a tourist resort.

Where Bath Street meets the Promenade was the site of the original hot and cold seawater baths of 1805. The foundation stone of this was laid by William Jameson (see p37 & p168), a builder and entrepreneur who was much involved in the town's early development and a shareholder in the baths company.

The baths were expensive and built to appeal to high class visitors in the spa tradition. Still there in 1853, they were most likely demolished for construction of the promenade. When this was completed, to cater for changing fashions, a pier was built in 1860, creating a new tourist attraction.

This was intended to provide a state-of-the-art set of Victorian seaside entertainments – a tearoom, camera obscura, and a concert hall. Once this opened, Portobello was no longer a genteel spa town where the gentry took a house for the summer, but a railway resort, attractive for visitors who came to lodge or just for a day trip.

18 After The Beach House, a large modern building with a bar and restaurant below and flats above, turn left into **Bath Street** and away from the sea. Just before the junction of Bath Street and Portobello High Street, on the left-hand side, is a mid-19th century building with a portico which in past times has been a hotel, the town's assembly rooms, and the place where Portobello council met.

Cross over, turn right and walk along **Portobello High Street** past the grand facade of **Portobello Town Hall** (Edinburgh City Architect James A.Williamson). This is the third of Portobello's town halls, but unlike the other two it was never the home of the local council having been constructed after the administrative merger with Edinburgh in 1896.

Opened in October 1914 just after WWI had broken out, it was another of the facilities provided as part of the merger deal between the two burghs. Unoccupied for a few years, an ambitious project has been proposed to repurpose the building as a major community-owned and community-managed venue for the town.

Section 7 ends at the town hall and there are bus stops just beyond it. **F**

(First stop) Lothian bus 26 to Princes Street, (second stop) Lothian bus 42 to The Mound, 49 (via Leith) to North Bridge

PORTOBELLO PIER

Portobello Pier was designed by Thomas Bouch, who was also a major investor in the company building the pier. Bouch also designed Granton's roll-on / roll-off ferry seen in Section 2, but he is probably best known for designing the first (and fatally flawed) Tay Railway Bridge a decade later.

The project cost £10,000 and the completed 380m long pier opened in May 1871. Its popularity was instant, aided by Sunday opening at a time when there was generally nothing else to do on the sabbath apart from going to church.

In Edinburgh a special public holiday on 12 August that year marked the centenary of the birth of Sir Walter Scott and it was reported that 2,500 people spent their holiday at Portobello Pier, paying a penny each. The railway companies quickly adapted to tap into this popularity offering excursion trains from all over central Scotland.

In 1892 the North British Railway Company bought out the company that ran the steam boat excursions from the pier. The pier closed during WWI when the excursion steamers were requisitioned by the navy and the visitors dried up.

The pier quickly fell into disrepair and was demolished in 1917. Plans were drawn up for a replacement in 1939 but were scuppered by WWII. Further plans for a contemporary version of a pier were unveiled in 2015 but so far have not progressed.

The south gate of the Palace of Holyroodhouse

Section 8
CROWNING HEIGHTS

Route: Portobello to the Palace of Holyroodhouse
Distance: 8km; 5 miles
Grade: Strenuous – While most of the route is Moderate, the ascent and descent of Arthur's Seat is steep and rocky and some will find it physically and mentally challenging. Good footwear is essential and the climb is not advised in wet or icy weather, or low cloud
Access: Lothian bus 26 from Princes Street, 49 (via Leith) from North Bridge, 42 from The Mound (*Portobello Town Hall bus stop*)

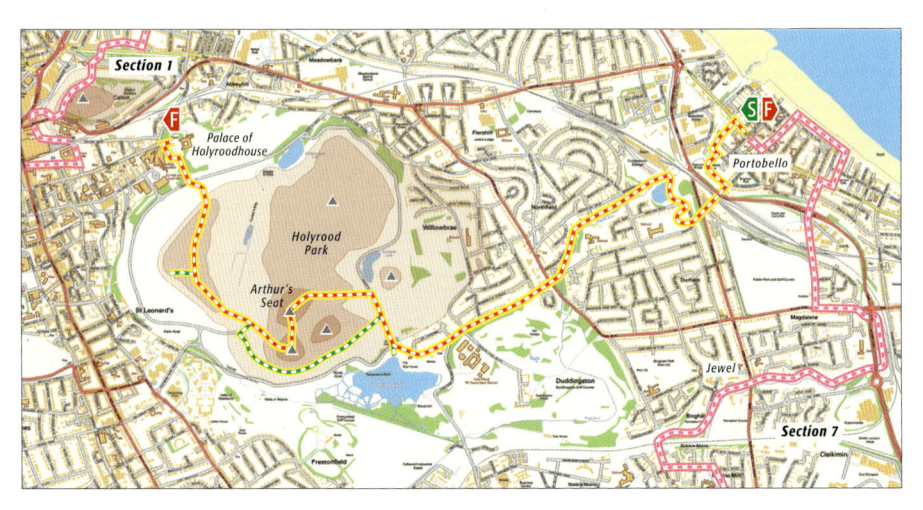

Starting from a seaside resort where sand and deep clay deposits encouraged industry and nurtured developments in the science of geology, this section progresses to a village nestling beside a loch, before reaching Arthur's Seat, the tantalising landmark seen from so many points on the route. Perhaps not technically a mountain, it certainly feels like one from the summit, topping all the hills climbed so far and offering a truly panoramic view of the city. Fittingly, the route ends at the foot of the Royal Mile; bookended by Edinburgh's principal historic buildings – the Palace of Holyroodhouse and the castle

S Start in front of Portobello Town Hall (see p165) and walk north-west along **Portobello High Street**. The road is very wide at this point with a curious intermixing of two-storey Regency buildings and higher Victorian tenements. Portobello lies just south of where the road from Edinburgh to London meets the road from Leith to Musselburgh. The monthly stagecoach to London was passing here before the first house was built in the 1740s, but the catalyst for growth from a hamlet to a town, was the start of a dedicated Edinburgh-Portobello stagecoach in 1806 (three times daily, cost 10 pennies). The stagecoach service

167

Section 8 CROWNING HEIGHTS

Bottle-shaped kiln on Bridge Street. One of the last surviving in Scotland and remnant of Portobello's once thriving pottery industry (see p171)

survived till the tram service began in 1875.

Cross the end of Rosefield Avenue, the second Portobello street to be laid out and originally the route to Rosefield House, home of William Jameson who is considered to be Portobello's founding father. As well as building for himself, Jameson built seven other villas and, although these were all modest in size they were set in generous gardens. When demolished these large garden plots offered development opportunities such as the 1960s local authority shop and housing development at the corner of **Rosefield Avenue** and the High Street, which was the site of a villa called Williamfield. Behind it on Rosefield Avenue was another villa called Jessfield, the name of which survives in the bowling green now on its site, behind Portobello Library.

> Portobello High Street has a variety of cafes, supermarkets and shops. There are toilets at the High Street end of Bath Street and in Portobello Library on Rosefield Avenue

The over-scaled police station on the other

WILLIAM JAMESON, THE FATHER OF PORTOBELLO

Born in 1737, William was the son of a well-established Edinburgh stonemason Patrick Jameson, who held the post of Deacon of the Incorporation of Wrights & Masons in the city. As William came of age, Edinburgh's New Town was being discussed and many improvements were being undertaken in the Old Town, so times looked auspicious for builders.

Entrepreneurial William could see that these developments would require vast quantities of bricks as well as stone. Bricks were used in the hidden sections of buildings, cellars, supporting arches, flues and internal walls. The same material used for bricks could also make chimney pots, pantiles and drainage pipes.

In 1763 he took something of a gamble when he purchased the feu of just over 16 hectares of land beside the sea to the east of Edinburgh at a spot known as Figgate Whins. Poor quality land, exposed, covered in gorse (whin) and fit only for grazing, its attraction was not its seaside location, but the clay deposits which lay in a thick bed under the sandy soil.

Jameson's first clay pits were by the mouth of the Figgate Burn with flimsy workers' housing constructed alongside (now all gone) and a village known as Figgate (or sometimes Brickfield) became established. In 1776 Jameson built himself a villa about 300m upriver called Rosefield. This stimulated a demand for summer residences in the locale and Jameson sub-feued several large plots for similar residences – modest two-storey detached villas, set within generous plots – for which he also acted as builder.

The brickworks thrived, producing three million bricks a year, not just for use locally, but also for export to Norway, the West Indies, Gibraltar and North America.

Section 8 CROWNING HEIGHTS

The Scots Baronial style police station on Portobello High Street

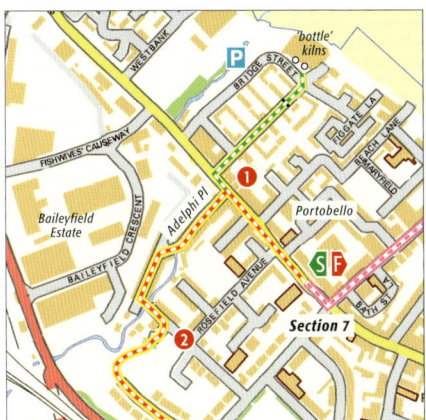

the North. The building was designed as a municipal and police building but within 20 years it was outdated when council functions moved to Edinburgh with the merger of the two burghs. The upper floors became the

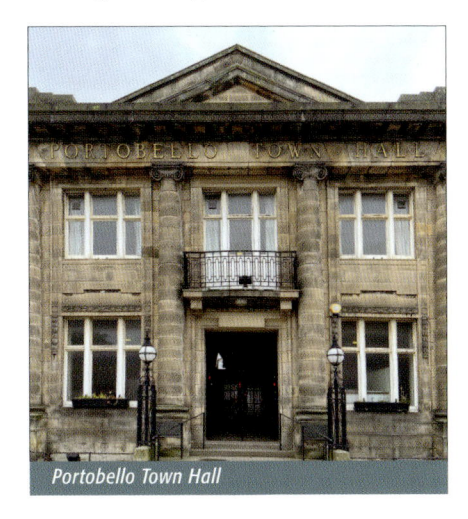

Portobello Town Hall

side of the High Street was actually designed as Portobello's second town hall and opened in 1878. The architect was an Edinburgh man Robert Paterson, who also designed the Café Royal in the New Town. His Scots Baronial style building was described in a contemporary building journal as worthy of the Brighton of

169

Section 8 CROWNING HEIGHTS

HUGH MILLER, THE SUPREME POET OF GEOLOGY

Unlikely as it seems, when Hugh Miller died in 1856 the 54-year-old, six-foot tall, flame haired, evangelical Christian stonemason turned newspaper editor and writer of books on geology, was something of a superstar. Despite his death being by suicide, his funeral procession was 40 coaches long, shops closed out of respect and thousands lined the route.

Originally from Cromarty (his birthplace is now a National Trust for Scotland museum), Miller lived in Portobello for only four years. For a decade before that, he had been living in Edinburgh and editing the large circulation Christian newspaper the Witness (through which he had been influential in the formation of the Free Church of Scotland in 1843).

His intimate knowledge of geology came from his apprenticeship as a stonemason and years of fossil collecting, making field observations and detailed drawings in his spare time. Despite being at the heart of Edinburgh's religious and scientific life, Miller always stood a little apart from it and was considered a man of the people. Portobello attracted Miller because at Shrub Mount there was a large garden where he could build a museum to hold his fossil collection. Also, like Jameson before him, he was attracted by the clay, which he came to understand as sedimentary rock in the making. He obtained permission to make a detailed study of the working clay pits and the preserved shells, tree and plant remains they contained.

His contribution to geology was two-fold, his thinking and his books, which were best sellers. In early-Victorian Scotland perhaps only a staunch Christian could have said that the evidence of the rocks disproved the Biblical account of the creation of the earth. He was explicit that it was the fossil record of the clays – 'younger rocks' – that had caused him to 'yield' to 'evidence' and say conclusively that 'the days of creation were not natural but prophetic days' which had been very long indeed; each 'day' representing a different geological epoch.

The headaches and paranoia which led to Miller's suicide have been put down to a combination of extreme overwork, anguish at having to reconcile his belief in God and the truth of the Bible with the evidence of the rocks, and a rapidly progressing brain disease, possibly a tumour.

Following Miller's death, a public subscription fund raised money to buy his collection of over 6,000 fossils for the nation. The British Government added £500 to the fund and Miller's fossils now form the basis of the collection at the National Museum of Scotland.

public library until 1960, when that moved to the new building on Rosefield Avenue.

Continuing up the High Street, cross Adelphi Grove and at the pedestrian crossing look to the other side of the street. An unprepossessing two-storey Regency villa, much altered with a bay window above and restaurants below, sits between a late Victorian three-storey tenement on the right and a red sandstone gabled hall on the left.

❶ This villa, formerly called **Shrub Mount**, was home to the geologist Hugh Miller. Behind the villa a museum housed his collection and was accessed through the close door of the adjoining tenement. A small plaque above the close door commemorates Miller's occupation from 1854-56.

Beyond this villa and over to the right, between the High Street and the sea, was the 'working' end of Portobello, site of brickworks and potteries, Georgian workers' housing and a small, short-lived harbour – all have gone to be replaced behind the tenements with low-rise 1970s housing which has breached the original street pattern. On **Bridge Street** towards the northern end of the Promenade, two

Section 8 CROWNING HEIGHTS

Shrub Mount, the two-storey Regency villa, once occupied by pioneering geologist Hugh Miller

PORTOBELLO POTTERY

The pottery industry developed in the late 18th century after William Jameson began to exploit the clay beds for making bricks and tiles. It continued down to the early years of the 20th century and did not dent the growth of Portobello as a holiday destination. Old photographs show a curious scene of a beautiful beach filled with fun seekers against a backdrop of tall chimneys and brick kilns.

In a shrewd move, Jameson set up two potteries to generate more income from exploiting the clay without creating competition for his brickworks. To use the local clay for pottery, as opposed to bricks, it had to be mixed with a finer clay. At first this came from flint ground in a mill powered by the water of the Figgate Burn, but later china clay from Cornwall was used.

The potteries were close to the mouth of the burn where his first clay workings were and around 1788 Jameson built a small harbour using local stone from Joppa. This could only take a few boats, but it was sufficient to allow the white china clay and the coal for firing the kilns to come in and bricks and tiles from Jameson's brickworks to be exported.

After Jameson's death, the potteries changed hands with varying economic success till the mid-19th century when the industry seemed to stabilise. In one, Thomas Rathbone produced fine decorative earthenware – tableware and ornaments – but this got into financial difficulties and the site was taken over around 1857 by William A.Gray who made more general stoneware.

The change in product may have been linked to the decline of the harbour, making the import of the finer clays required for decorative ware less viable. Gray's continued in existence till the Great Depression in the 1930s. By this date the local clay was all worked out and fashions had changed; the old brown stoneware was no longer popular.

In 1867 the other pottery came to be operated by Murray & Buchan who initially made plain utilitarian stoneware; later this partnership dissolved and Alexander Buchan worked under his own name. Rebranded as the Thistle Pottery and now making decorative ware, it survived to be the last pottery operating in Portobello before closing in 1972. Two of Buchan's kilns from the early 1900s can be seen on Bridge Street near the Promenade (see photo p168).

Section 8 CROWNING HEIGHTS

Single-storey brick cottages on Adelphi Place, built for workers in Portobello's potteries

bottle kilns, remnants of the pottery industry, have been preserved. They are scheduled ancient monuments and worth the short diversion if time allows.

Turn left up **Adelphi Place** which is wide at first with a mixture of architecture; some low housing circa 1830 on the left and a 1960s council scheme on the right making use of the site of the former Portobello Tram Depot. As the street narrows, the scale changes and it is lined with single-storey cottages. These were built by local businessman Thomas Tough, owner of one of the potteries (he sold to Murray & Buchan in 1867), for his workers in the 1860s.

On the right, the Mission Hall of 1863 indicates that the middle class churchgoers of the town felt the need to bring religion into the lives of the working population. Note the cottages on the right are built in brick – this was common in Portobello's early housing, but in grander houses the brick would have been covered in harling.

The road bends as it crosses the Figgate Burn, the renamed continuation of the Braid Burn followed for much of Sections 6 & 7. Go left at the T-junction then just beyond the last house in the terrace, turn left again onto a narrow path and cross back over the burn to emerge onto **Rosefield Place**. Behind the stone wall on the right is an old villa called Burn House; partly covered in harling it is most likely constructed of local brick.

❷ Continue ahead to reach the railing and gates to **Rosefield Park** and turn right into it. This small and peaceful park of just 3.1 hectares encompasses the grounds of the villa which William Jameson built for himself in 1769, and the centre of Portobello's subsequent development.

In 1920 Edinburgh's Parks Committee recommended the council purchase Rosefield for £1,400, perhaps recognising that the community had suffered a loss of outdoor amenity space with the demolition of the pier a few years earlier. At this date the town was at its industrial peak and the benefit of open spaces in what, by then, had become densely occupied working class areas, would have been much appreciated.

As the path bends right, it passes a section of old wall pierced by an arched opening, presumably constructed with Jameson's own

Section 8 CROWNING HEIGHTS

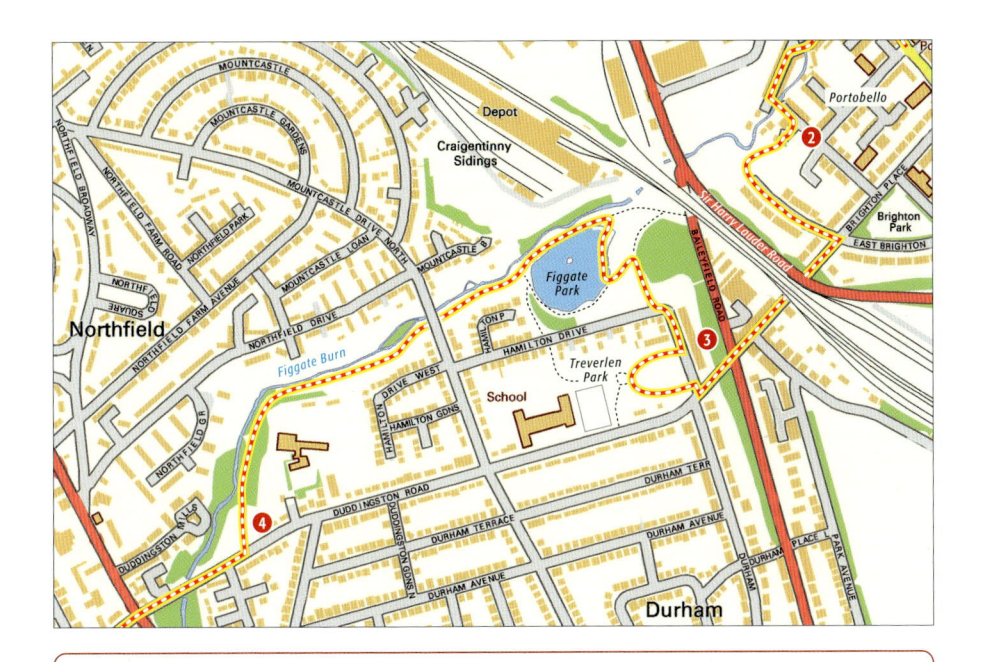

PORTOBELLO – A STRUGGLING BURGH

Rosefield House, William Jameson's home, had been central to the birth of Portobello and it was to play a small part in its struggle to become a fully functioning mature town.

Portobello came of age in 1833 when it was made a parliamentary burgh but this was a mixed blessing. Its new status gave the small qualifying population the vote but the legislation creating the burgh initially failed to give the new Portobello Corporation the power to raise any money. The council was also hampered by owning no property so, in its short existence of just 63 years, till the merger with Edinburgh in1896, the burgh struggled to acquire the trappings of Victorian civic pride, especially a town hall and a public park.

From the middle of the 19th century the council's functions grew – gas street lighting from 1846, a piped water supply in 1850 (from Crawley Springs through an agreement with Edinburgh) and a sewer system following a cholera outbreak in 1851. The council needed more space and took over Rosefield House, which by then had become a boarding school.

But Rosefield House soon became too cramped and remote from the centre of town, so the first purpose built town hall (now the Baptist church on the High Street) was commissioned from a specially constituted private company. It was a disastrous arrangement which dragged through the courts for years. The premises were not fully occupied till 1867.

As the town grew substantially with the burgeoning tourist trade, the council finally had the funds required and built its own town hall in 1878 (the Police Station passed on the High Street). At last, Portobello had a symbol of civic pride, but the struggle to get a substantial park took longer and it was only after the merger with Edinburgh that the gardens of Rosefield House became a park. (See also Portobello Park, Section 7, p161-2).

Section 8 CROWNING HEIGHTS

One of the old garden walls of Rosefield House

bricks. Note a small bridge on the right which crosses the Figgate Burn and leads to the new Baileyfield housing estate. The history of this site tells of the area's journey from remote site for early noxious industry to dormitory suburb.

In the late-18th century, the Earl of Abercorn granted two leases here; the nearer part became a brickworks with the portion behind being leased to a maker of sulphuric acid which in 1826 was purchased by William Bailey who converted it for glassmaking. The brickworks closed around 1910 but glassmaking continued until the final owners, bottle makers United Glass, closed in 1967. Subsequently, the whole site had been a light industrial estate.

Continue on the path through Rosefield Park to exit into **West Brighton Crescent** and follow this to a T-junction with Brighton Place. Note the street's setts, the stone blocks which were once the traditional urban road surface and still line Edinburgh's 'genteel' areas. These were recently replaced but the original setts would have been from local dolerite quarries.

Turn right into **Brighton Place** and pass under the bridge. Built for the North British Railway's main line, this bridge was enlarged over the

---

PROVOST BAILEY & BOTTLE MAKING

William Bailey hailed from Newcastle, but soon after his arrival in Portobello he began producing cut glass crystal and flint glassware in a factory on the far side of the new Baileyfield housing development. The main ingredients for glass making are sand, soda and lime, so it is no coincidence that the industry thrived in Portobello.

Bailey became a big player in the town, being elected its first Provost in 1833. Towards the end of his life, he took on Richard Cooper as a partner and the business switched to the production of bottles. The Portobello bottle-making industry was inextricably linked to Edinburgh's brewing industry, so it suffered as breweries closed. Following Bailey's death, Cooper took on a new partner Thomas Wood who, like Bailey, would serve a term as Provost. This partnership was dissolved in 1866 and the works were split in two.

Over the decades, both businesses kept abreast of technical improvements in the industry and even brought in craftsmen from Germany and Sweden to help with this. At its late-19th century peak, Wood's plant was producing around eight million bottles per year and Cooper had a similar sized plant. Cooper's works never reopened after closing during the General Strike of 1926, sources noting it had been badly affected by prohibition in the USA. Woods survived as a family firm until it was taken over by United Glass Bottle Manufacturers Ltd in 1937, closing 30 years later when that company consolidated manufacturing in Alloa.

In 1836 Bailey had built himself a large detached house to the west of the works called Baileyfield. Some 30 years later it was noted that this could no longer be used as a residence because of pollution from surrounding industry. The name Baileyfield continued to be attached to the site until the recent housing development, which has renamed it The Strand.

Section 8 CROWNING HEIGHTS

Wooden walkways cross the flooded claypits which are now a feature of Figgate Park

years to carry lines to the goods station. The final section, which was added for the Lothian Lines, has been rebuilt to carry the bypass road. Beyond the bridge on the left, a builder's yard occupies the former access to Portobello Station, which operated from 1846 till 1964.

At the crossroads keep ahead onto **Duddingston Road**. The high ground to the right is the remains of the embankment for the original historic Edinburgh & Dalkeith (Innocent) Railway line. This became redundant when the North British bought out the Edinburgh & Dalkeith Railway Company in 1845. There was a small station for the town slightly to the north from 1832 till 1846.

Turn right into **Hamilton Terrace** and cross this to reach a set of gates into **Treverlen Park**. This 2.5 hectare park, with its fine views, is the final resolution of the controversy surrounding the siting of the new Portobello High School. Beyond is the low-profile new St John's Primary, which is built on the site of the 1960s high school. Under the terms of the 2014 Act, which permitted the use of Portobello Park for its replacement, the council was required to construct this new park here after moving the primary school.

Take the path ahead to reach a junction. The landscaping has been done with input from the local community, which sought a park without a 'municipal look' featuring a skate park and artificial boulders for climbing on. There are wildflower meadows and tree planting and the water features are part of a sustainable drainage system which stops run-off water entering Figgate Burn. The boulders are a reference to the glacial erratics found across the city. The community has chosen a name for the park which predates the founding of Portobello to move on from all the controversies of the school rebuilding. Turn right and follow the path back to Hamilton Terrace.

❸ Turn left down Hamilton Terrace and where it bends to the left, keep ahead through a gate into **Figgate Park**. This opened in 1933 at a time when surrounding land was being developed for bungalows and low-density council housing, increasing the local population and putting further pressure on the area's ongoing need for public open space. It is one of the area's lesser-known gems.

At a junction of paths turn left then, in approximately 40m, turn right onto a wooden walkway which crosses the pond. At the end of the walkway, turn left onto the path which passes along the north-east side of the pond

Section 8 CROWNING HEIGHTS

Figgate Park and Arthur's Seat. The wheelset sculpture celebrates the park's relationship with the former railway

with the Figgate Burn now to the right.

The park was the vision of Provost Thomas Whitson and to create it, Edinburgh council purchased a worked-out clay pit from the Duke of Abercorn. Making this 11.3 hectare industrial site into a park took time and money as it was necessary to reprofile the clay pit and give it proper freshwater inlets and outlets, as well as landscaping the surrounding area. In total, this cost the council around £6,500, a substantial sum at the height of the Great Depression and just as the council was beginning its drive to clear slum housing.

At a junction of paths keep ahead on the left hand side of the Figgate Burn, following it upstream. Pass under the bridge carrying **Mountcastle Drive North**, then a footbridge and keep ahead on the left side of the burn as the path swings and rises up to an exit on **Duddingston Road**.

❹ Beyond Duddingston Road the Figgate Burn passes through a steeply wooded dell, then crosses Duddingston Golf Course – at which point it changes its name to the Braid Burn. Unfortunately, there is no path through the dell or along the route of the burn as it crosses the golf course, so a short section of road walking is required. Turn right and follow Duddingston Road to the crossroads and cross **Willowbrae Road** to Duddingston Road West.

On the north side of this junction is the hamlet of Duddingston Mills where a few old buildings remain. On the east side of Willowbrae Road are parts of a mill which was built on the Figgate Burn to harness the water-power as it passed through the dell. On the west side, a wall runs round the corner to Duddingston Road West, enclosing a neo-classical house which can be glimpsed through the railings on Willowbrae Road.

This was built by Louis Cauvin, a French teacher (noted for teaching Robert Burns) who, in his will, requested it be turned into a boarding school after his death. Louis Cauvin's Hospital (Charity School) duly opened in 1833. The building is no longer a school, but the charity still supports vulnerable young people.

❺ Keep ahead on **Duddingston Road West**. Here the route is leaving behind the Portobello clay and passing onto material that was deposited by melting ice; not the boulder-strewn deposits seen on the ascent of Corstorphine Hill in Section 4, but finer deposits of sand and gravel. With the movement to modernise agriculture in the mid-18th century, these areas of lighter soil were enclosed, drained and manured to provide good conditions for growing grains,

Section 8 **CROWNING HEIGHTS**

PORTOBELLO CLAY PITS

During his survey of Portobello's clay pits, the geologist Hugh Miller produced an estimate of their extent and depth. From his detailed observations, he hypothesised they sat within a larger bowl of glacial deposits about 1.5km in width and about 30m at their deepest by the outlet of the Figgate Burn, and petering out at the edges.

The remains of the plants and small marine creatures that he found, indicated the clay had been deposited in water with trees and vegetation nearby – a river or an estuary. His conclusion was that the clay belonged to a more recent geological time than the deposits in which they sat, which had been left behind after the ice sheet melted.

Between 1770 and 1936 the clay bed had largely been worked out, extracted for bricks while, in the process, providing employment for many in the town. While one pit slightly to the north was worked till the end, the pits around the Figgate Burn were largely lying derelict by WWI. Severe flooding on the Figgate Burn in 1907 may have hastened their demise because the banks between the burn and the pits were breached and the pits filled with water. As these pits were up to 20m deep, this made them both unsightly and dangerous.

The pits required filling in before the land could be reused and were not ideal for housing (filled land has to be left for a least a decade to settle), particularly when other farmland was available. Of the four large derelict pits in the area, three went to industrial uses. It was the last of these pits in the vicinity of the Figgate Burn which became Figgate Park.

potatoes and turnips, which became staple foods and improved the local diet.

Beyond the bungalows, the trees on the left side of the road screen **Duddingston Golf Course,** which occupies a substantial portion of the parkland surrounding the existing

Section 8 CROWNING HEIGHTS

The Watchtower of Duddingston Kirk – built to protect the graveyard from bodysnatchers

Duddingston House. This was once owned by the Dukes of Abercorn and is now a mixture of private dwellings and offices. This historically significant mansion, the only country house designed by Sir William Chambers in Scotland, was commissioned by the 8th Earl of Abercorn in 1760. The park was laid out in the style of Capability Brown and the house was complete by 1768; both were in a style new to Scotland.

It was being built just as construction was starting on the New Town and its influence can be seen there as Sir Laurence Dundas, a wealthy banker, also chose Chambers to design his house on the prime plot on the east side of St Andrew Square (later the Royal Bank of Scotland's HQ). Duddingston House and its stables are grade A listed.

Duddingston Golf Club was established in 1895 specifically for members of Edinburgh's financial industries and was known originally as the Insurance & Banking Golf Club. After WWI it changed its name and broadened its membership. Like other suburban golf clubs, its presence has preserved a large green space which could so easily have gone to house building.

6 When the houses end and the road begins to bend left, cross over **The Causeway**, and turn right into **Old Church Lane**. Follow the road, with an impressive rubble wall on the left, some attractive Regency villas on the right and growing views to the gorse-covered flanks of Arthur's Seat ahead, to arrive at a two-storey hexagonal structure at the entrance to **Duddingston Kirk**.

7 This Watchtower dates from 1824 and was built to prevent bodysnatching from the church graveyard. Duddingston Kirk has its origins in the 12th century and is where Sir Walter Scott was ordained as an Elder in 1806. The steps on the right-hand side of the churchyard gates are a 'loupin-on-stane', probably from the 1600s, to aid a rider mounting a horse. Return another day for a longer visit to Duddingston Village to explore the kirk, Dr Neil's Garden and connections to Bonnie Prince Charlie.

Section 8 CROWNING HEIGHTS

> 🍽 *Off to the right down The Causeway is the charming and historic Sheep Heid Inn which opens at 11 am, 12 on Sundays, and offers food, refreshments and the delights of skittles*

Follow the road as it bends gently downhill, to reach the entrance to **Holyrood Park**, which is marked by crown topped cast iron lampstands. This is a Royal Park and at 260 hectares it is by far the largest open space within the city's boundaries; it is also part of Edinburgh's official greenbelt. As a Royal Park it is not managed by Edinburgh council but by Historic Environment Scotland for the Crown. The park is also known as the Queen's Park or the King's Park depending on the monarch reigning at the time. Within its boundaries is Arthur's Seat, a constant landmark in the city landscape visible from many locations on this circumnavigation of the city.

Crown topped cast iron lampstands mark the Duddingston entrance to royal Holyrood Park

DUDDINGSTON WATCHTOWER & THE BODYSNATCHERS

Duddingston Kirk Watchtower was built in the early 19th century when Edinburgh University was at the forefront of medical teaching, which required dead bodies for dissection. This practice was controversial, particularly with religious leaders, and the legal supply of bodies was very restricted.

As interest in anatomy grew, the supply of legal corpses was never enough and teachers bought bodies without any questions as to how they had been obtained. So arose the lucrative, and for many very distressing practice of grave robbing. This was an era before modern policing and it was not a crime to take a corpse, as a dead body belonged to no one. Accordingly it was up to those who maintained graveyards to instigate a watch system to deter grave robbers. Hence the building of watchtowers in several of the city's graveyards – St Cuthbert's and Old and New Calton – and throughout Central Scotland, which date from this period.

The twin issues of grave robbing and the lack of corpses for medical dissection came to a very public head with the criminal trial of two men, William Burke and William Hare. This enterprising pair got around the difficulties presented by the watch system by simply murdering people to obtain good fresh corpses, killing 16 people before they were caught.

Hare turned King's evidence and escaped the gallows but Burke was hanged on the last day of January 1829 and his corpse was publicly dissected by Professor Monro (the owner of Craiglockhart Estate) at the university the following day. There was a minor riot as the number of students who wished to witness it was far greater than there was space for.

Three years later the law was changed to allow greater legal access to corpses for the medical schools and the need for watchtowers receded.

Section 8 CROWNING HEIGHTS

The gorse-covered southern flanks of Crow Hill from Duddingston Loch

DUDDINGSTON LOCH

At approximately 8 hectares of open water, this is the largest loch in Edinburgh and only one of two remaining freshwater lochs within the city (the other is Lochend visited in Section 1). There are other stretches of water which are lochs by name, but they are all man-made.

This loch is a post-glacial feature which formed when the ice sheet split to go round the hard volcanic rocks of Arthur's Seat, giving the ice at the side of the hill greater power to gouge out a valley – as happened with Castle Rock, creating the valleys to its north and south.

The loch was previously much larger and has been shrunk by partial draining on the south and west sides. Here there are now reed beds and marsh maintained as habitats for birds. Fed by natural springs, the loch drains through channels in this marsh into the Braid Burn. Most of the loch is an SSSI and is managed by the Scottish Wildlife Trust.

The loch is not especially deep (approximately 3m max) and from around 1650 to 1850, when the country was experiencing a run of very cold winters, the loch would freeze to sufficient thickness to allow the sport of curling to be played. Duddingston Curling Society was established here in 1795 and laid down the code of rules for the game in 1804.

Two decades later, the club engaged New Town architect William Henry Playfair to design a hexagonal stone clubhouse, which still stands in Dr Neil's Garden between Duddingston Kirk and the loch. The upper storey of this building was used as a studio by amateur landscape painter the Rev John Thomson, the minister of the Kirk for 35 years from 1805.

Other artists came to capture the scenery here and one of Scotland's most iconic paintings by Henry Raeburn circa 1795, shows the dourly dressed minister of the Canongate Kirk, the Rev Robert Walker, skating over a frozen Duddingston Loch. J.M.W.Turner is known to have visited twice and sketched the scene of Arthur's Seat seen from over the loch.

Section 8 CROWNING HEIGHTS

Once through the entrance, the route turns sharp right to follow a path beside the stone park keeper's lodge and the high hedge. Before making this turn, it is worth taking a moment to enjoy this spot by turning down left for the views over Duddingston Loch. The appreciation of the landscape of wild loch and hillside (and of Scotland generally) as beautiful rather than threatening or challenging, belongs to the Romantic movement in art which followed on from the Classical.

As seen in Section 1, on Calton Hill, the planners of the Third New Town had tried to fashion the landscape into a Classical ideal, but here it became appreciated for its wild naturalness. The novels of Sir Walter Scott were full of this Romantic sensibility and a general acceptance that wildness was beautiful would influence the development and preservation of Holyrood Park.

Return to the road, cross over and follow the path to the right of the lodge. This path is called **Jacob's Ladder** as it turns into steps – 210 in total – quickly gaining height. Here the route passes over a rock called tuff which is formed of volcanic ash. As the path emerges from the trees keep uphill on a muddy grass track with a further 18 steps to reach **Queen's Drive**, where a bench allows a stop to look back and enjoy the views over the loch and appreciate the height climbed so far. The road was created between 1855 and 1858 when the park assumed its current character under plans devised by Prince Albert.

❽ Turn right and follow the road round to another car park before **Dunsapie Loch**. The

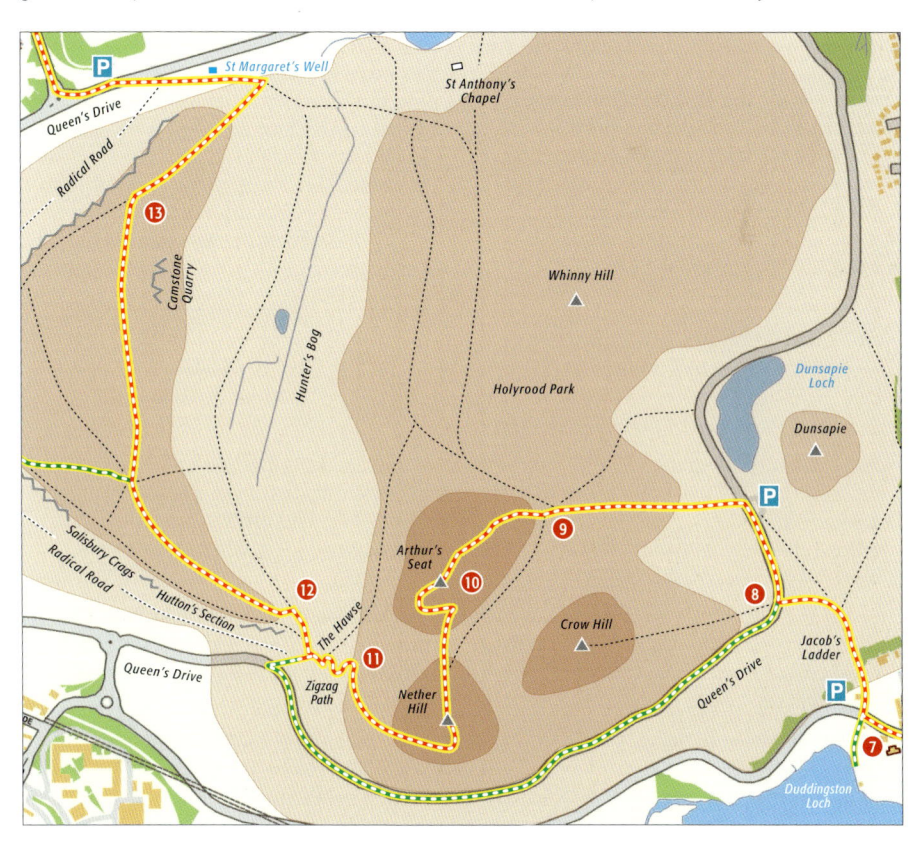

181

Section 8 CROWNING HEIGHTS

The chain handrail and pitched path leading to the final rocky scramble before the summit of Arthur's Seat

road is one way so traffic is oncoming. From the car park take any of the various well-trodden grassy paths leading towards the summit of Arthur's Seat. The underlying rock is agglomerate made up of material spewed out in an explosive volcanic eruption. Small ridges running across the grassy slope are not natural, but are evidence of medieval cultivation on this side of the hill.

❾ After a while a chain handrail and stone-pitched path are gained and followed to a point just short of the summit. From here the final section is steep and rocky with a lot of unstable gravel, so the route has to be picked out carefully but it's worth the scramble. The rock here is a harder dolerite formed in the neck of the volcano and, like many of the hills already ascended on this route, more resistant

ARTHUR'S SEAT

Arthur's Seat is the main vent of the extinct volcano which erupted 350 million years ago and, at 251m, it is the highest point of a large area of ground with several named tops – Dunsapie, Whinny Hill, Crow Hill and Nether Hill.

These summits, except Nether Hill, are comprised of hard igneous rocks which formed when the magma in the main vent of the volcano cooled. Nether Hill and the gentler slopes of the east side of the high ground are the remains of the lava flows and volcanic ash. Salisbury Crags to the west and north-west is a dolerite sill which formed 25 million years after the main volcanic eruptions.

By the time the last ice sheet passed over Arthur's Seat the whole structure had already been tilted to the east, allowing the harder cliffs of Salisbury Crags to shield much of the sandstone – now visible in the valley of Hunter's Bog – from erosion, while the volcanic core shielded the eastern lava flows and volcanic ash.

The landscape here may look like nature in the raw but it has seen many human uses through the centuries, both spiritual and practical, some of which have left their mark on the landscape. There are over 100 archaeological sites in the park including four Iron Age forts.

JAMES HUTTON THE FATHER OF GEOLOGY

Among those who have been inspired by the landscape of Edinburgh perhaps none has a greater claim to importance than James Hutton whose observations changed human understanding of the age of the earth and way it had formed.

He was born here in 1726 and educated at the university before completing his medical studies in Leiden. Initially he set up a chemical works, which would give him an income, and then he applied his intellectual curiosity to the vogue for improving farming; for more than a decade overseeing two family farms in the Scottish Borders. This experience drew him into the discipline of Natural Philosophy (later termed geology) as he observed at first-hand the slow natural processes of the erosion of rocks, and transportation and deposition of soil.

He began to develop the theory – later called uniformism – that these processes had been happening forever and, although slow, over a vastly long period of time they were the processes that created and destroyed rocks in a never-ending cycle. The visible layers in sedimentary rocks (bedding planes) were to him evidence of the process of deposition. In identifying places where horizontal bedding planes were clearly visible sitting on top of vertically arranged bedding planes (an unconformity), he explained that the forces of nature had lifted, tilted and exposed the rock which, over time, sank again and new sediment was deposited on top beginning the cycle again. As these processes are so slow, he concluded that the Earth must be very much older than the 6,000 years that Biblical scholars had calculated. This is the concept of deep time.

Hutton returned permanently to Edinburgh to a house on St John's Hill just across the valley from Salisbury Crags from where he gazed out daily for 37 years on this amazing landscape, pondering its origin. Living so close by, he was able explore the whinstone quarries, which were then operating at the crags, searching for proof of his novel theory that the subterranean heat that erupted from volcanoes was the source of power which lifted up the sedimentary rocks.

To prove it, he needed to find evidence of liquid rock flowing and distorting the bedding planes in existing sedimentary rock. This he found at Salisbury Crags South Quarry, at what is now a preserved exposure known as Hutton's Section.

The summit of Arthur's Seat is rarely quiet

Section 8 CROWNING HEIGHTS

Arthur's Seat and the gravel-covered path curving down the south face, seen from the flanks of Nether Hill

to the erosive force of the ice sheet.

10 Once at the summit of **Arthur's Seat**, take time to enjoy the achievement and the spectacular views, not only over the city but further afield. Unless it is very early in the morning, there are certain to be others on the top. It is an exposed spot surrounded by cliffs and the rock can be very slippery, so great care is needed, especially in wet or windy weather.

South of Arthur's Seat is the flatter grassy summit of **Nether Hill**, the next objective on the route. From the west, the two hills resemble a reclining lion, with Arthur's Seat the head and Nether Hill the haunch.

The route now involves descending some steep and slippery paths, but these can be avoided by returning back down to Queen's Drive and following it west, then ascending past the famous Radical Road path (currently closed) at the east end of Salisbury Crags, to rejoin the route. The map on p181 shows this option in green.

To continue to Nether Hill, gain the most westerly part of the summit area of Arthur's Seat. From there, a steep path of slippery gravel descends the south face, bending first left then back right down a rocky section, to reach a grassy saddle. Continue ahead to rise gently over the summit of Nether Hill and descend again on another slippery gravel path. Soon the path bends sharp right and the descent gets steeper. In approximately 200m, a tightly bending, very steep section known as the **Zigzag Path** begins.

11 This is a popular route of ascent so be prepared to give way to walkers puffing up the hill. These stops give opportunities to enjoy the views along the angular escarpment of **Salisbury Crags**, stretching ahead and directing the eye to the castle on its rock. The crags are a dolerite sill like Corstorphine Hill, but dipping in the opposite direction so the cliff face received the full force of the ice sheet.

In 16 switchbacks, the descent is rapid and the path soon becomes less steep. A path joins from the right and ahead, the path begins to rise gently to reach a section of

The descent is steep – but the views west across Salisbury Crags are stunning

184

Section 8 CROWNING HEIGHTS

> ### *CALSAY STANES OF SALISBURY CRAGS*
>
> *It is often noted that the Radical Road was constructed at the suggestion of Sir Walter Scott after the political unrest of 1820, when impoverished handloom weavers protested about their perilous economic conditions; the idea being that creating it would give them work in return for financial relief. But a track existed, at least along part of its route, well before that, leading to two quarries.*
>
> *In these quarries, the hard dolerite was extracted in small blocks known in Scots dialect as 'calsay stanes', a name which probably derives from one of their old uses, paving the raised causeways (such as The Causeway in Duddingston) that were frequently constructed across boggy areas in many Scottish places at that time. In English, the more common name for such stones was setts or cobbles.*
>
> *Making up the surfaces of streets and roads this way was rare before the mid-18th century but, from then, paving streets to match the elegant Georgian architecture and make coach travel possible in all weathers and seasons, became much more widespread. Consequently, demand for the stone increased dramatically and it was also shipped out through Leith to London.*
>
> *The Earl of Haddington, as the Hereditary Keeper of Holyrood Park, had been leasing out the quarries on Salisbury Crags for decades without anyone questioning his right to do so but several factors came together in 1819 to change this. Firstly, Edinburgh scientists and thinkers who were aware of the theories of Hutton, made expeditions to Salisbury Crags to see the rocks for themselves. Secondly, the spot was mentioned in Walter Scott's novel Heart of Midlothian as the perfect location to watch the sunrise or the sunset. Lastly, with the increasing demand for 'calsay stanes', the Earl of Haddington allowed explosives to be used in the Salisbury Crags quarry to increase output. These factors together alerted the general public that something valuable was being destroyed and a court action was brought to challenge the Earl's right to engage in destructive quarrying. The case was not resolved until 1831 when it was found that the Earl had exceeded his rights and quarrying ceased.*
>
> *Following the visit of Queen Victoria and Prince Albert to Edinburgh in 1842, the Earl of Haddington's rights were bought out for £30,000, opening the way for Albert to draw up plans for Holyrood Park. These plans made it more accessible to the public and appreciated the value of the landscape, rather than seeing it as a commercial resource, and essentially created the park as it is today. The Radical Road is currently closed due to risk of rockfall.*

pitched stone path. This leads to a low-point on the crest of Salisbury Crags known as The Hawse, where the alternative route round Queen's Drive rejoins the main route. Ascend to The Hawse for a fine view west over the city, then return and descend the path north for a short distance, to reach a flight of steps.

[12] Turn left up these and begin the climb up the flank of Salisbury Crags. Continuing the descent beyond the steps leads to Hunter's Bog beween Salisbury Crags and Arthur's Seat (see map p181).

Beyond the stepped section, keep to the right where the path forks and becomes less distinct but still gently climbing. Then, in approximately 300m, there is a meeting of several paths. The second path on the left heads west up to the 151m summit of the crags and is worth a diversion for those with a head for heights. Continue heading north, slightly descending but not losing much height, to reach bumpier terrain above clumps of gorse bushes, which skirts along the top edge of the old **Camstone Quarry**.

On this side of the valley the route is crossing a bed of sedimentary rocks which lies

185

Section 8 CROWNING HEIGHTS

above the harder rocks of the crags. Quarrying took place here over hundreds of years, including extracting stone for the building of Holyrood Palace.

Exposed rocks here can show distinct 'ripple beds', which capture, in stone, the moment wind or water moved the sand millions of years ago. Rounding the top of the quarry the path reaches the cliff edge (take care in poor visibility).

13 Turn right onto a path (often muddy) to head downhill. Panoramic views of the Firth of Forth open up with Fife beyond.

> ### PALACE OF HOLYROODHOUSE
>
> *Seeing the Palace of Holyroodhouse from the path descending Arthur's Seat, the impression is of a regular, square, grey, stone building. This form resulted from a major building programme to the designs of architects William Bruce and Robert Mylne in the 1670s, creating three long buildings around an internal courtyard.*
>
> *This was done in the expectation that the restored King Charles II would visit but he never did. However, his brother James Duke of York would spend some time living in the palace when he was appointed Lord High Commissioner of Scotland. These buildings were originally constructed in rubble but were refaced in ashlar, completing the current look, by Robert Reid ahead of the visit of George IV in 1822, although he too did not stay in the palace.*
>
> *Close up, viewed through the south gate, the older origins of the palace can be seen. The far (north-west) tower was built c1530 by master mason John Ayton in a pinkish rubble stone for James V. This was the part of the palace occupied by Mary Queen of Scots during the turbulent years of her reign – two of her three marriages were conducted here and her secretary Rizzio was murdered in front of her. The mirroring south-west tower was added by William Bruce in the 1670s and the building between was remodelled in line with a new desire for symmetry in architecture.*
>
> *When viewed through the main west gate on Abbey Strand, the ruins of Holyrood Abbey can be seen to the left of the palace. This is all that remains of the 12th century abbey founded by King David I which began the thousand-year connection between the royals and this site. Although not technically a royal residence till later, Scottish Royals were known to have stayed in the abbey from an early date: James II was born there in 1430 and James III was married to Margaret of Denmark there. It was James IV who took the Royal connection to the next step and began to build a palace next to the abbey.*
>
> *Bonnie Prince Charlie made a short stay during the siege of Edinburgh in 1745, but the Hanoverian monarchs did not visit Holyrood (or Scotland for that matter) until the visit of George IV in 1822. During this time it was in poor repair and the roof had fallen in. Repairs were made for Queen Victoria and Prince Albert, whose grand ceremonial entry was made on the north side so they could enter from the private station on Abbeyhill and avoid the slum that the Old Town was becoming and the industry growing up around the palace.*
>
> *However, Victoria rarely visited after Albert's death preferring to stay only at Balmoral when in Scotland. It was the unveiling of the Edward VII Memorial Gates in 1922 which reignited the monarchy's interest in reclaiming this as their principal residence in Scotland.*
>
> *Built, altered and repaired over many centuries, the palace is a museum to the quarries of Edinburgh, containing stone known to have come from Dumbiedykes and Camstone, the old long built-over quarries at Broughton, Leith Hill, St Cuthbert's, Niddrie and Stenhouse as well as the major 19th century quarries at Craigleith and Craigmillar.*

Section 8 CROWNING HEIGHTS

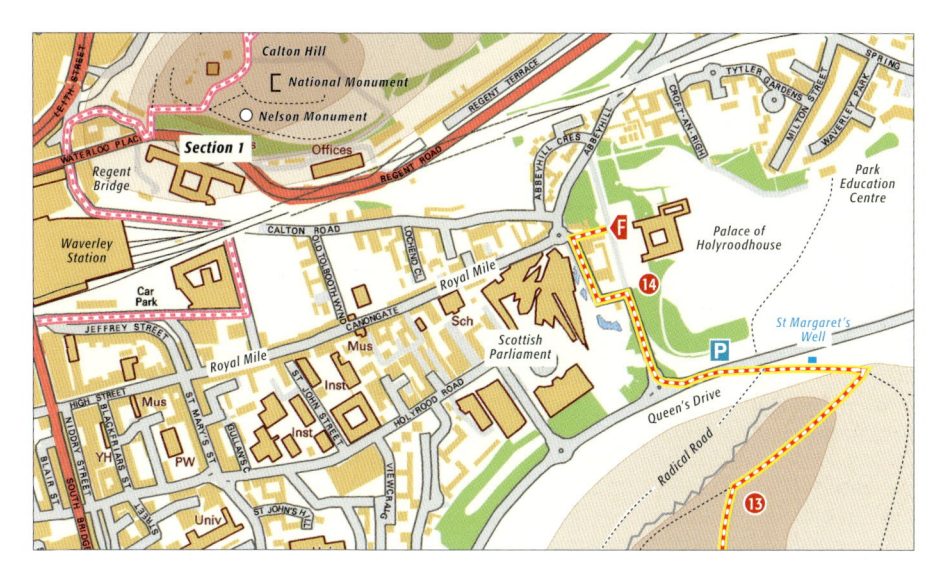

To the right, the view is across Hunter's Bog to the striking, exposed angled lava flows and beds of tuff which form the lower slopes of Whinny Hill. Many springs arise in the valley and from the mid-19th to the mid-20th century the loch that was here was drained. The natural wetland habitat has been reinstated in recent decades as it is now managed as a valuable wildlife habitat.

Ahead is St Margaret's Loch which looks perfectly natural but is in fact man-made, part of Prince Albert's landscaping. High above it stand the picturesque ruins of the medieval St Anthony's Chapel.

Keep descending to a junction with a well-surfaced path, then turn left heading

The 1670 south-west tower of the Palace of Holyroodhouse and Arthur's Seat

187

Section 8 CROWNING HEIGHTS

down to the flat ground below — way back in time the site of a post-glacial loch. Ahead now are views of Holyrood Palace, the Scottish Parliament building and the collection of monuments atop Calton Hill. Railings to the right indicate the site of **St Margaret's Well**, just one of the many springs which abound near Arthur's Seat because of the particular geology.

The excellent quality of the water in these springs gave rise to the city's large brewing industry and there was a concentration of breweries here at Holyrood, at St Leonards below the western flanks of Arthur's Seat and particularly at Craigmillar just south of Duddingston – a location that developed after the opening of the Suburban & Southside Junction Railway in 1884.

The expanse of flat ground to the east of Holyrood Palace and right of the car park is known as The Parade Ground and was added to the park in 1877, when the Crown purchased and demolished Belle Ville House and Estate (where there had once been a botanical garden) to save it from development.

> ♂♀ *The Park Education Centre has toilets. This low, metal roofed building is reached by a path which starts from the far corner of the car park by the wall and leads diagonally right across the grass. There are toilets in the Mews at the Palace of Holyroodhouse (and a cafe) which don't need a ticket to enter*

Cross over **Queen's Drive** and walk left past the car park, following the pavement and road round to the south gate of the **Palace of Holyroodhouse**. Along with two other sets of gates around the palace forecourt, these

---

NEW SCOTTISH PARLIAMENT

In 1707 an Act was passed in the Scottish Parliament just off the High Street to dissolve its powers and transfer them to a new Parliament of the Kingdom of Great Britain in London. In a referendum of 1997, the people of Scotland voted to have these powers devolved back and the quest was on to find a suitable building and site.

Seven years later, the Scottish Parliament Building was opened by the Queen. The process of its creation was not smooth and every aspect generated controversy; its location in Edinburgh, its site on a former brewery, the choice of Spanish architect Enric Miralles, the hard to read post-modern design, and above all the cost which came in at more than ten times the original estimate.

The building reflects neither Edinburgh's Old nor New Town style, but Miralles created a building for all Scotland by going back to the rugged landscape for inspiration in what has been termed a new 'National Romanticism'. The roofline is often compared to upturned boats but, in adopting a jagged profile and complex plans, it seeks not to compete with the hills but mimics the complexity and forms of the natural surroundings. There has even been a suggestion that Miralles was inspired by Raeburn's painting of the skating minister for some of the surface decoration.

The elements of the building are tightly grouped on its Royal Mile facade, but splay out on the side facing Arthur's Seat where a new public garden has been created. Here, stone terraces look from above like geological fault lines.

While it remains divisive, there is no doubting the craft and quality of the build. The old Parliament Hall, built in 1641, stands just off the High Street and is still used (as part of the legal quarter). The test for the new parliament building will be if it too can last for 380 years.

Section 8 CROWNING HEIGHTS

The Scottish Parliament Building – a £400 million break from traditional Scottish architecture

immense gates were erected in 1922 as a memorial to Edward VII. A statue of Edward stands beside the north gate but can only be seen from inside the forecourt.

14 The 1911 competition for the design of the gates was won by George Washington Brown (who also designed the Caledonian Hotel and the Central Library among many other late Victorian buildings in the city), but as built they are a trimmed down version of his design. The design proclaims this as a British royal residence and features the symbols of Scotland and England. The piers, displaying the coats of arms of Scotland and the UK, are topped with a crowned unicorn and lion holding a saltire and the cross of St George respectively, while the wrought iron gates are adorned with St Andrew, thistles and roses. The memorial was paid for by public subscription.

Continue past the gates, following the pavement as it bends right passing the palace stable block, to arrive in front of the **Scottish Parliament Building** which opened in 2004. For the final few steps of the route turn right down **Abbey Strand** to the west gate of the Palace where the route ends. **F**

Before leaving, turn around and look up the Royal Mile to where the route started at the Castle Esplanade, almost exactly one mile away. In the intervening 69km (43 miles) the route has gone through 410 million years of geological and 874 years of human history, from the castle's construction and the founding of the Royal Burgh by King David I in 1130, to the opening of the new Scottish Parliament Building in 2004. Along the way, a story has unfolded of how the modern city has been shaped, not just by geography and geology, but by its thinkers, writers, builders, engineers, architects and planners.

The route has crossed the city's hinterland where its natural resources were exploited to generate wealth through its harbours, riverside mills, quarries, coal mines, sand and clay pits. It has passed country houses built with this wealth, suburbs opened up by railways and social housing giving poorer inhabitants the chance of a healthier life. But, most of all, it has shown what a wonderful range of parks and open spaces the city has within its boundaries, how they were created and how they came into public use.

REFERENCES

GENERAL INFORMATION, MAPS, GUIDES & STATISTICS

A Dictionary, Geographical, Statistical, and Historical, of the Various Countries, Places, and Principal Natural Objects in the World *John Ramsay McCulloch*
Edinburgh And District *Ward Lock Red Guide*
Edinburgh, Bedrock & Superficial Deposits (Scotland Sheet 32E) *British Geological Survey*
Edinburgh from the Air *Malcolm Cant*
Edinburgh, Lothians And Borders *John Baldwin*
Edinburgh: The Making of a Capital City *Brian Edwards & Paul Jenkins*
Edinburgh Urban Nature Map *Urban Good*
Secret Edinburgh – An Unusual Guide *Hannah Robinson*
Short Guide to Edinburgh *(1953 Blue Guide) Russell Muirhead*
The Edinburgh Encyclopedia *Sandy Mullay*
The Evolution of Scotland's Towns *Patricia Dennison*
The First Statistical Account of Scotland (1791/99)
The Second Statistical Account of Scotland (1834/45)
The Third Statistical Account of Scotland (1951/92)
111 Places in Edinburgh That You Shouldn't Miss *Gillian Tait*
www.curiousedinburgh.org
www.ed.ac.uk/visit/city/basics/did-you-know
www.edinburgh.gov.uk
www.edinburghguide.com
www.edinburghlive.co.uk
www.edinburghmuseums.org.uk
www.edinburghnews.scotsman.com
www.google.co.uk/maps (Street View)
www.historicenvironment.scot
www.mapapps.bgs.ac.uk
https://maps.nls.uk/
www.openstreetmap.org
www.scotsman.com
www.scottish-places.info
www.undiscoveredscotland.co.uk
www.visionofbritain.org

LOCAL HISTORIES

Annals of Liberton *Rev Campbell Ferenbach*
Annals of Duddingston and Portobello *William Baird*
Leith History Tour *Jack Gillon & Fraser Parkinson*
Leith Lives: the Old Kirkgate *Leith Local History Project*
Leith Through Time *Jack Gillon & Fraser Parkinson*
The Illustrated History of Edinburgh's Suburbs *Sandy Mullay*
The Iron Mills at Cramond *Patrick Cadell*
The Life and Times of Leith *James Scott Marshall*
The Private World of Cammo *Simon Ballie*
The Story of Leith *John Russell*
The Stranger on the Shore: A Short History of Granton *James Gracie*
The Water Mills of the Water of Leith *Graham Priestley*
The Water of Leith, Source to Sea *John Geddie & Joseph Brown*
The Water of Leith *Stanley Jamieson*
Traditions of Trinity and Leith *Joyce Wallace*
Villages of Edinburgh Vol 1 & 2 *Malcolm Cant*
www.allaboutedinburgh.co.uk/restalrig-and-craigentinny
www.cramondassociation.org.uk/
www.grantonhistory.org
www.ourtownstories.co.uk (Corstorphine & Zoo)
www.portobelloheritagetrust.co.uk
www.porty.org.uk/local-history/

BUILDINGS & ARCHITECTURE

Craigmillar Castle *Historic Scotland*
Edinburgh: An Illustrated Architectural Guide *Charles McKean*
Historic Houses of Edinburgh *Joyce Wallace*
Lost Edinburgh *Hamish Coghill*
The Builders of Edinburgh New Town 1767-1795 *Anthony Lewis*
The Buildings of Scotland: Edinburgh *John Gifford, Colin McWilliam, David Walker, Christopher Wilson*
The Making of Classical Edinburgh *A.J.Youngson*
www.edinburgharchitecture.co.uk
www.scottisharchitects.org.uk
www.thecastlesofscotland.co.uk
www.thefreelancehistorywriter.com (info on Craigmiller Castle)

DEVELOPMENT, PLANNING, CONSERVATION, HOUSING & HISTORY

Calton Hill and the plans for Edinburgh's Third New Town *Kirsten Carter McKee*
Rebuilding Scotland: The Postwar Vision, 1945-1975 *Miles Glendinning*

REFERENCES

Renewing Old Edinburgh: The Enduring Legacy of Patrick Geddes
Jim Johnson & Lou Rosenburg
Scotland's Homes Fit for Heroes: Garden City Influences on the Development of Scottish Working Class Housing 1900 to 1939
Lou Rosenburg
The Transformation of Edinburgh: Land, Property and Trust in the Nineteenth Century
Richard Rodger
www.municipaldreams.wordpress.com/category/edinburgh/

RAILWAYS, HARBOURS, SHIPS, CANALS, TRAMS & ROADS

An Illustrated History of Edinburgh's Railways
W.A.C.Smith & Paul Anderson
Edinburgh – the tramway years *Alan Brotchie*
Edinburgh's Trams & Buses *Gavin Booth*
The Union Canal: A Capital Asset *Guthrie Hutton*
The Union Canal *RCAHMS (Royal Commission on the Ancient and Historical Monuments of Scotland)*
They Once Were Shipbuilders: 1 (Leith-Built Ships) *R.O.Neish*
Yesterday's railway, Edinburgh
The Railway Correspondence and Travel Society, Scottish Branch
www.edinburghtrams.com/
www.grantonhistory.org/harbour/harbour_handbook_1955_text.htm
www.grantonhistory.org/harbour/harbour_handbook_1937_text.htm
www.jamescanalpages.org.uk
www.leithbuiltships.blogspot.com/2009/12/henry-robb-shipyard.html
www.networkrail.co.uk/who-we-are/our-history/iconic-infrastructure/the-history-of-edinburgh-waverly-station/
www.sabre-roads.org.uk

GEOGRAPHY, GEOLOGY & QUARRIES

A Sketch Of The Geology Of Fife And The Lothians, Including Detailed Descriptions Of Arthur's Seat and Pentland Hills
Charles MacLaren
Edinburgh: A Landscape Fashioned by Geology
Scottish Natural Heritage & British Geological Survey
Edinburgh And Its Neighbourhood, Geological and Historical *Hugh Miller*
Edinburgh and West Lothian: A Landscape Fashioned by Geology *David McAdam (SNH & BGS)* Edinburgh Rock *Euan Clarkson and Brian Upton*
Edinburgh: Landscapes in Stone *Alan McKirdy*
Lothian & Borders *RIGS (Regionally Important Geological Site) Group leaflets*
Lothian Geology: An Excursion Guide
A.D.McAdam & E.N.K.Clarkson
The Building Stones of Edinburgh
Andrew McMillan, Richard Gillanders & John Fairhurst
The Evolution of Scotland's Scenery *J.B.Sissons*
The mineral resources of the Lothians
A.G.MacGregor & BGS (pdf)
The Nor Loch: Scotland's Lost Loch
Malcolm Fife
The Water-bearing Strata of the City of Edinburgh *John Horne*
https://blogs.agu.org/magmacumlaude/2014/04/06/edinburgh-arthurs-seat-and-salisbury-crags/
www.edinburghgeolsoc.org/edinburghs-geology/
www.geowalks.co.uk

PARKS, GARDENS & GREENSPACES

Park management & regeneration plans where available online (Princes Street Gardens, Calton Hill, London Road Gardens, Lochend, Victoria Park, River Almond Walkway, Cammo Estate LNR, Corstorphine Hill, Water of Leith, Easter Craiglochart Hill LNR, Braidburn Valley, Craigmillar Castle Park, Little France Park, Rosefield Park, Figgate Park)
Assorted Wikipedia entries for parks & open spaces
www.edinburgh.gov.uk/directory/10204/a-to-z/W
www.edinburgh.gov.uk/parks-greenspaces
www.edinburghoutdoors.org.uk
(park events & closures via twitter)
www.elgt.org.uk (New Little France Park)
www.greenerleith.org.uk
www.mypark.scot
www.scottishwildlifetrust.org.uk/reserve/johnston-terrace-garden/
www.theparksalliance.org/portfolio-items/forth-quarter-park/
www.treverlen.org.uk
www.woodlandtrust.org.uk

REFERENCES

MISCELLANEOUS

An Edinburgh Alphabet *J.F.Birrell*
Industrial Archaeology of Scotland *John Butt*
Kidnapped *Robert Louis Stevenson*
Mining The Lothians *Guthrie Hutton*
Monumental Edinburgh *Jack Gillon & Paul McAuley*
Monuments and Statues of Edinburgh *Michael Turnbull*
The Buttercup: The Remarkable Story of Andrew Ewing and the Buttercup Dairy Company *Bill Scott*
The Civil Engineer & Architects' Journal, Volume 22 p380, 1858 *(Duke of Buccleuch's architectural competition for houses at Granton)*
The Making of Urban Scotland *Ian Adams*
The Prime of Miss Jean Brodie *Muriel Spark*
The Richest of the Rich *Philip Beresford & William Rubinstein*
The Rise of the British Coal Industry *J.U.Nef*
The Scottish Marine Station and its work *William Hoyle*
The Story of Calton Jail: Edinburgh's Victorian Prison *Malcolm Fife*
Trainspotting *(the book) Irving Welsh*
Trainspotting *(the movie) directed by Danny Boyle*
Wish You Were Still Here: The Scottish Seaside Holiday *Eric Simpson*
www.bathsandwashhouses.co.uk/archive/your-local-buildings/edinburgh/
www.britannica.com/sports/ice-skating
www.casemine.com
   (Edinburgh & Dalkeith Railway v Wauchope)
www.cycling-edinburgh.org.uk/bike-paths.htm
www.edinburghcurling.co.uk/history-of-curling/
www.engineering-timelines.com
www.gracesguide.co.uk
www.johnmuirway.org
www.roe.ac.uk/roe/history.html
www.scottishbrickhistory.co.uk
   (useful info about William Jameson)
www.scottishmining.co.uk
www.sites.google.com/view/historicalcurling places/scottish-places
www.talesofonecity.wordpress.com/2015/08/25/saughtons-glorious-summer-of-1908/
www.sustrans.org.uk/
www.workhouses.org

GOLF

Edinburgh Evening News 5 September 1889
Glasgow Evening News 9 May 1892
The Scotsman 30 May 1889

PEOPLE

History And Genealogy Of The Family Of Wauchope Of Niddrie-Merschell *James Paterson*
www.britannica.com/biography/John-Murray
https://www.thefriendsofhughmiller.org.uk/
www.patrickgeddestrust.co.uk
www.napier.ac.uk/about-us/our-location/our-campuses/special-collections/war-poets-collection
   (War poets at Craiglockhart)
www.ucl.ac.uk/lbs/person/view/8961
   (John Gladstone)
www.wikipedia.org/wiki/Walter_Scott

HISTORIC PHOTOGRAPHS & IMAGES

Edinburgh as it was: The People of Edinburgh Vol II *Norma Armstrong*
Edinburgh in the Nineteenth Century *Thomas Shepherd*
Edinburgh in the 1950s: Ten Years that Changed a City *Jack Gillon, David McLean, Fraser Parkinson*
Edinburgh Since 1900: Ninety Years of Photographs *Paul Harris*
Edinburgh: The Fabulous 50s *Evening News*
Edinburgh Then *Evening News*
Old Newington, Grange, Liberton & Gilmerton *Robin Sherman*
South Edinburgh in Pictures *Charles Smith*
Views in Edinburgh And Its Vicinity, Vol 1-2 *James Storer, Henry Sargant Storer*
www.archiseek.com
www.britainfromabove.org.uk
www.canmore.org.uk
www.nls.uk/digital-resources/
www.edinphoto.org.uk
www.geograph.org.uk
www.nationalgalleries.org

REMINISCENCES

www.edinphoto.org.uk